...went on to become a comic, ...V personality, Rowland Rivron won ₤8 membership of the Groucho Club in a game of cards in 1984 and never looked back. Well known for his outrageous antics both on and off the screen, among many others he appeared in *Groovy Fellers*, *The Tube*, *The Last Resort with Jonathan Ross*, *French and Saunders* and worryingly played Alf the Pizza Chef in a children's science programme.

ROWLAND RIVRON

WHAT THE F***
DID I DO LAST NIGHT?

The memoir of an
accidental comedian

PAN BOOKS

First published 2011 by Sidgwick & Jackson

This paperback edition published 2011 by Pan Books
an imprint of Pan Macmillan, a division of Macmillan Publishers Limited
Pan Macmillan, 20 New Wharf Road, London N1 9RR
Basingstoke and Oxford
Associated companies throughout the world
www.panmacmillan.com

ISBN 978-0-330-51161-2

Cheers very much to James Rampton!

The acknowledgements on page 339 constitute
an extension of this copyright page

1 3 5 7 9 8 6 4 2

A CIP catalogue record for this book is available from
the British Library.

Typeset by Ellipsis Digital Limited, Glasgow
Printed in the UK by CPI Mackays, Chatham, ME5 8TD

Visit www.panmacmillan.com to read more about all our books
and to buy them. You will also find features, author interviews and
news of any author events, and you can sign up for e-newsletters
so that you're always first to hear about our new releases.

TO MON AND THE KIDS

(I JUST WISH I KNEW WHERE THEY LIVED)

SIMON TRACEY BRINT

(1950-2011)

CONTENTS

INTRODUCTION:
WHAT IS IT ABOUT MEMORY?

What is it about memory? How the bloody hell does it work? How come there are bits you remember as clear as day and other bits that are seemingly gone for ever, until a key word or name is mentioned and then – Bosh! – you're back in the thick of it? Some people have the ability to recall anything from their past: places, dates, names. What they were wearing, eating, thinking. How they felt, what they felt, who they felt. Others – that'll be me, then – can only ever remember stupid things, like what they were drinking. OK, that's not strictly true but I do, for instance, have total recall when it comes to my tipple of choice going as far back as my early teens. When I say 'teens' I must add here that my counting, as a kid, wasn't great: I am dyslexic, left-handed and word-blind – some say I have the full set of ailments in that department. After the numbers seven, eight and nine came the double figures, so I was straight off with tenteen, eleventeen, twelveteen, then thirteen and so on.

Anyway, I would race home in time to get comfy in front of the telly for my weekly fix of BBC TV's flagship (quite literally) kids' show, *Blue Peter*. From the cut-glass ship's decanter on the antique marching drum, which doubled nicely as a side table in our compact lounge, a largish Harvey's Bristol Cream Sherry would be poured and, together with a smallish bowl of salted peanuts, thoroughly enjoyed. Don't worry, I never overdid it; one bowl was always enough. Pissed? Maybe. Fat? Never.

Yesterday, in my early fifties, I had a very palatable Welsh cream liqueur going by the name of 'Merlyn', after the mighty wizard of Wales according to the blurb on the back of the bottle. See what I mean? Total recall. Of course, I have no idea where I was. And I see what they've done there – very clever. Substitute the 'i' for a 'y' and suddenly you've got a very convenient 'Welsh' wizard that an advertising team can muck about with.

I don't think I'm alone here but it's fair to say that over the last thirty-five years my career has been both helped and hindered by the 'bottle', in what I'd like to think panned out as an even fifty-fifty split. Some of the people I caught up with to help me put this book together see it differently. More like seventy-thirty, some said . . . or as much as ninety-'tenteen'. But in which side's favour, the helped or the hindered?

In writing this book, I have attempted to piece together the shards of my memory, like some medieval craftsman painstakingly repairing a shattered stained-glass window. To help me with the very tricky task of recollecting what on earth I was doing most of the time, I have invited a series of old friends out to lunch. (I considered calling the book *Out To Lunch With Rowland Rivron* but that sounded like I was reviewing restaurants and made me look far too responsible.) They have reminded me what I was really like and their recollections are scattered throughout the book. What picture emerges of me? I'll leave that for you to decide . . .

1: THE CALL OF THE DRUMS

Our school was different from most. Rather than run an achingly awful classical orchestra with children scratching badly on violins while they struggled with Schubert, Abbotsfield Secondary Comprehensive School in Hillingdon, Middlesex, had a big band. A big swing band.

We had a very charismatic French teacher called – no word of a lie – Mr Bean. This was a good thirty years before the name was hijacked by the talented Rowan Atkinson, a man to whom we'll come back later. Out of nothing and virtually single-handedly, 'Bean', as he was known, created an eighteen-piece school jazz orchestra. And from that grew my passion for performing. I got the itch as an eleven-year-old – and I've been scratching it, one way or another, ever since.

My older brother of three years, Raymond, already played saxophone in the band, so when I joined the school, being a lazy bastard, I said I'd play drums because drummers didn't have to read music – or so I thought. I took to it immediately. When it comes to learning an instrument, there's no point trying to force kids of that age to do something – they've got to want to do it. And, very quickly, drumming was all I wanted to do. We lived in what was laughably called a three-bedroomed house, in which the third bedroom was referred to as the box room, to give you some idea of its size.

I used to practise endlessly in that box-room facing onto the road, initially drumming along to *The Good, the Bad and the Ugly* – arguably the easiest thing to play on a kit cobbled together from second-hand bits and bobs. I'd recorded the soundtrack on to a reel-to-reel tape machine and would sit for hours banging away and driving everyone in the house and street mad. There's always one old dear who's the exception to the rule. She lived a little way down the road from us and on her way to the shops would stop outside our house to listen to me thrashing away. She loved it in that odd way old people take to the strangest things – skydiving springs to mind. She was, technically, my first fan. I was soon to learn the ladies love a drummer. What a pity she was easily in her early eighties.

The school big band had been up and running for six years when, aged fourteen, I inherited the drum seat. I was the youngest in the band – being the youngest of three brothers I'd pretty much always hung out with older people, so this wasn't quite as daunting as one might imagine. In fact, I forged stronger friendships with the older guys in the band than I ever did with anyone in my year group, the downside being I never really bonded with anyone in that 'best mate' kind of way. I honestly don't think I ever had a 'best mate'. Don't get the hankie out yet, although it might come in handy later.

There was a natural turnover in the members of the band, as once they'd done their A levels they had effectively left school and weren't eligible to play any more. It was quite a juggling act for Bean. He had to make sure the band was never short of players, so he would actively steer new kids starting school towards whatever instruments were played by those he knew would be leaving in the near future. I loved being in a band – the teamwork, the camaraderie, the showing off. As soon as I joined, I thought: 'This is it. This'll do me!'

Academia? Erm . . . how are you spelling that?

As a fourteen-year-old kid it never occurred to me, but what was amazing about the band was that it was completely self-sufficient – it didn't rely on anything from the school. We generated our own income, performing at paid functions all over London. The band even played in Paris, but that was with a chap by the name of Ian Mosley on drums, the bloke I was to replace. After leaving school, Ian promptly turned his back on jazz and eventually joined the progressive rock band Marillion, the band he's with to this day. Before joining forces with the great Fish, Ian worked in a drum shop on Shaftesbury Avenue, and naturally that would be my shop of choice whenever I wanted anything relating to drums. He would invite me out on to the street so a deal – at cost, basically – could be done on whatever it was I was after. Thanks for that, Ian. You were not only a family friend but also a very generous man, and I'm sure you had nothing to do with the shop eventually falling into receivership.

Fish appeared on my Radio 2 show, *Jammin'*, a few years back and was a joy. The compulsory pre-show 'tea and biscuits' in the Marlborough Arms, a pub round the corner from the Drill Hall, the gay and lesbian theatre in London where the show was recorded, was interesting. There's no hiding Fish. He's a big man, so it wasn't long before attention was drawn. Several drinkers, or possibly drunks, began calling out the word 'Fish' for no apparent reason other than to create a scene. This was water off a duck's back for Fish (what?). Apparently it happened wherever he went and was recognized. He sympathetically referred to these people as his 'Fish Heads' and thought nothing of it. As his proper name was William Dick, it occurred to me these 'Fish Heads' looked much more like 'Dick Heads' to me, but hey, never knock your fan-base. I did get to play in Paris eventually, but much later on and under laughably different circumstances, which we'll get to in good time.

All schools try to raise money. They have to, and it's usually a half-hearted pain in the arse. At Abbotsfield, school functions put on to raise money became major local events. They held dinner dances where people actually danced to an eighteen-piece orchestra. One year the Maynard Ferguson Orchestra (an international big band with a be-kaftanned, ear-splitting, rotund trumpeter at the helm) played, with the school band doing the first half and Maynard blowing us away in the second half. God knows how Bean did it, but on another occasion Dudley Moore turned up with Chris Karan on drums and Pete Morgan on bass and entertained a packed school hall. Not bad for suburban comp PTA fundraiser!

Around this time, Bean entered the band for a talent competition sponsored by a brewery. Think *X Factor* – but in a shitty pub. It did have its own Simon Cowell, however, in the shape of Tony Hatch, a composer best known for the *Crossroads* theme tune and a whole bunch of annoyingly catchy but slightly wet pop songs. Take a look at any pic-

ture of him from the seventies and, even without listening
to any of his music, you'd have to agree with me.

We didn't win the talent show but we suspected the
whole thing was rigged! Thirty-three years before phone
vote fixing became the norm, the art of cheating in talent
competitions seemed to be alive and kicking and happening
in a cavernous pub in Harrow-on-the-Hill. The Abbotsfield
School Jazz Orchestra came second to 'London's Liberace!',
a fresh-faced pianist called Bobby Crush. The winner was
assured a bunch of prestigious gigs and a recording contract. After all, we reasoned, if you were holding the
brewery's purse strings, who would you rather go with? An
eighteen-piece orchestra of children or a bloke who can play
the piano, any piano, anywhere, on his own? We suspected
economics had won out, although to be fair Bobby Crush
did win *Opportunity Knocks* (6 times!) and went on to
fame as 'the UK's favourite piano entertainer' (. . . surely
that's a man who entertains pianos – Ed.) and, no word
of a lie, has recently finished a limited run at London's
Leicester Square Theatre playing Liberace in *Liberace –
Live from Heaven!* Staying power or what?

Our Big Break came, rather incongruously, in December
1975, on the anniversary of Glenn Miller's death. For some
reason, in-between making rubbish toys out of household
items with sticky-back plastic and telling a far from funky
dog, Shep, to 'get down', *Blue Peter* thought it would be a
good idea to draw to the attention of twelve million kids the
death of the great Second World War band leader Glenn
Miller. The tribute would take the form of a big band,
similar to Glenn Miller's, performing his most famous tune,
'In the Mood', which topped the US charts for a staggering

fourteen weeks. That was, of course, in 1940 and probably the only record one could buy at the time. But what would be better than getting a kids' band to recreate that really old and outdated sound?

It occurred to me some time later that rather than play 'In the Mood' (a tune, apparently, about getting ready to have sex, for Christ's sake!), we should have played the very little-known tune 'In the Channel', as that's where he was at the time, his plane having gone down on 15 December 1944, somewhere over the English Channel. His official status as 'missing' leaves his sad fate open to suspicion. Some are convinced he died in a Parisian brothel; in which case, 'In the Mood' is easily the better choice of song.

This was a time when television really was king, and as far as kids' TV was concerned my top three were *Blue Peter*, *Animal Magic* and *The Flintstones*. They were the staple diet of conversation in every school playground. I would sometimes sneak a peek at the much trendier *Magpie* over on ITV, which was frowned upon in our house.

It's hard to believe now, but *Magpie* was very racy. On *Blue Peter*, you just knew that good old spinster Valerie Singleton could always be relied upon to be sporting an 'everything to the imagination' Platex bra and a girly slip under a frilly blouse and a neutral-coloured, unisex cardigan. I was convinced that Sue Stranks, the sexy woman fronting *Magpie*, wore absolutely nothing under that jumpsuit. The *Blue Peter* presenters all had nice, respectable hair – no hint of rebellion there – while on 'Magpie' they boasted much wilder and more anarchic hairstyles. One of the two male presenters, Mick Robertson, was sporting long curly hair and clogs way before Brian May made the combo really unfashionable. There was also a great contrast between the shows' signature tunes. One was a staid, traditional old sea shanty, the other a rocking contemporary number oozing sex and . . . magpies. *Blue Peter* was just altogether worthier, always saving the planet, while *Magpie* didn't appear to give a monkey's, teaching us how to tie-dye or make stink bombs.

Even so, I loved *Blue Peter,* and when we heard we were to appear on the show, everyone at school was over the moon. Everyone in the band, that is – everyone else was, obviously, insanely jealous and I was on the first bus to Coventry.

Television back then was a magical place, located far, far away. It seemed way out of reach for the likes of us. I thought, 'Blimey, I'm going to get a *Blue Peter* badge without having to pay for a Seeing Eye dog or bring a sparrow back to life.' A *Blue Peter* badge was a very big deal back then, and for children today it may still be. I'm not too sure about their exclusivity, though. A BBC wardrobe lady I once knew had a fishbowl full of them in her flat. I think the idea was you could help yourself to one whenever you were there. Then again, maybe you did have to earn one, in which case I am profusely sorry that I nicked a bunch from her.

The short journey to the BBC Television Centre up the A40 from Hillingdon remains a blur, but I do remember the feeling of nausea and the urge to go home the minute I got into the studio. The way they'd set the band up was a little odd, to say the least. Traditionally, the drum kit is right in the middle or to the side of the rest of the players and always within inches of the bass player and pianist. It makes for a more cohesive sound, as eye-contact between the piano, bass and drums is always a good thing.

For a reason that was never really explained, the drum kit in the *Blue Peter* studio was set up on a round podium about fifteen feet in front of the orchestra. I was completely cut off from the rest of the guys, unable to see anyone, communicate or have anything to do with them. It was as if I'd done something wrong and had been banished from the band, but was still required to provide the rhythm. Paranoia quickly set in, as I figured I wasn't even going to be seen playing on the bloody show – maybe Biddy Baxter, the show's producer, had been involved in some weird alter-cation with a drummer in her youth and consequently wanted nothing to do with them. As I said, I never got to the bottom of it.

A clip of our appearance on *Blue Peter* cropped up the other day on some TV show, and you can actually see me squinting off to one side at a monitor on the studio floor, trying desperately to see if anyone was pointing a camera at the kit. They were, and frequently, as it happened, so no harm done.

Random memories from that day have lodged in my mind. I remember the great John Noakes had a fag on the go the whole time in the studio. Over one or other of his shoulders there was always a 'No Smoking' sign to be read, but John had no truck with that and would only put the fag out when he was required to be in front of the camera. Odd that it was the complete opposite with me. In the very same studio, fifteen years later, while working with Dawn French and Jennifer Saunders as 'Duane', the pissed, bongo-playing younger half of the father and stepson duo Raw Sex, I would have a fag on the go the whole time he was in shot and then immediately spit it out as soon as the little red light on the camera went out.

The *Blue Peter* pets were kept in big cages and released at the last minute. As viewers, we always had the impression that the animals were allowed to roam around as if at home in the Noakes' rambling farmhouse. Thinking about it, though, there are a lot of electrical cables lying about in a TV studio. You only needed one of the animals, busting for a piss, to slip away and make a puddle in the wrong place – before you knew it they would be dropping the item on 'easy-to-make gift ideas for Fathers' Day' and relocating for a bit of live outside broadcast in the *Blue Peter* garden to bury either Petra, Patch, Shep, Goldie, Bonnie, Mabel, Lucy, Meg or Barney. And that's just the dogs! By the last count, they'd also got through nine cats, five tortoises and two parrots. Is it just me, or is that a bit excessive? Suddenly I'm seeing the show from a different angle: I'm looking at a bunch of kids playing a forty-year-old song about sex, dedicated to a dead bloke, while animals are being sacrificed left, right and centre for the sake of vanity and the ratings.

What made the experience completely surreal was that we recorded the programme at about one o'clock in the afternoon, on the same Thursday that it was to be broadcast. This meant there was a frantic dash to get home in time to watch it on telly at five o'clock. This was way before VHS machines, so we really did only have one crack at watching ourselves on telly, which of course made the whole thing that much more imperative. To us, anyway.

Television, especially the BBC, fascinated me. I loved it, couldn't get enough of it. Ten years later, one chilly Christmas night, the BBC would find they'd had more than enough of me . . .

2: 'HOB-KNOBBING' AT THE BEEB

To a restaurant in Soho, the heart of London's heady West End, to begin the 'Out to Lunch with Rowland Rivron' series of meals with old friends in order to piece together my splintered memories. It's probably best I don't mention the name of the restaurant, as the person I was to have lunch with had a slight misunderstanding there, years ago. A meal for two that came to a very reasonable £70 cropped up on his credit card bill later as £700. It seemed neither the card company nor the restaurant could help. Had this happened to me back then it would have been tantamount to financial ruin or would have resulted in imprisonment due to the ham-fisted torching of said restaurant. But that's John Lloyd all over: 'Don't make a fuss, dear boy. It's only money.'

After several false starts I managed to corner John *The News Quiz, To The Manor . . . , Not the Nine . . . , Blackadder, Hitchhiker's . . . , QI* Lloyd for a bowl of pasta and a bottle of Limoncello. He complained, 'I know what you're like, you're like David Frost. Whenever I have dinner with him it's the same. I'm going to say things I'm going to regret and don't want my children knowing about . . .'

He'd grown a beard since we'd last met. The beard, the

watery David Essex 'cow eyes' and the receding blond hair made him vaguely resemble a dashing German U-boat commander. A big, thick, white woolly roll-neck would have clinched it, but he's always been a shirt-and-tie man. Over the twenty-five years I've known John, unlike many, he doesn't seem to have developed a bitter and twisted view of the business. Obviously, his renowned dogged persistence with much-cherished projects has paid off. Dogged persistence? I must give that a try some time.

I was keen to talk to him, as I distinctly remember it was he who managed to talk Jasper Carrott out of punching the crap out of me years ago in the lounge bar of the Hilton Hotel in Holland Park. A whole bunch of people ended up there after the 1983 BBC Light Entertainment Christmas party, held just up the road at TV Centre earlier that evening. Everybody who was anybody in light entertainment and comedy at the BBC attended the Christmas party – an invitation to the event signalled you'd arrived and were part of the corporation. The invite wasn't one to pop on the mantelpiece and promptly forget.

John was there in the *Not the Nine O'clock News* camp, as he produced the show. I was there in *The Young Ones* camp, completely fraudulently of course, as I had absolutely nothing to do with the programme. Alexei Sayle, Nigel Planer, Ade Edmondson, Ben Elton, Rik Mayall and Lise Mayer comprised *The Young Ones* camp that night; I just happened to live with Rik and Lise, his girlfriend and co-writer, at the time so was invited along for the ride. It happened quite a bit in those days. I think I was playing the 'Jimmy Five Bellies' role to Rik's slightly more abstemious 'Paul Gascoigne'. Lise found it easier and safer to have me standing at the bar with Rik, matching him pint for pint, and as long as we stayed on the beer and didn't move on to the spirits, she knew there'd be few tears . . .

John was originally first choice to produce *The Young Ones* and fondly remembers the script 'turning up on his desk', stained with semen and Marmite, and covered in scribble (the script, not his desk; I don't think John likes Marmite . . .). All very anarchic, of course, which was how everyone regarded the show.

He didn't take the show because, as he freely admits, back in the day he was genuinely scared of the new alternative comedians when they arrived on the scene. I think the die was cast when he showed up at one of the early Comedy Store nights. Originally, the Store was above a dodgy strip club in a poky side street in Soho, and access to the venue was by way of a small, rickety old lift. Curiously, it was considered by many as the birthplace of alternative comedy and yet – no sexist jokes here – I remember, for a time, the barmaids being topless, a legacy of the building's former strip club status . . . John had gone along to see Clive Anderson, who I think was a friend of his. By day Clive was a fully paid-up barrister and by night an aspiring comedian. He bounced on stage and promptly announced that the ex-Oxbridge, very important BBC Radio 4 producer of comedy, John Lloyd, was in the audience. Not a good move, especially the Oxbridge reference. Things were shouted – not very nice things – but John did the three-quarter stand, nodded, sat back down and tried as best he could to blend in and become invisible.

The evening moved on very agreeably until it was time for the poor man to leave. He quickly found himself trapped, alone, in the rickety old lift, the only means of escape from the club. The main perpetrator of the barracking John had received that night, Keith Allen, had deftly torn a knackered old radiator off the wall and, somehow, wedged it in the lift gates so that the whole thing ground, quite dangerously, to a halt. In most films when something like that happens, you can put money on the baying crowd, in this case the alternative comedians, carting the captive off, parading him around on a stick for a bit and eventually eating him alive. That didn't happen because he was now sat opposite me tucking into lobster pasta, and anyway alternative comedians are all big softies, even the professional heckler and self-appointed Godfather of alternative comedy, Tony Allen (no relation to Keith).

At the Light Entertainment Christmas party, John was surprised at how glamorous *The Young Ones* camp looked. He'd expected the new comedy anarchists to arrive on ropes, crashing through windows dressed in army fatigues, with shaved eyebrows and laughing manically. As it was, Lise always looked good, but Rik and I had pushed the boat out with a couple of Moss Bros' finest for the occasion. Some people didn't initially recognize Rik, to which Rik, being Rik, didn't take too kindly. Something had to be done and, unfortunately, Rik left it up to me, as usual. On my return from the gentleman's lavatory, Gareth Gwenlan, the head of comedy for the BBC, was the first one to spot the small oversight. We were all standing in a circle giggling when Gareth joined us. This was the man who okayed all the comedy on the BBC at the time, so the giggling stopped and the pleasantries came thick and fast.

John claims it was a good minute or so before Gareth

clocked the 'old man' hanging out of my very sharp tux. Wow! You got it! Anarchy or what!? Looking for an exit from this embarrassing and quite frankly childish situation, Gareth asked if anyone wanted a drink. Not waiting for a reply, he turned on his heels and disappeared, and I followed him muttering something about me having a large one . . . (It pains me to recount this story but I really think it's better out than in, fnarr fnarr.) Luckily, I was virtually wrestled to the ground by Rik and Lise, who were looking forward to a long and illustrious career with the BBC and didn't want to nip it in the bud quite yet. Me? I just fancied another free drink.

Fully refreshed and with the 'old man' back in bed, I attempted to circulate, only getting as far as Ronnie Corbett's wife, whom I very nearly talked into buying a painting I had removed from the wall minutes earlier. I was getting into my stride. There were two huge televisions, one either side of the impressive Christmas tree, both showing clips from the BBC comedy archive. All very good but just a bit predictable – so after a little fiddling about we were soon enjoying *The Sweeney* on ITV and whatever was happening on the fledgling Channel Four (at that time of night, probably a test card and a continuous, electronically produced E sharp).

My parents were big fans of it, and so were the BBC. No, not proper English – vinyl wallpaper. When it was first launched, the adverts for it on TV were bonkers. A happy, smiley couple bounded into their drab living room with an armful of wallpaper. Seconds later, the room's had been wallpapered and looked, to their mind, fantastic! A few seconds on, the same couple were effortlessly removing the wallpaper with one simple tug. The big selling point for vinyl wallpaper was that you could remove each 'drop' in one go: 'It's vinyl! It's simple! It's, quite literally, off the wall!' Basically, buy some wallpaper you have so little confidence in that you'll want to remove it the minute it's up.

Even if you half-liked the look of it once it was on the wall, the temptation to have it off the wall 'in one easy tug!' never went away. In the very swanky executive boardroom where the BBC party was being held, I managed to remove one-and-a-half 'drops' before I was moved on. I offered to Sellotape it back on to the wall, but this fell on deaf ears as the person who had moved me on was now desperately trying to re-tune the two giant TVs either side of the Christmas tree.

John seems to think Leslie Ash was there as the then girlfriend of Rowan Atkinson. I'm not so sure as she went to leave the party, not with Rowan, but with a girlfriend neither of us can place. Much like the original Comedy Store, it seemed the only way to come and go from the fifth-floor party was via a lift that opened straight into the room and didn't stop at any other floors. It was a bona-fide executive lift, the type you only saw in American films. By now, I couldn't be held responsible for my actions. As the two women entered the lift, I pleaded with them not to go, but they were insistent that they'd had enough and anyway it was really boring. Boring? Right! As the two inner doors of the lift began to close, out came the 'old man' again, which I offered up and positioned between the two outer doors as they too began to slide shut. Lesley and her friend, realizing what was about to happen, began screaming just before the inner doors of the lift closed. A second later, I began screaming as the outer doors came, silently, together. I'll never forget the sound of those two gorgeous women getting fainter and fainter as the lift descended directly to the ground floor.

'I have to say, every moment, every minute I've been in your company, it's been an exquisite pleasure. I'm struggling to think of anyone else I've ever met that I can say that of. We've never had a cross word,' says John Lloyd (Limoncello'd).

If you were a big enough name, the Hilton Hotel at Holland Park was where the BBC put you up as long as your journey home after a bash was more than sixty-two-and-a-quarter miles – they were sticklers like that. Having, justifiably, been kicked out of the party, I found myself along with a group of others in the lounge bar of the Hilton. This was where Birmingham's finest, Jasper Carrott, had been 'put up' as London to Birmingham is 101.5 miles. Not so for myself, Rik and Lise – London to Islington is nothing, 'so sod off home!' Technically, we were in the bar as Jasper's guests, as it was the middle of the night, and we all had a drink in our hand. This was a very magnanimous gesture from a man I only knew as the bloke responsible for the annoying, 1975 novelty top-five single, 'Funky Moped'. What better way of expressing my thanks for his generosity than by offering him a cigarette from the solid silver cigarette box I had nicked from the party? I lunged towards Jasper who was sitting next to John on a huge sofa. I opened the box and offered it to Jasper, completely forgetting that I had soaked all the fags in brandy while still at the party – I was convinced I'd invented a way of smoking and drinking at the same time. The contents of the beautiful, mahogany-lined, solid silver cigarette box were now a stinking, syrupy fag-goo that dripped on to Jasper's sofa, dangerously near to the arm of his immaculate, cream dinner suit.

With good reason, Mr Carrott threatened to punch me full in the face if I came any nearer with my gooey cigarette box, and it was only the intervention by John that averted a horrible end to what was a very happy evening, I thought.

The meal over, the wrong side of two bottles of wine and a bottle of Limoncello, John made his impeccably polite excuses and was gone within a matter of seconds. I got the impression I'd been very privileged to have spent nearly two hours with a man who was a force to be reckoned with in the business. It took a while for the penny to drop. Seduced by his natural charm, I had failed to spot that because of his experiences in the very same restaurant all those years ago, he obviously has no intention of ever paying for a meal again in his life. And who can blame him? When you're as lovely as John Lloyd, surely it's almost a God-given right to have someone else pick up the tab. So I was left to settle the bill. Note to self: must buy a good magnifying glass to scrutinize the next credit card statement.

3: SCHOOL AFFAIRS

If I was prostrate on the psychiatrist's couch, he'd be steering me back to my childhood and blaming my desire to trap my knob in an executive lift on something that happened when I was a toddler. I remember once mentioning to someone I was fond of a lady's high shoe and they came straight back with, 'That'll be because you used to play around with your mother's high heels when you were a little boy.' But then, I used to play around with my mum's fags as a kid and I'm not fond of women who smoke particularly. Having said that, something did happen when I was about four years old and it was to do with my mum's fags . . . Shit, there might be something in this.

Mum and Dad, Pete and Ruth to you, were smokers. But then again everyone was when I was a kid. We won the World Cup in 1966, and I'm sure I remember watching the game on our grainy twenty-one-inch black and white television set and seeing the England goalkeeper having a crafty fag whenever the ball was down the German end. My mum and dad were sucking on forty a day when I was a kid, so cigarettes were part of the scenery. We had an Austin A40, hand-painted black by my father with a two-inch brush. Whenever we went anywhere in it, the heady combo of Mum's Elnett L'Oréal hairspray, Dad's Old Spice aftershave and the fag smoke that quickly built up in the cramped confines of that little car was incredible. You could have flushed out the most persistent of Taliban rebels with what was happening in that car. Nobody thought smoke was dangerous – on cold mornings, my Dad would go out and start the car to let the engine warm up before heading off to work. We kids would follow him out and have a whale of a time playing in the exhaust 'fog' the Austin belched out – we'd think it was just like floating around on a cloud up in heaven. Playing out there on those frosty mornings, none of us realized how close we were to actually ending up in heaven. Not only were we allowed to 'go and play in the car's exhaust fumes, kids', but go and play in the road, in the exhaust fumes.

So, back to my mum's fags. I'm the youngest of three brothers, and we're all three years apart in age. Our names all start with an 'R', end with a 'D' and have seven letters. Our parents maintain it was not engineered, but I have my doubts. They were always cagey about it when questioned and would quickly throw the focus to other names. Suddenly, they'd be talking about the bloke who lived next door to us and how odd it was that he was Scottish and his second name happened to be 'Bruce'. And how even odder it was that his first name – wait for this – was 'Jock', for Christ's sake. The thing was that Mum and Dad were dead right. It was true; we did live next door to a Scotsman who answered to the name Jock Bruce – 'uncle' Jock as I remember. He wasn't any relation, of course, but anyone Pete and Ruth were close to and had known for a long time automatically became an honorary uncle or aunt to us three kids. It wasn't as if we were short of them, either; my dad was one of eleven brothers and sisters, every one a smoker and most of them barking mad, in the nicest possible way. Whenever we visited my aunty Ida, she would always sport a bandage on one or other of her perfectly healthy legs – as she would say, 'just in case . . .'

So there we were, Richard, Raymond and Rowland (aah, of course . . .) all playing happily at home when I decided to show off to my brothers – I'm told it happened quite often. Much like a rat in London today, in the sixties at 19 Keith Park Road, you were never more than nine feet from a packet of fags. I started mucking about with Mum's fags, pretending to smoke one, probably in a very camp way – it never really worked if you tried to do the moody, James Dean look. I'd managed to command their attention flouncing about with a fag in my hand when Mum came into the room, not best pleased at my antics. Suddenly it was a case of 'if you want a cigarette, you're going to have a cigarette'. Out came the lighter and before I had time to scream 'social services!', I was puffing on a John Player King Size. Even though I was turning green, she made me smoke all of it in front of Rich and Ray who were crying their eyes out and screaming, 'Mummy, make it stop!'

Apart from actually having me, I can honestly say making me smoke that cigarette was the best thing my mother could have done because, try as I might, I have never been able to get the hang of smoking since. The one addictive drug you can buy in a sweet shop and I snap shut like a book every time I take a drag. Raw Sex toured for a year with French and Saunders and as Duane, the fag-smoking piss head, I would regularly get through fifteen fags a night but, like Bill Clinton, I 'never inhaled'.

I really thought I would get the taste for them. I played for a while with the brilliant jazz pianist, Simon Wallace, and remember being envious of the effect Simon's first fag of the day had on him. I would ask him to describe the feeling and try to equate it with something I had experienced – a warm bath, sex, a pint – but he couldn't, or wouldn't for fear of being held responsible for my eventual lung cancer. I know what you're thinking, 'You don't know how lucky you are, not being a slave to the death sticks', but he did look cool playing the piano with a cigarette hanging out of his mouth. A cigarette is the only thing I've ever turned down – and that was when I was four!

Apart from the fag incident, life at 19 Keith Park Road was pretty idyllic. We lived in married quarters on a sprawling Royal Air Force base in Uxbridge, Middlesex. 'The camp', as we called it, was home to the grand-sounding Central Band of the Royal Air Force. My dad was in it, playing the clarinet.

My kids are babysat by a sixteen-year-old girl from up the road, but when I was a child the only babysitters I can remember were members of the band Dad was in, obviously looking for a few extra bob. One of them, Herbie Flowers, then playing tuba for the Central Band, went on to provide the iconic bass line for Lou Reed's 'Walk on the Wild Side', amongst other things. Forty-two years later, when he kindly appeared as a guest muso on my Radio 2 programme, *Jammin'*, he pretty much stole the show with embarrassing anecdotes about my time in nappies.

The Central Band was where Pete and Ruth met, my mother being in the Women's Royal Air Force Band. She played the cornet and marching drum, but never at the same time – that would be showing off. They married in their lunch break at the registry office in Uxbridge and rented a flat a couple of hundred yards from the band headquarters where they worked. That just doesn't happen these days, does it? Once we kids started coming thick and fast, not literally, they set up home in the married quarters within Uxbridge RAF Camp. From a small, loo-in-the-garden, dingy house in the aptly named Grays Road, they moved up in the world and settled in Keith Park Road where I spent the first ten years of my life.

I use the word 'idyllic' because life in married quarters on an RAF camp wasn't like living in the real world. For a start, I don't think I saw, smelt or came into contact with a granny or a granddad until I was about seven. This was at my first 'play date' with a friend after school and his grandmother lived with the family. She sat motionless in a high-backed chair in the corner of the living room, latching on to fragments of conversation, fruitlessly trying to keep up with what was going on around the house. Because of dear old gran's frail, confused state, the family didn't have a lock on the loo door, and while it was bad enough actually going to the toilet in someone else's house when you are a shy seven-year-old, to attempt it in a loo with no lock on the door? Per-lease!

The RAF camp 'didn't do' old people. All the 'grown-ups' were in their thirties or forties, roughly the same age as my mum and dad. Most of the dads worked alongside each other as bandsmen. We had a different, 'no lock' policy in the married quarters thanks to the nine-foot perimeter fence we lived behind and the security checks on the gates we came and went through. No one locked anything, no one had need to, as we were completely protected from the outside world. This also meant there was no through traffic, so we didn't have the worry of big lorries or buses hurtling past our front garden, which, I suppose, goes part of the way to explaining Mum and Dad's relaxed attitude with the Austin A40 toxic 'fog fun'.

Maybe it's the way everyone looks back at their early schooldays and I'm being mind-numbingly predictable, but St Andrew's Primary School was something straight out of a fifties' feel-good British movie. True, I was there in the early sixties, but Richard, my eldest brother, started there in 1955 and, to the best of my knowledge, nothing had changed by the time I was old enough to attend eight years later. There was the kindly, white-haired, old and almost unnaturally small first-year infant teacher called Mrs Bees, whom you'd hug all morning until Mum arrived to pick you up and take you back to sights, sounds and smells you were more comfortable with.

By the fourth-year juniors, there was the classic, tall, spindly, pointy-nosed dragon – her name? Mrs Cutter. Talk about names painting a picture. I was hopeless at reading, but dyslexia didn't exist in the sixties. So she just had me down as thick, and Mrs Cutter didn't like thick people, people who couldn't read out loud in front of the class from a 'Janet and John' book. Each morning before school, while Dad was downstairs making a cup of tea, I'd climb into bed with Mum for a bit of 'hot-house' reading in the hope I could go unnoticed in class later that day. I'd read the same page over and over again until I'd almost learnt it off by heart – to this day, I can still remember the opening lines of that bastard Janet and John book: '"My brother John can ride a pony," said Janet . . .' Gripping stuff.

The caretaker was straight out of Central Casting with his broad grin, shuffly gait and tweedy woollen trousers held up by a thick leather strap that had no use for belt loops. Even on the coldest days his collarless shirt, sleeves rolled to the elbows, would suffice. For the nicest, kindest old bloke you could ever wish to meet to fit perfectly into my feel-good British movie, the caretaker's name would have to be something contrary like Mr Savage – which it bloody was! It must be a killer, being a teacher with an odd 'sir name'. Mrs Ouching, there's another one – the head mistress at St Andrew's; lovely lady, crazy name.

St Andrew's Primary School and the adjacent St Andrew's Church were both built in 1864. The church was an impressive building that survives to this day, unlike the school buildings, which were ruthlessly knocked down in the early seventies to make way for a better road system. As you'd expect from the tactless march of time, I think the church is now located in the middle of an impenetrable five-lane roundabout. The school was rebuilt in a field nearby, all continuity with the church, sadly, gone forever. Well done, guys.

I'm not a religious man, but I have spent a fair amount of time in church, having married into a Catholic family with more than its fair share of nuns and priests. My first brush with the Lord's house, however, was at primary school where every Friday assembly was held in St Andrew's Church adjacent to the infants' playground. I quickly sussed that it was possible to miss most of the first lesson after the Friday church assembly if you had a job helping the vicar during the service. You could string out the tidying, putting stuff away and hanging cassocks up, before eventually ambling back to class. I got the gig as one of the two processional candle-bearers. We wandered around with huge burning candles fixed into even bigger brushed-chrome candlesticks, which were nearly as big as us. My mate Richard Penny and I were easily the macho element of the whole show. No poncing about holding books or fetching things for the vicar for us – we were in charge of the big fiery things. If there was any trouble, I got the impression it would be us people would come to for help. The vicar eventually had to 'let me go'; he was a stickler for getting things right – which is fair enough – and was never keen on spontaneous laughter in church.

No two Friday assemblies seemed to be the same (he 'supposed' with 'sibilance'); there was always a new angle to each service. One week, a special candle was set up in the pulpit, which had to be lit at a given moment – all very symbolic. Seeing as I was the candle-bearer nearest the elevated pulpit, accessed by some wooden spiral stairs, I was going to do the lighting. This had to be done with what was basically a small taper candle, wedged at an angle on the end of a wooden pole. It was the same pole used to snuff the candles out, so I could see the logic in using that. What I couldn't get the hang of was when to get up and light the bloody thing. The first time I got up off my knees, I lit the taper and headed for the pulpit. Thankfully, the vicar was able to intercept me, merely with his eyes, and let me know that this was not the time and that I should go back and kneel down. The natural reaction to cover embarrassing situations like this is to break out a little smile or maybe a fleeting giggle – I *was* only ten.

The second time I got up to go, I fired up the small taper and made it as far as the bottom of the spiral stairs so, unfortunately, had lost eye contact, momentarily, with the vicar. Just as my head appeared over the banister of the pulpit, I spotted the vicar shaking his head furiously and waving me back. 'Not now?' I muttered. I then caught a glimpse of the kids in the pews below me and tutted to the audience – a mistake. I headed back down the spiral stairs and emerged only to be confronted by the whole of the first row giggling uncontrollably, shoulders going nineteen to the dozen. Third time lucky, and this time with the blessing of the vicar waving me towards the pulpit, I headed up the spiral stairs to light the special candle. Sadly, it wasn't to be – the taper on the end of the stick had finally burnt down to its base and gone out. I sheepishly re-emerged at the bottom of the spiral stairs and pointed to the smoking taper. There was now audible laughter from the congregation. The vicar handed me a box of matches and, stepping out of the reverential moment, barked, 'Use these, boy!'

The vicar didn't bear a grudge. Later that year, he invited all the boys who were going on to secondary school and had helped in church down into the vicarage cellar. He was in the process of bottling his homemade sherry and very kindly let us give him a hand. And very good sherry it was, too.

* * *

Moving on to secondary school coincided with the family moving off the RAF camp and into Civvy Street, to 47

Merton Avenue, to be precise. This was a semi-detached forties' house in a sprawling estate adjacent to Abbotsfield Secondary Comprehensive Boys School. On a good day it was a twenty-minute walk to school, and on a bad day, four minutes in Dad's British racing green Triumph 1300 Toledo. Unlike his first motor, the Austin A40, Dad was obviously happy with the paint-job British Leyland had done on the car, as there was no need for the two-inch, natural bristle brush and pot of all-weather paint.

I was quite fortunate in that my two brothers had attended the same school. By the time I got there, I pretty much knew everyone which, rather embarrassingly, meant pretty much everyone knew me. Richard had left with flying colours the year I joined. After a false start with an apprenticeship at a professional football club, he was training to become a teacher. He had quickly become disillusioned with the world of professional football. Although he spent a brief time in the England Amateur Youth Squad, he wasn't too happy about some of the things they were being taught at the club where he regularly played – how to commit fouls without the referee noticing certainly rubbed him up the wrong way. The amount of daytime the players spent in the bookies or bingo halls when not training also got to him, so he changed tack and headed for York College and academia, emerging a few years later a PE teacher. (OK, he became a PE teacher.)

Raymond was still at Abbotsfield being a genius at everything as long as it was indoors. Unlike Rich, sport eluded our Ray. You name it and he could turn his hand to it. Art, music, languages – he even made a gun once that actually worked! The house he lives in today, in the shadow of Castle Coch in Wales, is an astonishing shrine to his DIY aptitude and imagination. It wouldn't surprise me if, one weekend, he razed it to the ground and then simply rebuilt it again, in time for Monday, on a slightly different angle, this time so the living room got less sunlight. A pallid man despite his name, Ray was never good with sunshine. Rich and I were always slaves to the tan, but Ray's got all the wide-brimmed hats and takes the ribbing in good spirits, probably because he knows full well he'll have the last laugh.

Before I had time to misbehave at Abbotsfield, Raymond had become head boy, which meant any plans I had for mucking about at school went straight out the window – brother of the head boy getting into trouble? No chance. Getting the shit kicked out of me? No problem. I think the kicker's name was Dennis. Everyone knew him as the school's trouble-making nightmare. He set about my face with his hands in a similar way a top chef at Benihana would set about a raw prawn with a pair of sharp knives.

Teachers didn't know what to do with him and he didn't know what to do with himself, so he would regularly go bonkers and lash out. As with the yet to be diagnosed dyslexia I suffered from, this poor chap probably had something that, today, would be succinctly classified and comprehensively understood, and have generated its own cabinet full of concoctions and tablets to alleviate the problem. In 1975, he was just a nutter – who happily kicked the living daylights out of me for no better reason than the fact that my brother was the 'Perfect Peter' head boy.

Once, as I left the last lesson of the day, someone approached me and calmly said there was going to be a big fight in the 'quiet' playground – schools don't have them nowadays for health and safety reasons, as it's the ideal place for someone to get a surreptitious kicking – and that I was going to be one of the people fighting. Naturally, I thought he was pulling my leg. He wasn't. Dennis was more than ready to push my face in. When I got there, the young, psyched-up Dennis was being very quiet in the 'quiet' playground; it was the other fifty kids that were making the noise I could hear yards before I turned the final corner into the now heaving playground.

It didn't take long. To be honest, I don't think I really had the 'fight' in me. I was being punched in the face because my older brother was the head boy. I had no idea what Dennis's older brother did – whatever it was, I'm sure it didn't warrant me trying to break his little brother's nose. On my walk home, the throbbing in my face grew progressively worse as bits began to swell and by the time I was home one eye had closed completely. Mum took one look at me and assumed I'd fallen out of a tree – under a truck would've been closer to the mark – and I quickly put her straight and mentioned Dennis's involvement. Like mums do, she went berserk and was all for marching up to school there and then. I managed to talk her round as I didn't want my mum fighting any of my battles. Perversely Dennis was all smiles the next day, even asking if I was OK. I lied, telling him I was fine and asked after his welfare. He confessed to a slight soreness on the knuckles of his right hand. 'Oh well, that's not too bad then,' I replied, but his mind had moved on. I left him screeching obscenities at a foreign exchange student teacher making her way across the play-ground.

* * *

Richard had not only done fairly well on the academic front – passing whatever paper he put his mind to – but was also the team captain in just about every competitive sport the school had to offer. Ray took all the 'easy' A levels a year or so before everyone else in order to free up enough time in the sixth form to do a bunch of exams that no one had ever heard of or seen before. These would enable him to move seamlessly into medical school, we were told. I have to take my brimless hat off to him: he was one of only a handful of people fast-tracked from a secondary comp sixth form straight into first-year medical college. It cost Mum and Dad an arm and a leg to get him through med school, which was ironic, as he became an ear, nose and throat doctor. So no pressure on the third son, muggins here, bringing up the rear, to do well. To shine.

What the pitiless Mrs Cutter had perceived as thickness in my third year at St Andrew's hadn't gone away and was alive and kicking at Abbotsfield. I don't think dyslexia existed round our way until the late seventies, certainly not before the massive, long hot summer of 1976, the year all my O level revision took place in the garden of 47 Merton Avenue, flat out on a sun lounger. Even at secondary school, I was still considered a little thick. Beautifully tanned, but a little thick.

In order to blend in at school and create the impression that the third Rivron wasn't going to disappoint, I had to employ a degree of ingenuity. I quickly sussed that some of the subjects at school were taught in a two-year cycle. You can understand that; teachers would turn bonkers going over the same topics year in, year out. They'd get demoralized, lose interest, turn to drink and probably end up marrying a pupil, convinced it was the best thing that had ever happened to them. This only happened once at our school and I wouldn't mind but for the fact it was my first girlfriend who was the pupil in question – the cow. Anyway, cycles. This meant, for example, some people at school had done exactly the same History course work I was doing for my exams, but two years earlier. See where I'm going?

The school jazz orchestra was made up of students from all years. During my time drumming for the band, there were three guys in the trombone section who were all older than me. Gary Lewis, although a good friend, was only a year older, so was of absolutely no use to me on the academic front. Clive Robson and Steve Berry, however, were both two years ahead and one of them had taken History with my teacher, Mr Phelps. Perfect! When it was my turn to sit the History mocks, I simply smuggled Clive's entire mock History exam answers into the classroom and pretty much copied them out word for word. In the perfect world of comedy, I would now go on to report that, unbeknownst to me, Clive had spectacularly failed his mock History exam. But we both passed with flying colours! I lived to impress for another day.

If Mr Phelps did smell a rat, he didn't mention it. He was the friendliest, most 'down with the kids' teacher you could ever wish to meet. Not every lunchtime, but often during my O levels I would find myself squashed in the back of someone's mum's car and on the way to a pub for a quick pint and a packet of crisps. It was thirsty work, this learning business. A pragmatic Mr Phelps thought it very amusing that, on occasion, I'd turn up for his afternoon lesson slightly the worst for wear. 'Go and sit at the back, Rivron. Take in what you can and try not to fall asleep.'

Over the years, a handful of the teachers had become family friends, all very unprofessional, I know, but they had witnessed more than ten years of Rivrons come through the school with unblemished records. Mr Phelps was one such teacher. Often after the school fundraising dances the jazz orchestra played at, Mum and Dad would invite a few people back to our house. Seeing as the school hall would only have been granted a drinks licence until half past ten, it wasn't the cosiest of places for a lock-in. I, of course, would be sent straight to bed, but the sound of some of the nicer teachers from my school having a great time downstairs in our front room, while I drifted off to sleep, made my years at secondary school all the more disarming.

Mr Phelps was one of the lovable odd ones. He wore dark-coloured velour jackets and was the sort of man who could carry off a bow tie without being laughed at. With an olive complexion, very high cheek bones, pointy nose and slicked back hair, he could easily pass for the love child of Mr Burns, the nuclear-power-plant-owner from *The Simpsons*.

My brother Richard fondly remembers the time he was in Mr Phelps' A level History class, when a schoolmate, Robin Hill, known affectionately as Dobbin – I think he had once, very briefly, resembled a horse – locked Mr Phelps in the History room store cupboard. There were not many, if any, teachers you could do that to, knowing they weren't going to go ballistic and thrash you to within an inch of your life – remember, it was the 1970s. Mr Phelps took it in his stride. When he was eventually let out, he saw the funny side of it and made a big thing of doing a 'note to self' along the lines of 'never leave keys in store cupboard door during lessons'. The students loved him all the more for it. Clever man.

For a time he ran the school photographic club and would often be seen wandering around the school in the lunch break taking pictures of some of the more photogenic pupils. Nothing wrong with that. It was the mid-seventies – obviously, one couldn't do that today. I'm not even allowed to take a picture of my own flesh and blood in the nativity play at his infant school these days, for fear I might catch some other kid's elbow in the picture and then that's it – 'Would you mind coming with me, sir? I'm afraid we suspect that photo of your son dressed up as what we can only assume is a sheep has the tip of Child A's elbow clearly visible in the background, if viewed through an electron microscope.' Apart from the bastard long-haired teacher running off with my very first girlfriend, this was a simpler, more naive time. Or so I thought . . .

Mr Brady was an English teacher who joined the school when I was in the fourth year, so was a bit of an unknown quantity. He had similar qualities to Mr Phelps, in as much as he never seemed to get annoyed or lose it with anyone. We later learnt they had both been at the same boarding school, so that all made sense. Mr Brady can be best described as looking like a prime contender for Hasbro's 'Flip 'N' Find Face Game' called 'Guess Who?' He had a distinctive haircut, a distinctive goatee beard, wore distinctive, thick, pebble glasses and would often be seen in one of those very distinctive Alpine-style trilbies, the ones with the little feather on one side. Weirdos wear them.

I clearly remember that once during English he very matter-of-factly described, in far too much detail, what tugboat sailors got up to with semen – and no, I haven't misspelt it. It's not fair that I should have to remember what he said and for you to be left blissfully unaware – why should it just be me who has to try and get through life saddled with this sort of 'information'? If you really can't bear to be enlightened, please look away now:

Apparently, the semen is collected and stored until it solidifies.

And then it's carved into figurines.

Good God, I feel better for that, now I've said it. And, as we're all up to speed on the tugboat skipper front, it means I can get on with my life – and with a bit more of a spring in my step.

Still trying to maintain the deceit to my parents and teachers that I was everything my two brothers were and more, I pulled off a beautiful fast one – I can't believe I've just written that straight after the tugboat revelation – and it was Mr Brady who I conned.

We'd been given an assignment to write a poem using 'analogy', which I couldn't really get my head round. That night I asked our resident genius, Raymond, what I was supposed to do. He deftly explained that it was a form of logical inference, reasoning that if two things are taken to be alike in a particular way, they are alike in certain other ways.

'Yeah, right . . . but what the bloody hell does "analogy" mean?'

Rich was a big fan of Jethro Tull, the electric-folk-rock band fronted by singer/songwriter and flautist, Ian Anderson, who was famed for standing on one leg when playing the flute. Rather than try to explain what 'analogy' was, Rich played me a track from Tull's 1971 album, *Aqualung*, in an attempt to hammer home the concept. I listened intently to the track and gave a perceptive nod but was still none the wiser. I handed in the assignment and Mr Brady gave me a very commendable sixteen out of twenty. OK, when I say 'me' I mean, 'Ian Anderson got a very commendable sixteen out of twenty', as I'd copied the lyrics word for word from the sleeve notes. The track was called 'Locomotive Breath', but I nimbly threw everyone off the scent by calling it 'No Way To Slow Down' by Rowland Rivron (yeah, right!).

> *In the shuffling madness*
> *Of the locomotive breath,*
> *Runs the all-time loser,*
> *Headlong to his death.*

It goes on like this, interminably, using several words I didn't even know the meaning of.

So well done, Ian: sixteen out of twenty. Not bad, my English teacher Mr Brady obviously thought. However, there was some improvement to be had and as far as he was concerned, you could have done better. As far as I was concerned, once again I'd lived to lie another day.

* * *

Mr Brady and Mr Phelps's time was soon to come to an end. It must have happened over a half-term holiday, or maybe the police waited until then, as they needed a few days when they knew there wouldn't be any kids getting in the way and the place would be deserted. Abbotsfield School was located at the top of Clifton Road, and the first, tantalizing morsel of news filtered through from my mate who lived at the bottom of Clifton Road. He'd seen it all – loads of police had suddenly descended on the school. What could have happened? I'd been at the school nearly five years and had never seen a single policeman there. We immediately went into supposition overdrive. A pupil who had left school under a cloud had obviously returned to seek revenge by wrecking the place. Or a couple of villains 'on the run' were hiding out in the school and we were all in for a juicy siege. Or a lethal gas was escaping from the chemistry lab and the locals were dropping like flies. We were all way off the mark.

Mr Phelps and Mr Brady were found together in a wood somewhere in Wales. They'd poisoned themselves, apparently. They did this as soon as they heard the police were going to search the teachers' classrooms and lockers. Suddenly, everything made sense: Mr Brady's canal barge weekends organized for the third-year boys; Mr Phelps' photo sessions in the media studio with a bunch of second-year kids, all dressed up in fetching togas. It all seemed fairly harmless stuff at the time, but what happened in the wood was to blow it all out of the water. By the time half-term was over and we were all back to school, it was as if 'that chap who taught History' and 'that other bloke, the English teacher' had never worked at Abbotsfield. Mr Phelps and Mr Brady never existed. Which was a real shame.

Loads of people pointed to the fact this wouldn't have

happened at a mixed school. Abbotsfield Boys was a single-sex school and mixed with Swakeleys Girls only in the sixth form, arguably the worst, most distracting time a hormone-pumping boy could be introduced to the female sex. There you are, sixteen years old, having only really come into contact with girls in a 'let's throw conkers at that bunch of girls walking home from school as we like the idea of them, but this is the only way we know how to communicate' kind of way. Suddenly, they're in our classroom, being really sensible, stinking the place out with their heady perfume and sitting next to us! All day!

I'm citing the fact that the all-boys arrangement at Abbotsfield found me, for the briefest of moments I hasten to add, fancying a lad in the year below me. Thankfully, I've since learnt that all boys of a certain age go through the same thing and if you don't, well, aren't you just the strutting alpha-male lady-killer with your great big antlers and your rock-solid sexuality? I obviously wasn't gay. The attraction must have only lasted about five minutes and I didn't fancy any of the other boys – and there were some corkers at Abbotsfield, I'm telling you. Maybe if I try to describe what he looked like, you'll understand where I was coming from.

Then again, I don't want to start unlocking any 'closet' in the back of my mind that might get me going. It was all of thirty-six years ago, but it would be like playing with fire; a lot of laughs, but really dangerous. Let's just say this chap I was briefly besotted with wasn't a million miles, in looks, from a teenage Ronald Allen, the very handsome matinee idol who for sixteen years from the late sixties managed a motel near Birmingham called Crossroads.

I could never work out whether my school was rough or not. We did have the comp school chip on our shoulder and each year had a class full of kids who only ever seemed to do brick work and gardening lessons, never carried satchels and weren't allowed anything sharp like pencils. But it was nowhere near the bedlam that some schools have been tagged with. Maybe I caught the school just as it had got its act together, as there had been an incident, way before my time, to which Richard would occasionally allude.

There are certain qualities a teacher needs if he is going to succeed in his chosen career. Tragically, we know 'taking a good picture' isn't one of them. The ability to relate to children helps, confidence is good and the ability to induce interest in the given subject comes fairly high up the list. Being able to command and retain the high ground in a classroom is, surely, also a must. Mr Shepard, the physics teacher, sadly possessed not one of these qualities. A nervy man at the best of times, he would have been far better suited to a long-term research post in the middle of nowhere, working alone in an environment where contact with the outside world would have proved detrimental to his invaluable conclusions. That is to say, Mr Shepard wasn't a people person. He was a very, very slight man who, looks-wise, had let himself go. Think Dustin Hoffman, but more *Midnight Cowboy* than *Rain Man*.

His inability to control a room full of kids came to a head when, one afternoon during a fifth-year physics class, he noticed through the picture windows that ran down one side of the classroom his beaten-up Vauxhall Viva rolling into view. He was unaware that a few of the kids from his class had not only nicked his keys, but slipped out of the classroom, unlocked his car and pushed it all of fifteen feet on to the grass area outside his physics lab. He pleaded with the kids in the class to ignore what was happening out on the grass, as he didn't want to give oxygen to their antics. This all changed when smoke began billowing from the car. Mr Shepard then made a hollow request for everyone to carry on working while he legged it out of the classroom with a fire extinguisher to try and save his car. Incidents like this did nothing for his morale or his nervous disposition. When he got to the car, it wasn't as bad as he had first thought. The oiks had only let off a smoke bomb on the passenger seat. In typical Shepard fashion, in all the confusion he was unable to apprehend the culprits, so he came down heavily on the whole class. No afternoon playtime for the lot of them. You can't help feeling the class had already had their playtime, and as usual it was at poor Mr Shepard's expense.

4: DRUMMING AT THE BLITZ

Once Ray had left Abbotsfield and disappeared off to med school, I think it's fair to say that whatever academic ability I did possess quickly tailed off. Without an older brother's presence keeping me on the straight and narrow, the temptation to arse about became too great. When I say arse about, I wasn't getting into trouble – I just wasn't getting into too many lessons. I'd managed to keep my head down and get a bunch of O levels, which kept everyone happy, just about. It was the A levels that completely exposed me for what I was at heart: a bloody drummer.

As I entered the sixth form, Mr Bean, the man responsible for the school jazz orchestra, left under a cloud due to some altercation with the borough jazz orchestra. The Hillingdon and Uxbridge area, it seemed, wasn't big enough for two bands. Mr Bean, justifiably, got the hump and buggered off to a magnificent boarding school on Vancouver Island, Canada, where he created another impressive school jazz orchestra and lived happily ever after. But that meant the Abbotsfield orchestra sadly disbanded. And no longer having a school orchestra to drum for, I found I could broaden my horizons and was soon playing outside the comfort of school and actually earning money.

Uxbridge's newly built precinct was an abomination of

concrete and windy walkways. I'm sure the artist's impression, on the drawing board, looked lovely, but this was a time when brutalism in architecture was all the rage. Nice red bricks were 'sooo' 1940s and out, while grey, shitty concrete was 'sooo' in and 'sooo' incredibly cheap. The one saving grace was that Morgan's Record and Organ shop arrived in a town where, previously, if you wanted to buy a record, you had to go to Woolworths. But Woolies didn't really do jazz – unless you regard Acker Bilk and his Paramount Jazz Band as jazz. Well even if you do, it's *not*, and that's not his real name, either (but then Bernard Bilk and his Paramount Jazz Band doesn't have the same ring to it somehow).

Morgan's was a specialist record shop run by Chris Morgan, who happened to be a keen Hammond organ player. Together with a few guys from the school jazz orchestra, the ones who were really into jazz, I would spend hours in there on a Saturday, meticulously searching through the jazz section and taking an age to decide which album to buy. Chris, noticing that the majority of records I brought were fronted by drummers, quickly deduced I played drums and one week asked if I fancied a gig with him and a guitarist mate. Up until then, the only 'gigs' I'd done were in the safe, familiar, cotton-wool surroundings of the eighteen-piece school orchestra. This was going to be a gig with virtual strangers, and not very many of them – it was just a trio. Shit!

I played it as cool as a fifteen-year-old boy could – which was probably lukewarm at best – and said I'd have to have a look in my diary. That would be the non-existent diary I didn't have at home, then. I left the shop, did a couple of circuits of the precinct and returned to tell Chris I'd had a look at the 'diary' and yes, I was available Saturday fortnight to play at what was to be my first ever paid gig.

From the off, I hadn't really thought it through. For a start I didn't have a decent enough drum kit, which is the one thing that's vital if you're doing a gig on drums. The only kit I'd ever used had belonged to the school music department. Then there was the transport situation again; the school had taken care of all that too, with the aid of the minibus. After assuring the music teacher, Mr Evans, that I would return the kit first thing Monday morning and sweet talking my Mum into giving me a lift to the gig, it looked like I was all set.

Thankfully, this landmark gig, the birth of my drumming career, was only up the road at the Hilton Hotel, just off the M4 near Heathrow Airport. Mum had only recently passed her driving test in her cherished Hillman Imp, the 874cc two-door coupé people tended to purchase if they couldn't afford a Mini Cooper. So puny was the Imp's car horn, people about to be run over would just stand there and laugh whenever it was brought into use. The one flaw with the Imp was the rear-mounted engine. All cars with a rear-mounted engine come with drastic and unavoidable oversteer – particularly the Hillman Imp. And loaded to the gunwales with a drum kit? Forget it.

While this was never going to be the best of vehicles for carting a drummer and a kit about, as Dad was also gigging that Saturday it was all I had at my disposal, so I had no option. I felt sure Mum and I had unintentionally achieved some sort of Guinness World Record by not only installing ourselves in the two-door Imp, but also squeezing in a twenty-four-inch bass drum, three tom-toms, a cymbal case and a huge traps case, which is the thing on wheels containing the snare drum and all the stands. Imagine a medium-sized tumble-dryer and you can see the problems we had.

Having only recently ripped up her L-plates and got her full driving licence, Mum was in danger of losing it again almost immediately as she sat behind the wheel of a seriously overloaded Hillman Imp doing about eighteen miles an hour down at least two dual carriageways. To say the journey erred on the side of caution was an understatement, but I couldn't have done it without her, for which I will be forever indebted. We got there in the end and she gamely returned later that evening to pick me up. This was a routine that would carry on with increasing frequency, until eventually I passed my own driving test on the fifth attempt, the sticking point being that I was completely unable to tell my lefts from my rights, which to this day, ridiculously, remains a bit of a nightmare for me.

But once we finally reached the Heathrow Hilton Hotel, my first paying gig went alarmingly well. Sure, it was a hotel lobby gig and no one was listening, but we felt we stormed it. Chris had brought with him a massive double-tier Hammond organ with bass pedals that he played with his feet. It was a remarkable thing to look at – a bloke sat at a keyboard, playing with his hands and feet. I know it's what drummers do all the time, but on some of the faster numbers Chris was like Georgie Fame from the waist up and Lord of the Dance Michael Flatley from the knees down: incredible to witness. The third member of the trio was an amazing guitarist called Freddie Phillips. An old bloke, he played a semi-acoustic Spanish guitar. There's no denying it was a pretty odd combo, but it seemed to work perfectly for the cavernous hotel lobby. The music we played was virtually indistinguishable from the 'muzak' that was playing as we were setting up and that kicked in again the minute we finished.

Here's a fascinating fact that stopped me in my tracks when I heard it. Every note of background music you hear in hotel lobbies and lifts emanates from one place: Fort Mill, South Carolina. It's all beamed round the world via satellites, which means the person getting into a lift in London is listening to the same piece of muzak as the chap getting out of a lift in participating hotels, anywhere in the world. I need to get out more . . .

When we took a break at the Heathrow Hilton Hotel and the muzak struck up again, Chris proudly mentioned we were in good company, as Freddie had played with the BBC Symphony Orchestra, the English National Opera and the Royal Ballet. I think he thought I'd be impressed – sadly, I wasn't. Not being big on symphony orchestras, opera or ballet, I inquired if he'd done anything I would have actually heard of. He went on to tell me Freddie was responsible for all the music on the kids' TV classics *Camberwick Green* and *Trumpton*, two programmes I, and pretty much everyone else of a certain age, grew up with. This put Freddie in a whole different light – Pugh, Pugh, Barney McGrew, Cuthbert, Dibble and Grubb! He was no longer the old bloke with a Spanish guitar who didn't say much; in my eyes, he was '*Trumpton*'s Freddie Fluid-Fingers Phillips!' I felt like shouting, 'Everybody! Stop checking in or out!

Listen! It's Bloody *Trumpton*'s Freddie Bloody Phillips playing and you're taking absolutely no bloody notice!'

I think this was the one and only time I could own up to being starstruck. I sat in on congas with Jools Holland's big band for Comic Relief a few years ago, and Eric Clapton suddenly showed up and did a number. But that wasn't a patch on the gig with *the* Freddie Phillips all those years ago in the lobby of the Heathrow Hilton Hotel. The other great thing about that gig was that the moment I tapped out my first beat, I was instantly bitten by the performing bug. I knew, there and then, that I wanted above all else to be in showbiz. More fool me!

My mum continued to be a fantastic help to my embryonic drumming career. She would drop me off at a regular gig I had in the basement at the Troubadour Café in Earls Court, a coffee house of some repute. My mum would have got the wrong end of the stick, completely, so I didn't mention that the Black Panthers used to meet there when they left Paris after the 1968 riots. It was, however, the first place Bob Dylan performed in London and was also where Richard Harris fell in love with his wife Elizabeth – she was doing the washing-up. Ken Russell and Oliver Reed became friends there, too, apparently. Quite what some of London's fiercest boozers were doing in a 'teetotal' coffee house escapes me. Maybe it was all a front, maybe we were being duped and those famous hard-drinking hell-raisers were just pretending all along – but I do hope not.

By the time I started working in the basement of the Troubadour, they'd all long gone and it was peopled by old men playing chess and what I assumed were hippies – certainly people with very little money, very long hair and too much to say. The audiences downstairs were real hard-nut jazzers. I'd be playing with a bunch of guys twice my age, doing fourteen-minute versions of 'Autumn Leaves', while my mum would be outside in the car – ferocious be-bop jazz didn't sit too comfortably with her – genuinely content, reading a book or watching the flotsam and jetsam of Earls Court shuffle by.

Once I'd passed my driving test there was no stopping me. I was working more and more in town, which didn't go down too well at school. Apart from the jazz gigs, there were the four nights a week in the house band backing the burlesque duo, Biddie and Eve. For a time, outrageously extravagant presents were the order of the day at family Christmases, much to the embarrassment of my student brothers. We had a residency at the legendary Blitz Club on Great Queen Street in Covent Garden. This meant I wasn't getting home much before three or four in the morning. Trying to get into school for 8.45 a.m. was proving difficult, if not impossible. And the sticking-point was that half the A level exams were in the morning. If they'd all taken place in the afternoon I would have been fine – it would only have been all the revision I hadn't done that would have let me down . . .

Everyone in the sixth form had to meet with the careers adviser. This was the man who was going to create the blueprint for the rest of our lives. To make matters worse, we had to drag our parents along, and to this day I can remember sitting there with Mum and Dad as this chap jotted down the A levels I was taking and then asked what I wanted to do with myself. I told him I was already doing it, thanks, and that it was going quite nicely, I was earning good money drumming in the West End.

This didn't compute with the careers adviser. You obviously weren't meant to turn up with a career already under way. He thought for a while, reassessed my O levels and my A level choices and, obviously completely at a loss as to what to suggest, gave us his stock line: 'Have you thought about hotel management . . . or maybe the police?' A career in the police force would have been perfect. Richard was a teacher and Raymond was fast becoming a doctor, so obviously the third son has to forge a career in the police force. That way Mum and Dad could sit back and relax, happy in the knowledge all three of their kids had landed butter-side up. As it was, two out of three's not bad.

Everyone really did think the drumming thing was just a phase I was going through. They felt it wouldn't be long before I revealed that I'd got the calling and joined the clergy or enrolled in one of the forces and became a credit to the family name. Thing was, at seventeen and still at school (just), I was probably earning nearly as much as the guy who saw my future as running a Best Western hotel or feeling people's collars. The string of gay clubs I was working at with Biddie and Eve meant the pink pound featured significantly in my early career. I think it took my family a little while to come to terms with the fact they were never going to know exactly what I was up to, where and with whom, so they could never fully relax.

* * *

The residency with James Biddlecombe and Eve Ferret, better known as Biddie and Eve, at the Blitz Club was fairly full-on. We were soon doing four nights, Wednesday to Saturday, every week with gigs all over the country slotted in as and when. The Blitz Club itself was a bit of an eye-opener for a sixth-former from Hillingdon. This was where the New Romantic movement was born, and Biddie and Eve were the burlesque double act that entertained them. Brendan, a laconic Irishman with a curly perm and a 'tache, ran the place and couldn't believe his luck when his Second World War-themed licensed burger bar was hijacked by Steve Strange and Rusty Egan for their Blitz Kids nights.

By day, it was a fairly run-of-the-mill Covent Garden eatery. But by night it became the place to be, if you were dressed up to the nines and covered in make-up. Some of the girls looked good, too. For a time, before becoming 'Boy George', George O'Dowd worked there as the 'hat-check girl', taking the coats in the little closet to the right as you went in. Rusty Egan would be DJ-ing, and Steve Strange would wander around making sure everyone was behaving outrageously. My abiding memory of that period was of how much the punters stank, a stink that's not dis-similar to the fug that hits you when you enter an Oxfam or Sue Ryder shop today. This was so cutting edge 'New Romantic' that nobody had actually started making the clothes which were to become a fashion statement in their own right. Everyone was adapting old clothes or just wear-ing outrageous vintage stuff. Biddie was the double of Joel Grey, the MC of the Kit Kat Klub in *Cabaret*, a thin, hand-some, peroxide blond man who complemented perfectly London's answer to Mae West and Eartha Kitt – Eve Ferret.

When I joined, they were performing with a cherub-faced female double-bass player, Erica Howard, and a stick-thin punk on piano called Richard Jones. I only did a handful of gigs with Richard, as he had his sights set on greater things, directing plays and operas in the main. Over the years, he's won just about every award going, and as I write this he is getting rave reviews for *The Gambler* at the Royal Opera House. Richard lived in a minute top-floor flat on Ledbury Road right in the heart of Notting Hill Gate. His piano lived in the kitchen where we would rehearse for hours. I'll never forget Richard, fag on the go, dressed in skin-tight black jeans and an achingly trendy sleeveless, zipper-trimmed black vest, cowering against the piano while trying to accompany Eve as she sang a song she believed would be enhanced by the flailing of a huge bull-whip she had absolutely no control over. There was genuine fear in his big, saucer eyes.

I hadn't been playing long at the Blitz – I think I was just eighteen – when I met a beautiful nurse at the club and did the classic drummer's thing of moving in with her. I had to be on my best behaviour as I was now living the drummer's joke: what do you call a drummer without a girlfriend? Homeless. She and a few mates were renting a flat in Clapham. It was massive, so one more person wasn't too much of a problem. If it was, there was ample compensation in the fact that the flatmates suddenly had unlimited access to what was becoming the club to be at.

So not only was I still playing the drums and quids in, but I was now living in London with a very attractive nurse. For a time, the family relaxed and it looked as if they were finally accepting what I was getting up to. And what a bloody result, living with a nurse! If only she had been there to administer tender loving care when I had my first of two rather serious forays into hospital . . .

I was walking through Leicester Square late one evening, carrying a canvas holdall on my shoulder. It contained some kit I needed for a gig I was doing with Biddie and Eve at the 'wholly appealing' gay club, the Mine Shaft. This venue was the white-knuckle end of London's gay club scene, spread over three underground floors. The further you descended, the more debauched it became. Four floors below street-level, there was just a room, mattresses and one of those small, red, rotating police lights. The entrance was a single door in an alleyway that ran down the side of the Odeon Cinema from Leicester Square to Charing Cross Road.

As I walked towards the club I accidentally bumped into someone, not difficult to do at 11.30 on a Saturday night, and thought nothing of it. I arrived at the club and rang the bell to be let in. As I was waiting there, the chap I must have bumped into approached me and, without stopping, punched me square on the jaw. Thankfully, I think I was as drunk as he must have been, as there were no shooting pains round my face. I just felt my lower jaw an inch or so out of alignment with my upper jaw. The door to the club opened, and I shuffled in a little dazed. When I attempted to tell Biddie and Eve what had happened, they immediately assumed, from the difficulty I had forming my words, that I was seriously pissed. Once I'd convinced them that, although merry, I had just been punched really quite hard in the face, it was thought best that I get along to a hospital – and sharpish. Eve very kindly ran me up the road in her green half-timbered Austin A40 to a hospital behind

Millbank, where she dropped me off before disappearing back to the gig.

I was immediately admitted on to a ward where I was to remain for four days. I'd suffered a double fracture of the lower jaw. My first full day in hospital was taken up with a six-hour operation to wire the jaws together. This entailed putting a small loop of wire around the base of each tooth and then wiring those loops together, top to bottom. For a day or so I was kept under observation, just in case anything wasn't right. But everything was just peachy because every time I pressed the bell on the end of the cord hanging from the ceiling by the side of my bed, a nurse would arrive at my bedside and jab a needle into my bum. Pretty quickly, everything was beautiful, the world was a gorgeous place. Blissful . . . Jaw? What jaw? I felt fantastic, the lights were sooo shiny and my body tingled with a delightful contentment.

To complement the badly broken jaw, I'm sure I developed a little tiny callus on my thumb from the incessant bell pressing. Like Pavlov and his dogs, it wasn't too long before simply ringing the bell did it for me. Just think what that would be like, going through life completely off your face every time you heard a bell ring. The money I would have saved. Thinking about it, that's obviously what every church-bell-ringing junkie is up to. From where we're standing it's a cacophony of noise – I challenge anyone to pick a tune out of that racket – but from where they're standing, of course, the peal of bells is seeing them off on another mother-of-all trips. Do not ask for whom the bell tolls – they're too busy having a whale of a time.

So it was with a degree of sadness and a very sore arse

that I had my final meeting with the doctor who had so comprehensively wired my jaws together. He told me not to do anything too strenuous, as my ability to take in oxygen was severely compromised. On this list were the usual suspects: competitive swimming, marathons, squash, mountaineering and then he casually slipped in sex. I don't mean he literally slipped over on some sex he hadn't spotted on the lino in his office; he advised me against having strenuous sex. I assured him that the sort of sex I got up to couldn't be put on a par with climbing a mountain or running a marathon. Running upstairs, maybe – and on my own . . .

Just as the wired jaws meant I would be unable to 'gulp down' extra oxygen for the strenuous sex, I would also be unable to 'throw up' anything suddenly through the same aperture. So the doctor strongly advised me against drinking alcohol for the six weeks the wires were in, as this increased the chances of me vomiting. He then produced from his desk drawer a toffee hammer, one of those little solid brass hammers with the rounded ends you can easily fit into the palm of your hand or a back pocket. I was to keep this on me at all times. If I felt I was going to be sick, I was to offer the toffee hammer to the nearest person and ask them to knock my two front teeth out, as this would greatly increase my chances of not choking to death on my own puke. I'm surprised the doctor wasn't aware that it's physically impossible for the adult human body (well, mine, anyway) to go six weeks without a 'sharpener', so the toffee hammer was diligently carted everywhere with me. It became something of a humorous talking-point and then, very quickly, a worry at dinner parties. Once I'd filled up on soup, I'd be into the first bottle of wine and forcing the responsibility for the toffee hammer duties on to the assembled guests.

It was during my time wired up that I discovered the delights of Guinness, as this both filled me up and got me where I wanted to be. Despite sinking pints of the stuff, over the six weeks I lost about three stone and never had to call on the toffee hammer, thank God. My brother, Doctor Ray, told me they once had some really drunk bloke in Accident & Emergency who was wired up in a similar way. Just for their peace of mind, the medics knocked his teeth in – just in case, he said. The poor guy was in agony and suddenly completely covered in blood.

Somewhere on the internet, there is some amusing footage of Biddie and Eve performing on *Lift Off with Ayshea!*, a popular kids' music show. We played the Kinks' 'Lola', and the camera very kindly started on the drummer counting the band in. Because you couldn't actually see the wires in my teeth, it just seemed like I had the most disturbing speech impediment – not a good look. I wouldn't have wanted the presenter, the beautiful Ayshea Brough, to get the wrong end of the stick about my inability to communicate. I sensed she thought I was incredibly attractive, but the perceived speech impediment was to ensure that we were never to become an item.

The first McDonald's in the West End of London had just opened in the Haymarket, and everyone was going bonkers about how fantastic the burgers were. I still had a week or so to go before I was back with the carnivores and couldn't wait to sample my first quarter-pounder with cheese. I had it all planned; go see the doctor in the morning, whip out the wires and then straight up the West End for a McDonald's with fries. Not chips: fries. I'd never eaten fries before either; this was going to be unbelievable! Who was I bloody kidding . . . ?

I turned up at the hospital full of the joys of spring – 'today's the day!' The doctor told me he'd be cutting the wires that connected the jaws together and removing as many of the wire loops around my teeth as possible. As possible? This didn't bode well. But he did assure me I could eat with the individual tooth wires in place. Great, I thought, McDonald's here we come!

Or not. I'd badly overlooked the basic workings of the body, in as much as I hadn't realized that muscles which haven't been used for six weeks aren't going to be in good shape. And the muscles that worked my jaw weren't in any shape at all. My lower jaw fell open about half an inch and just hung there. I looked like a village idiot. I had to use my hand to close my mouth; this wasn't part of the plan. Six weeks I'd waited for this moment, only to find, if I was lucky, I could just about squeeze a French fry into my mouth, but I couldn't entertain the idea of actually chewing the bastard. That was weeks away.

This disappointment soon paled into insignificance when the doc began trying to remove the little wires that were tightly wound around each tooth. Over the six weeks, all the wires had become embedded into the gums and as the teeth were narrower at the base, the wire couldn't just be lifted up over the tooth, no, it had to be pulled around the tooth with a pair of pliers. What made matters unbearably worse was that as the doc unwound each wire there was left at each end a curly pigtail length of sodding wire which was going to be pulled around the root of each tooth before leaving my face.

As I've never before worked in a paddy field, stopped growing rice for a moment to give birth to a child and then carried on working, I can safely say that what happened in that doctor's office was the most miserable and painful thing I have ever experienced. Sure, we tried anaesthetizing each tooth, but to no avail as the little piggy wires laughed in the face of anaesthesia. At one point, the doctor said, 'If I give you any more anaesthetic and someone finds out, I could be struck off.' On a good day, we could get two of the bastards out. Most days, using the knee-on-chest, hand-on-forehead, pliers-tightly-gripping-on-to-one-end-of-the-little-piggy-wire method, it was only ever the one we could liberate. The doc's idea of telling me he was going to count to three and then pulling on two quickly got my goat and really wasn't doing me any favours. The pain was unbearable. One day I actually fainted, and I'm not a fainter. My body obviously said, 'That's it! Enough is enough already!' and stepped in to help by either killing me there and then, which I would have been quite happy with, or at least getting me to a better place where no one could hurt me – unconsciousness.

What an amazing, painful thing my body is.

5: GAY PAREE

I wasn't working exclusively with Biddie and Eve. I was doing a number of jazz gigs around town and for a while found myself as the house drummer in the original 606 Jazz Club, a dingy basement in the King's Road. It's now a very salubrious venue and has moved round the corner to 90 Lots Road, but in the late seventies and early eighties it was a tinderbox of a place with wine corks stuck all over the ceiling. It actually relied for heating on an open fire during the winter months and boasted seven incredibly cramped tables. The whole place could hold no more than thirty people, ideally all very good friends. It was a real musicians' haunt, and nobody got there much before ten-thirty, eleven o'clock. I never left there much before five in the morning. Drummers: first in, last out.

Some nights, a number could easily last twenty minutes, as musos would turn up after their money gig and want to jam as soon as they negotiated the rickety steps and got their horns out. We'd just be coming to the natural end of a number and we'd suddenly hear a trumpet or sax fire up, signalling another two or three times round the same bloody tune. The place was run by a guy called Steve Rubie. Being small helped down at the 606 in the sort of beautiful, shambolic way that you don't see today – they've probably been health-and-safetied out of existence – but they were so much fun. I probably got to play with some of the country's best musicians down at the 'Six', but I'd be pushed to remember a handful of them.

To the Shoefactory in Rushden, Northamptonshire, an amazing arts space created by Nick Weldon and Andrea Sparks. I'd come to meet Nick as part of my series of lunches. He is one of the writer Fay Weldon's kids. He is the most amazing pianist who also speaks fluent French and is an incredible chef. He's currently professor of jazz music at the Royal Academy of Music. I think he's probably a bit like my brother, Raymond – good at anything he turns his hand to.

I hadn't seen him for twenty-five years, and when I caught up with him he was effortlessly preparing lunch for the pair of us and enthusing about his new passion, playing the double bass. I first met him when he deputized at a few Biddie and Eve gigs, and we went on to do a whole bunch of jazz gigs together.

He was also a regular down the 'Six' and reminded me of some of the other nightmare musos who would turn up and want to play. They included the valve trombonist who played all his achingly long solos in measured quavers, managing to rinse out any passion or fire from the be-bop we were supposed to be playing. There is nothing worse than mediocre, listless jazz. I'm sure that's why all those guys who invented the form dropped like flies, smacked off their faces, as soon as they heard what people were doing with their 'baby'. This guy would turn up to the 'Six' on his Honda 90 with his trombone securely chained to the back of the moped. If you were playing and you heard the rattle of the chain above you in the street, it didn't matter where you were in 'Autumn Leaves', the bandstand would empty and we'd all be on a break, having a drink, when the poor guy shuffled in.

Jeff Castle was another one I dreaded showing up at one-thirty in the morning. He was a lovely bloke and really incredible pianist – almost too good. He was so talented that he was also very self-absorbed, and that was the sticking point. He would have a habit of sitting in and then suddenly producing these five-page charts he'd written for us to sight read, really tricky jazz-opus stuff Frank Zappa would have had trouble getting his head round. We played a piece he'd composed for Bill Evans one night, and he was very excited about it. It wasn't bad, the first time we played it. But it did begin to pall after the third time he made us play the same bit of music, to the same people, on the same evening.

Working with Nick was a joy, not least because he was the most gentle, mild-mannered, laid-back bloke you could ever wish to meet. All of those traits were tested to the full during our time gigging in Paris together. Nick had been working with a cool black American singer called James Brockington who had gone to live in France. He called Nick and asked if he fancied putting a trio together for a residency he had set up in Paris. He got bass player Erica Howard and myself on board, and before we knew it we were heading for Dover in my Ford Escort Estate, musos and drum kit packed in the car with Erica's huge double bass strapped to the roof.

Everything was going well until we landed on French soil. We had overlooked the small problem of applying for and filling out a document called a 'Carnet'. Apparently when you take a musical instrument abroad, the authorities assume you will sell it, so a deposit has to be in place. It is returned when you leave the country with the same instruments you entered with. At Calais, we could go no further unless 350 quid was left with the uniformed strangers at border control, money we were sure we'd never see again. Being able to speak fluent French, Nick was left to sort it out, which meant he ended up reluctantly agreeing to leave a personal cheque for the full amount that he would pick up on our return.

The accommodation James had arranged for us was in a lovely part of Paris, but was basically his room in the flat he shared with a part-time catwalk model called Ginette. Nick had arranged to go and stay with one of his male friends. We quickly got the impression Ginette had been left in the dark about the arrangements James had made. There was a frostiness that gave no sign of thawing while we were in her way. I, haplessly, managed to turn the thermostat down a few more degrees by ending up in bed with Ginette one night. Not a good move – French women are very feisty, aren't they? – and Ginette didn't take kindly to the toe-curlingly casual way I treated the whole situation. But it did mean we all got one good night's sleep. OK, I got one very good night's sleep. The next day I was full of remorse, as Nick and Erica weren't best pleased. What had I done? And why didn't somebody stop me? Nick, in a very sanctimonious way, looked at me and said, 'Mate, now you shall stew in your own semen.' Erica promptly let out howls of laughter at another fine sexual mess I'd gotten myself into.

As Erica and I could speak little or no French, Nick was

in the unenviable position of being on call the whole time we were there. I honestly thought our stint in 'gay Paree' was about three weeks, but Nick assures me it was no more than a week – it just felt three times as long. The gig was in a dank jazz cellar beneath a cafe, which attracted very few punters. James' promise of a packed house didn't material-ize until four or five gigs in, when one night the place was heaving. There was almost a party atmosphere to the place, it was fantastic. Everyone was offering each other wine and laughter, and James was in his element as mine host.

That night his rendition of 'Surrey with the Fringe on Top' was supreme, the best we'd ever heard. Suddenly everyone was happy, at last. Obviously, word had got out and the rest of our time there was sure to be a success. It wasn't till the following night with the usual six or seven people in the audience that Nick managed to get the truth out of the cafe manager. What money we had taken on the door so far, James had spent throwing last night's party for us and all his friends. We were responsible for inadvert-ently drinking the profits. This took its toll on all of us, apart from James, who seemed to take it in his stride and even saw the whole thing as the beginning of a very fruitful, long-term project. A long-term project he was to pursue, solo, as the next night Nick, Erica and I played our last gig in Paris and at three o'clock in the morning, still in the dinner jackets we had worn all week, climbed into the Ford Escort Estate and headed for England.

As is the norm when leaving a gig you've not enjoyed, I nicked a full bottle of Cointreau Orange Liqueur from behind the bar for the 250-mile journey from Paris to

London. Wedged between my legs, I'd take a swig every few miles – it worked wonders.

The nightmare wasn't over for poor Nick who, when we got to the port at about seven in the morning, desperately tried to reacquaint himself with the £350 personal cheque he'd left at customs barely a week earlier. Wouldn't you just know it, the cheque was nowhere to be seen. The few custom officers who were there to greet us had no recollection of anything being handed over the previous week. Now, not only had the gig in Paris actually cost us money, but it looked like Nick was going to be a further 350 quid out of pocket. Once we were in England, I drove him to his place in Brixton where his wife and kids would be waiting with open arms to welcome the breadwinner home.

Erica and I drove straight on to Langan's Brasserie in Mayfair. We had a gig that evening, with a lovely but crazy seven-foot-tall Irish pianist, the fastest most frenetic keyboard player you'd ever seen, the last thing we needed after the day we'd just had. I went home that night and slept for two whole days. The upside to the whole debacle was that Nick managed to cancel the cheque before it was cashed, so he wasn't beaten up by his wife and kids. I, meanwhile, can boast that, like Phil Collins on Live Aid, I've drummed in two capital cities in the world on the same day.

The Blitz Club residency was providing the bread-and-butter money, but it was the private party gigs that really paid and made the difference. On a good New Year's Eve, there would be as many as five gigs happening. There'd be a couple of restaurants in town, early evening, then I'd toss the kit into the back of the car – no time for packing it down – and belt up to Hampstead for a thirty-minute set in a private house the size of a hotel, for someone with more money than hair follicles. Then back into town to Wedgies on the King's Road, a toffs' nightclub run by the notorious playboy, Dai Llewellyn, known affectionately as the 'Conquistador of the Canapé Circuit'. He was a fantastic, ruddy-faced man who was always laughing and never without a glass of bubbly in his hand – maybe the two are connected? He would greet people at the door dressed in stockings and suspenders and sporting a cowboy hat and holsters. Playing Wedgies was like being in the saucy 1978 film *The Stud*, not least because Joan Collins, the star of that movie, would often be there holding court and looking gorgeous. From Wedgies, it would be a quick flit across town to the Blitz Club, our spiritual home, in Covent Garden for a right old knees-up that would see us tipping out at about five in the morning. Biddie and Eve were always dressed to the nines and had got it into their heads that we could create more of a party atmosphere if the band dressed up, too. Nick was happy to don a tutu and dress up as a ballerina (I meant to talk to him about that), Erica was resplendent as a pink angel with gossamer wings and I'm sure I looked a million dollars in my green tights, green felt tunic, big floppy green hat and long pointy green boots with bells on. We gave the 606 a wide berth that night.

The number of nights we played at the Blitz meant that whenever anyone hired the place for a private bash, Biddie and Eve would be the first call as in-house entertainment. In July and August of 1979, the Boomtown Rats song 'I Don't Like Mondays' went to number one and stayed there for four weeks. Ensign Records hired the Blitz Club and Biddie and Eve for a party to celebrate the fact that one of their acts had done so well. This was an opportunity for the band to invite everyone and anyone they knew for the mother of all piss-ups. I seem to remember it took place, rather incongruously, one sunny Sunday afternoon. I don't remember anything about performing at the party, so that must have gone well. But what I do remember is cowering for our lives behind the bar, with Brendan the owner and a very giggly Bob Geldof, who had the good sense not to be 'hands on' as an enormous fight broke out. Almost on cue, one of the hammered Irish revellers tossed a bentwood chair into the air, the signal for the mayhem to commence. Within minutes, the whole place resembled the bar-room brawl scene from *Carry On Cowboy*, as chairs, then tables, glasses, then bottles were sent flying in all directions. Biddie, Eve, Brendan, all of us, were shitting ourselves – surely this was very dangerous? Surely someone's going to get hurt? Surely this shouldn't be happening, not on a Sunday afternoon, with the sun shining outside? And surely, shouldn't someone call the police?

It was all a bit odd. From the relative safety of behind the bar, Bob and a mate were now really laughing at the carnage that was unfolding in front of our eyes. Brendan took one of the record company people to one side and suggested it might be a good idea to call the police, as the place was now getting really trashed. The guy from the record label just looked at Brendan with a big grin on his face and said, 'Naarrr, this happens all the time – let's not spoil the lads' fun, it's not every day you get to number one!' Brendan nodded the half-hearted nod of a man resigned to the fact that the police were never going to come and save his club from total ruination. 'Don't worry, mate,' said the record executive. 'They're good lads, they'll pay for any damage. What's a couple of chairs and the odd beer glass?'

6: A RIGHT EYEFUL

We usually finished at the Blitz at about one-thirty, two o'clock on a Saturday night. This gave us plenty of time to carry the party on somewhere else, and Biddie and Eve were seldom short on offers. I never found out whose party it was on this particular Saturday. I couldn't even work out who the lesbians were who invited us when we came off stage at the Blitz that night, but all I do know is I still bear the scars from the lesbian party on the Vauxhall one-way system.

Having spent a large amount of time in Biddie's company, I'd become well-versed with the notion of homosexuals – indeed, some of my new best friends were complete arse bandits. When I first hooked up with Biddie, he was sharing a small garden flat with his childhood friend, Simon Doonan, who was shocking the Establishment by dressing windows in Savile Row with stuffed rats and generally pushing the boundaries wherever he went. It was at their completely over the top Moroccan-themed flat that Simon introduced me to the gentleman's cologne that I wear to this very day, Vetiver Guerlain. Simon had a bottle of it, the size of a portable television, which I think he'd 'acquired' whilst window-dressing a big, posh department store in the West End. I smelt gorgeous then, and I smell gorgeous today; ask anyone who knows me. These days, Simon is a columnist on the *New York Observer* and creative director of Barneys in New York and pretty much the toast of the whole place. His early life has been committed to film in the BBC2 sitcom *Beautiful People*, based on his bestselling book of the same name. Hanging out with those two, I was more than up to speed with the gay thing whilst remaining utterly heterosexual. My brother Richard did comment once that I had taken to elongating some of my words – bit of a worry, but that was as near as I came to handing in the antlers. Having said that, it was lesbians who were a complete mystery to me. Hillingdon didn't have lesbians, and if they did, I'd never spotted one. Television has had camp male icons since I was a small boy. I grew up with Larry Grayson, John Inman, Russell Harty and Dick Emery's outrageously camp 'Hello Honky Tonk' character, Clarence – all of them bent as nine-bob notes and accepted with open arms. But there was no sign of the female equivalent. I'm not running with the Valerie Singleton rumour here (I mean we've heard it denied from her own lips). And if anyone needs the proof running down their throats, cut along to the internet, click on 'images of Val'. The photo of the pair of us, entwined, should put anyone's mind at ease.

So, it was a party that was going to be heaving with lesbians, and I had absolutely no idea what to expect. Would it be a bacchanalian female flesh fest? It was quite late at night. Or was it going to be a bunch of women sitting around smoking fags, getting drunk and having a laugh? Either would be a result.

When we arrived I went straight to the kitchen with the bottle of champagne Biddie, Eve and I had 'acquired' from the club. For a lesbian party, everything was looking pretty normal from what I could see, but that wasn't to last. As I stood in the kitchen feverishly removing the foil and the wire from the not very cold bubbly, the cork suddenly shot from the bottle. The bottle I was staring down at. I've since learnt that insufficiently chilled fizz can be a volatile commodity. The cork went straight into my eye, but not before it had smashed through the glass lens of the spectacles I was wearing. This threw me a little, and I began stumbling around, initially in the kitchen and then the rest of the flat clutching my really quite badly damaged right eye. I was still valiantly trying to get a fix on what a lesbian party looked like with my good left eye, but it was proving increasingly difficult as the throbbing, pain began to register in my right. This wasn't going at all well. It was like some Greek tragedy: inquisitive man arrives at a remote island, full of woman, only to be struck blind the minute he gets off the boat, so is denied the joys of all he could have surveyed.

Eventually, I found Biddie and explained what had happened. His first response was to establish that the bottle of champagne was still intact. Once I'd assured him not a drop had been spilt, he then set about trying to sort me out. I was led into the bathroom and told to lean backwards over the bath, looking up – not the easiest of manoeuvres to execute with both eyes now tightly closed. As I balanced precariously over the bath in a limbo stance, Biddie asked me to, 'Open your eyes . . . NOW!' This I did, and he proceeded to pour a litre of freezing cold water straight into the damaged eye from a plastic lemonade bottle. He mentioned something about this being good for washing out any shards of glass that might be present. I was now soaking wet, freezing cold and blind. There's no denying Biddie is a faultless transvestite cabaret entertainer, but his first-aid skills leave a lot to be desired, especially when treating the body's delicate areas like the eyes, where a degree of finesse is imperative. It was quickly agreed that Biddie's 'treatment' had not helped matters and, without the aid of sight, I could sense the bathroom filling up with lesbians, all either eager to help or just point and laugh at the 'hapless man', I wasn't sure which. The next thing I knew I was holding Eve's arm and being lead down the stairs and out into the street. As with the now infamous 'Mine Shaft jaw incident', she realized the best thing for me was a hospital, and quick.

Within minutes, we were pulling up at St Thomas' Hospital A&E department on the South Bank opposite the Houses of Parliament, where without turning the engine off, Eve helped me out of the passenger seat, pointed me in the right direction and made her way back to the party. I baby-stepped into the waiting room and sat on the first seat I could find, figuring someone would come over to find out what was up. But, of course, it was Saturday night, and the place was heaving with drunks in pain and drunks that were definitely *being* a pain. It was a mad house. The staff on duty that night seemed to take it all in their stride, some even joking with each other while people bled all over the floor and idiots threw up. I suppose that's how they deal with it, gallows humour – never got it myself. I sheepishly wandered around in an attempt to find someone who could help and was eventually led up a corridor and into a small, dimly lit room, where I sat for what seemed like an age mulling over what had just happened and what the fallout was going to be this time. A young doctor arrived and quizzed me about events and clamped my face into what I can only describe as a head-shaped metal vice. Using what looked suspiciously like a really small pin, he began trying to remove the shards of glass he'd spotted floating about on the surface of my eye while looking through his big magnifying machine. This was all very uncomfortable, watching this pointy needle moving toward your eye and you not being able to do anything about it. People make horror films like this, don't they?

He was able to remove a total of eight – that's EIGHT! – tiny shards of glass from my right eye. He proudly showed them to me, but I was unable see what he was on about so I took his word for it. He then dropped the bombshell – the 'keep you in for observation' line, which I thought was a bit much as he'd done all he could with the nifty needlework. While bandaging me up, he said there was more to it than that, but at four o'clock in the morning he wasn't in a position to elaborate, as there was still a room full of walking wounded up the corridor and at least three hours left of his shift. A&E doctor: a vocation or what?

A nurse showed me to the men's eye ward, which was a bit spooky to say the least. There were eight beds, arranged in two rows facing each other with a curtain at the far end. What made it spooky was that some of the blokes were sitting up in bed with bandages or cotton pads over their eyes, so you couldn't tell if they were asleep or not. The one free bed that was obviously mine had no sign of a dangling button for the bell that summoned a nurse to your bedside armed with the happy needle, the one I'd enjoyed so much six or seven months earlier when I'd had my jaw broken. I gingerly inquired about what would happen if I couldn't sleep due to the discomfort and was told, in no uncertain terms, that I could have a couple of paracetamol, but only two and only every four hours. I put this down to NHS cutbacks since my last stay and tried to get some sleep.

The next day I was woken by the sound of visiting time. It must have been about midday. I peered over the bed covers with my one good eye to see a succession of people coming in with fruit and flowers. Everyone was now sitting up in bed with their eyes heavily bandaged, unable to see what was going on. As each person filed in, they took whatever gift they had brought for their blind, bedridden friend, plonked it on his bedside table and, oohing and aahing, made a beeline for the huge, panoramic window that stretched the whole width of the ward. We were about four floors up and had the most fantastic view of the River Thames and the Houses of Parliament directly opposite, and all these guys in bed were unable to see a thing. They could have been in the basement and they would have been none the wiser.

I left St Thomas' a few days later with a badly haemorrhaged eye, which to this day is still not right and isn't going to get any better. The doctor said it would have been much worse had I not been wearing glasses – I would have probably lost the eye. What's weird is that every time I close my eye I can see the burst blood vessels, a constant reminder always to chill the champagne before attempting to open. Biddie and Eve presented me with a very fetching diamanté-encrusted eye patch, but it was strictly for stage use only, you understand. Within the space of one year I'd spent two spells in hospital and nearly lost an eye. Now I was about to lose my coveted driving licence.

* * *

The reason escapes me, but Biddie was dressed as Alanasimova, an obscure Russian princess, in yards of flowing chiffon, stilettos and a three-foot-tall hat securely tethered to his head. He looked . . . I want to use the word amazing, but it's not quite right. 'Bizarre' might cover it better. But this uncompromising outfit meant the only way we could get him from home to the gig was if he lay down on top of the drum kit in the back of my car. He lived in Battersea and we were heading to Covent Garden, so we were swinging round Trafalgar Square. What we hadn't bargained for was the police road block on the north side of the square. They were stopping cars, supposedly checking people's tyres, but they were in actual fact looking for drink-drivers. This meant they would walk out into the middle of the one-way road and signal you to slow down and then pull over to the curb. Here they could get you out of the car to have a look at your tyres and quickly deduce whether you were pissed or not. They did this with me, and suddenly I was breathing into 'the bag' and watching the crystals turn green. I was able to provide them with exactly what they were looking for, and they very kindly invited me to climb into the back of a waiting paddy wagon. All the while Biddie remained motionless, prostrate, in the back of the car.

A policeman asked me for my car keys and as I handed them over I mentioned, rather facetiously, 'What about the Russian princess in the back of my car?' The copper came straight back with, 'Your girlfriend will have to get a cab or the bus home, mate.' As the paddy wagon pulled away, I glanced out through the window to see Biddie, high heels, tall hat, chiffon blowing in the breeze, teetering across the road and shouting, 'I have no pockets, I haven't got any money!'

It must have been about five in the morning when I asked about the car, to which the charge sergeant gave me a withering look and said, 'You're not going anywhere in that, mate. Come back tomorrow.' It's funny, the people who have been put on the planet to tell you off are all very free with the word 'mate'. It was a long walk from Whitehall Police Station to the flat in Clapham, and I felt like shit. What the hell was I going to do now? I was to report to the famous Bow Street Magistrates' Court, no less – nice to make an appearance at such a historical location, as it was to close down a year or so later. When the day came and I made my appearance, the policeman I'd last seen in Trafalgar Square stood up in court and maintained that, 'Mr Rivron was driving slowly and swerving from side to side, so I pulled him over.' What? The bastards! He was the very reason I was driving slowly – he stepped out into the middle of the road, and the swerving was me being told to pull into the side of the road, as he was 'very concerned' about my bloody tyres!

* * *

What do you call a drummer without a car? Nothing – because if he hasn't got a bloody car he isn't a bloody drummer! I really got it in the neck when I went home and broke the news to my parents. In my mum's eyes, suddenly I was a ten-year-old kid again and I'd just broken one of the small panes of glass in the French windows with a football. A long time ago, Ray and I were mucking about with one of Richard's big leather footballs that we didn't really have any control over, and it was only a matter of time before something went wrong. She heard the sound of breaking glass and came running out and declared, 'Right, Raymond, you're not going to Paris with the school jazz orchestra! And Rowland, you're not getting that Corgi Batmobile! Now both of you, get inside!' Of course, Ray did get to go to Paris with the school jazz orchestra and I did get the Corgi Batmobile, but in the heat of the moment we were both gutted, Ray probably slightly more so. Your first ever trip to Paris and a toy car? Is there any comparison?.

Dad was a little more philosophical about my conviction, stating, 'There but for the grace of God go us all, son.' It was a veiled admission that I wasn't alone when it came to drink-driving and, yes, he might have had the odd shandy and climbed behind the wheel, so let's not be too harsh. It didn't make me feel any better, though. I knew I'd done something wrong, and Dad could see I was really suffering. He took me to one side and said, 'Son, don't worry. Whatever happens to you, it'll never be as bad as what's happened to me.' I'm close to tears every time I think about what he said, and I think it really did change the way I viewed everything I did from then on. I didn't worry, because it was never going to be as bad. I was barely eighteen, what was I doing? Leading the life of Riley in London's heady West End, earning good money doing exactly what I wanted to do, in the company of some great jazz musicians and a bunch of crazy transvestites. By the time my dad was eighteen, he'd already been two years in the Army and was laid up in a British hospital in Singapore awaiting an appendix operation. On 2 February 1942, Japan invaded Singapore and my dad was captured.

He spent the next four years in the notorious Japanese prisoner-of-war camp that was to build not only the Burma railway but the famous 'Bridge over the River Kwai'. Dad didn't talk much about his time in the POW camp when we were kids. There obviously weren't many laughs. But over the years we got to learn a little about what he went through and why he was right when he said we had no need to worry. There were horror stories about when the prisoners were finally freed. Some of the POWs made use of the graves they had been forced to dig for their sick friends by burying alive some of the more sadistic Japanese guards. Also, a lot of the men, who had endured four years of imprisonment, accidentally killed themselves the day they were liberated by simply eating too much abundant food and bursting their stomachs. My dad watched, helplessly, as one of the planes that had been commissioned to fly the prisoners to safety crashed straight after take-off and burst into flames. Those sorts of tales very much put our trivial quotidian concerns into perspective.

Some of the stories were truly amazing. On one occasion, Dad and a mate decided to escape by swimming out to a boat they'd spotted a mile or so out at sea. They gave the guards the slip and began swimming. My dad was a keen swimmer and had played water polo for the Army. As they approached the unmarked boat, they noticed the crew's Japanese uniforms. Rather than give themselves up and get the shit kicked out of them for trying to escape, they made a hasty retreat and quickly swam all the way back to the mainland. They rejoined the other prisoners before anyone realized they had gone missing.

I remember that everyone marvelled at the fact that my dad didn't have a single filling, amazing when you think he didn't brush his teeth for four years. In the jungle they would use the cotton 'string' produced by the kapok tree and literally floss their teeth clean. And there's me thinking flossing was a stupid eighties American affectation! On the inventions front, my father maintained he thought up the idea of the button-down shirt while in the POW camp, and I'm inclined to believe him. Library books would have it that Brooks Brothers of, again, America introduced the button-down shirt collar in 1896. Originally it was for sportsmen, and then it was adapted for casual wear. At eighteen, how on earth would my dad have any idea what blokes in America were after when they were going for the casual look? He didn't nick the button-down collar from the Americans! He didn't know it existed! He thought it up himself – you ask my brothers! The number of scraps I got into as a kid while defending my dad's invention.

The most heart-warming, life-affirming story from his time as a prisoner is vaguely spiritual. In the same POW camp was Dad's brother, Malcolm. They were in the same regiment when captured. A religious man, Malcolm would carry a large Bible with him wherever he went, including during his time working on the Burma railway. Malcolm became very ill at one point, so ill that he had to be carried from one workplace to the next. This was usually the sign that it was only a matter of time before a prisoner died and was buried by the side of the railway line, one more burden lifted. But Malcolm didn't die – the Bible saved his life. Each night after his brother had fallen asleep, my dad would carefully remove a few translucent pages of the sacred book and sell them to the guards for use as cigarette paper. With the small amount of money he raised, Dad was able to purchase medicine that ensured Malcolm survived.

One of the odder by-products of Dad's experience at the hands of the Japanese was that after the war rice and cucumber were definitely off the menu round our house. Being anywhere near the stuff, seeing it, smelling it, would get Dad going as this was pretty much all they lived on for long years. Sightseeing in London with his three kids could also be problematical. Tourism was just finding its feet in the sixties and seventies, and the last thing my mum wanted to have to cope with was Dad bumping into the odd, innocent Japanese tourist.

My father truly was an amazing man. He could have so easily pulled the 'you don't know how lucky you are' card on us – and with full justification. He could have rammed that in my face, but he didn't. Every spat and galling tantrum we had as kids, he took on board as if it were the most important thing in the world. Whilst not being the most communicative bloke, he made sure, silently, that our childhoods were truly idyllic. All this from a man who had lived through horrors that none of us can begin to get our heads round. I thought my brothers' footsteps would be difficult to fill, but Rich, Ray and I could never even begin to fill the shoes our dad left behind.

7: COMIC STRIP

At home, the Ford Escort Estate had replaced the Hillman Imp as the family's second car, but it was no coincidence that it was perfect for carting my drum kit around. Mum was dead against the idea of replacing the Hillman. She hadn't driven anything else, and you always have a weird, almost maternal bond with your first-driven. Dad could see the sense in getting a new car for Mum and me to use. He was still reeling from the mechanic's bill, incurred when I blew up the engine of his pride and joy, the Triumph Toledo, on the way back from a gig in the Fawlty Towers Hotel, Beaconsfield. OK, it wasn't *the* Fawlty Towers Hotel, because that doesn't exist. This was the cash-strapped Woburn Grange Country Club, which was used for all the exterior filming – the opening shot, cars coming and going, people storming off. It conveniently burnt down not long ago, which must have come as a blow to the people who owned it . . .

Dad, Mum and I went to have a look at the Escort. Mum steadfastly refused to get in for the test drive; her face was a picture, she really didn't want to have anything to do with the car. As Dad and I climbed in and gingerly pulled away up the road, in the rear-view mirrors stood Mum with a face like thunder. We'd only got about twenty-five yards up the road when the car came to a stop. I climbed out first and collapsed on the floor in fits of laughter, and then Dad got out, laughing like a drain. In his hand was the gear stick; it had come off going into third. We walked back towards Mum, who was desperately trying to keep a straight face, but not for long – eventually she cracked up, too. We were all laughing our heads off when the man who was selling the car came and joined us. Almost triumphantly, Dad offered up the gear stick, to which the man said, 'Bit of a design fault, that, on the Escort. Were you snatching it into third?'

As soon as the responsibility for taxing and insuring the car could be laid at my feet, I was off. The cynic in me feels that maybe my parents thought, 'There's no way he will ever leave home if he's not behind the wheel of a car.' And that made up their minds. I could just see my parents going into a huddle and whispering, 'This is what we do . . .' It was a great car that was lovingly looked after – back then you could actually open the bonnet and tinker with a car. At weekends carburettors would be replaced, tappets fiddled with.

Some of the things Dad said, usually in passing, could stop you in your tracks. One time, he was helping me fix something on the car. He was lying on his back on the passenger seat, soldering something Vitally Important behind the dashboard, and, unbeknownst to him, his arm came too close to the soldering iron he was wielding. Some of the hairs on his arm began to singe. He stopped what he was doing, took a couple of sniffs and, slightly distressed, inquired as to what the smell was. Once he had realized it was 'only' his arm, he quipped: 'God, that smell reminds me of camp.'

'Come again, Dad?' I replied.

'The smell of burning flesh – takes me back, son . . .'

Nothing really was *ever* going to be as bad as what Dad had been through. (Christ on a bike! I am genuinely in tears as I type this.)

It was in this same blue Ford Escort Estate, driving home on the way back from a May Ball gig in Cambridge, that I finally realized I wasn't going to working for Biddie and Eve any more, but it wasn't the end of the world.

The May Ball circuit was a fertile place for a burlesque cabaret duo, and like New Year's Eve, Biddie and Eve would often do two or three gigs in one night. This was always very taxing on the liver; three gigs meant three riders to get through. It was our last gig of the night and we weren't due on stage until about four or five in the morning. The venue was a huge marquee with a stage at one end and trestle tables and benches at the other, where student revellers, all dressed up to the nines, were gallantly quaffing bottles of champagne and picking at the beginnings of breakfast.

I have to admit, I have a slightly jaundiced view of further education. I didn't go to university or college but, perversely, over the years have played in just about every one in the country. And just like the Queen can't avoid the unmistakable smell of fresh paint wherever she goes, I can't help associating seats of learning with the unmistakable stench of booze. I'm also slightly jealous that I missed out on what everyone tells me was a rollicking good time, and back then all at the taxpayer's expense. Every pint that passed my lips back then was paid for by the sweat of an honest man's brow – albeit in a gay nightclub.

Everyone at the May Ball looked like they were having a good time. I certainly was, I was completely pissed – in fact, slightly too pissed, as I was to discover to my cost. The first couple of numbers were fine, and then we launched into Louis Jordan's 1946 hit, 'Ain't Nobody Here But Us Chickens'. This required a particularly robust 'two and a four' on the snare. Suddenly my whole night's drinking – all three riders – caught up with me. I was on a drum riser, on a stage that was about four-foot high, so in total I was about six or seven feet from the ground. I reckon I must have passed out. All I knew was that, dazed and confused, I had got to my feet and discovered I was in the street, with cars whizzing past me, standing there in the pouring rain. The fact that I was completely unscathed was a miracle. I couldn't work out what had happened and had no idea how I'd got there. I could hear the song I was supposed to be playing coming from inside the marquee, but I was outside. What the hell was going on? Clutching both drumsticks, I must have fallen backwards off the drum stool and riser and slid down between the back of the stage and the tarpaulin end-wall of the marquee, under which I managed to roll. I'd fallen out of my own gig!

I wandered the fifty yards up the road and joined the queue to get in. Even though I was wearing a DJ and blended in remarkably well with the other punters, the bloke on the gate wouldn't let me enter without producing the '4 a.m. breakfast wristband'. I explained, as best I could, that I was the drummer in the band that was provid-ing the entertainment inside the marquee and, to hammer the point home, drew his attention to the drumsticks I was holding. He was, understandably, confused and actually went and had a look at the band to see if it was, as I'd pointed out, missing a drummer. I got the feeling he wasn't totally convinced of my claim, but eventually he let me in just the same. I legged it up to the stage and scurried round the back to reappear at the kit in time for the beginning of the next number.

The journey back to London after the gig was a sombre affair. There was none of the usual banter, laughter and bitching. Biddie left it about twenty miles before he sprung it on me. He and Eve couldn't go on with me like this, and they thought it was probably best if they let me go – this coming from the man I was giving a lift home to. I stopped the car, told Biddie to get out and drove on leaving him alone and forlorn on the side of the motorway. No, I didn't. He was right, though. Falling out of gigs – that's surely the beginning of the end, isn't it?

* * *

After parting company with Biddie and Eve, it wasn't long before I stumbled upon another, utterly accidental phase of what might laughably be called 'my career'. Quite by chance, I was there at the beginning of 'Alternative Comedy'. It was a genuinely electrifying time, and it really felt like we were breaking new ground.

The Comic Strip performed two shows a night, Friday and Saturday, at the Boulevard Theatre above the Raymond Revue Bar in Walkers Court, Soho. Rik Mayall and Ade Edmondson performed as 'Twentieth Century Coyote', Peter Richardson and Nigel Planer appeared as 'The Outer

Limits', and Dawn French and Jennifer Saunders were simply 'French and Saunders'. Alexei Sayle was the far from genial host, and Arnold Brown was, er, Arnold Brown. Everyone bar Arnold did at least one song, so they had Rod Melvin on piano, Simon Brint playing bass and a bloke called Martin Pig (honestly!) at the drums. But not for long. Depending on whom you talked to, Martin either went off with a band called Furious Pig or became disillusioned and gave it all up. So I stepped in behind the drum kit at the Comic Strip. Little did I know that the people I was to meet at the Comic Strip would change my life for ever. They took themselves rather seriously, but for all the ego trips and power games, it felt like the start of a revolution.

To play regularly every Friday and Saturday night in front of a baying audience was hugely exciting. There was a genuine crackle of electricity in the air. The house was always packed – everyone loved it and the Comic Strip soon became the hottest ticket in town. Sayle was a hugely confident compère, and every now and again someone like Robin Williams or Barry Humphries would turn up out of the blue and perform, arsing about with the audience and just winging it. Dawn and Jen were very quiet back then – they didn't ooze confidence like they do these days. They weren't long out of teaching and their comedy was new, different and really funny.

I couldn't believe I was actually doing a gig in the same building as the Raymond Revue Bar, London's foremost nudie emporium, but the incredible thing was, for the year or so I worked there, I didn't get to clap eyes on one professionally naked lady. From the pictures outside, they looked amazing – so near, and yet so far. As you entered the building, the sharply dressed doorman would direct you to, 'Turn right for the Festival of Erotica, upstairs for the Comic Strip.' Even so, we would often spot confused Germans in the audience politely waiting for something naked to happen on stage and eventually getting up to leave after Alexei's first set, a barrage of entertaining filth and abuse. Ian Hamilton wrote in the *London Review of Books* (3 September 1981): 'A rock version of the theme from *Crossroads* starts the show, and Sayle hurtles on to the stage, spraying the audience with saliva, sweat and a deluge of fucks, cunts and bastards.'

I think Mr Hamilton was being a tad creative with the term 'rock version of the theme from *Crossroads*'. Rod was playing a jangly old upright, Simon's bass was going through a practice amp and I was probably thrashing about on brushes. The most enjoyable number, the one I always looked forward to, was Rik as 'Wik', his alter ego in *The Young Ones*. His rendition of 'I'm Evil', the Elvis classic, was both hilarious and incredibly creepy at the same time. They weren't all covers. Jen would do a faithful and funny country-and-western number, 'Why Do Boys Always Marry Girls Just Like Their Mothers?' I know it doesn't sound like it scans, but she made it work. Despite being labelled the 'new, brash, alternative' comedians, there remained an endearing, faint whiff of traditional light entertainment whenever they lapsed into song.

Backstage, there was a boys' dressing room and a girls' dressing room. We never quite got to the bottom of why the band were required to share with the girls, although this did mean we actually got to know Dawn and Jennifer a lot better than the other guys. Everyone would keep themselves very much to themselves: turn up, do the two shows and disappear home. Rik was completely focused on his performance. Ade was, too, but a tad less obsessive. Peter is credited with getting the whole thing up and running and always seemed to be more preoccupied with his role as a producer than as a performer. So we only ever spoke when we wanted him to pay us, as he rarely offered. Nigel was being Nigel, appearing to worry about every single minute detail of his life. He took hypochondria to new heights and exploited it perfectly in the hippy character Neil that he went on to play opposite Rik and Ade in *The Young Ones*. A really scary bloke on stage, Alexei was, initially, also a really scary bloke off it. I got the impression he really didn't suffer fools gladly, so I kept a low profile. But as I got to know him and his wife Linda, that all changed. I'll forever be indebted to Alexei for providing the funds to replace a fine set of Zildjian cymbals that had been half-inched out of the back of my car. Arnold, meanwhile, inhabited a beautiful, slightly surreal world of his own, no matter where he was, on or off stage.

For me, the Friday and Saturday shows at the Boulevard were perfect, as it meant I could walk the 500 yards to Ronnie Scott's Jazz Club on Frith Street and catch the last set by whoever happened to be on. Ronnie's was the place to be. Not only did it have a fantastic vibe – everybody who was anybody played Ronnie's – but it was also where you'd be sure to bump into every other jazz musician in town. To turn up after you'd been gigging was great, a sure sign you'd arrived as a jobbing muso in London. Punk came and went while I was holed up at Ronnie's – I missed it completely. The ultimate sign that you'd made it, of course, was actually to play there. The first time I did it, I came in rather low under the jazz radar – appearing there with Simon Brint in the comedy music double act, Raw Sex, didn't really count. It was funny. But it really didn't count.

I had a slight problem with a lot of the other drummers at the 606 Jazz Club and Ronnie's. I was never very big on talking shop. To me, a cymbal stand is a cymbal stand and a pair of sticks is a pair of sticks! I once listened to a guy, for pretty much the whole of a Bill Evans set, whispering to me about just where I was going wrong with my drumhead dampeners. Some of the more fanatical drummers would regale you with tales of the five or six hours' practice they'd just spent, poring over various advanced drum-notation books. These were thick tomes of really complicated stick-work; one was not only meant to sight-read the bastard, but master it, too. Impossible. My practice regime was much simpler and not nearly as laborious: sitting astride the arm of the sofa, in front of the telly, knocking out a few para-diddles – left-right-left-left, right-left-right-right, left-right-left-left, right-left-right-right – while watching nothing longer than *Boss Cat* or *Blue Peter*.

It wasn't until the Comic Strip was offered a nationwide tour that I got to know Rik and Ade a little better. The combination of booze and suddenly living in each other's pockets did a good job of cementing the friendship. Rod, Simon and I were invited along to be the tour band. A typical example of how the musicians were initially perceived by some was the fact that we were moved to have a T-shirt printed up with the words: 'Nigel Planer thinks I'm Simon Brint'. I urge you to take a look at one of the photos of

THAT'S ME DURING MY
INCREDIBLY TOP-HEAVY
DAYS . . .

WITH MY BROTHERS, STILL NOT
GETTING THE HANG OF THE
'BLENDING IN' THING.

MY FIRST DAY AT SCHOOL,
HELPED IMMENSELY BY MY
MINDERS, MUM, RICH AND RAY.

SCHOOL FOOTBALL - WHEN SHIRTS LOOKED COOL TUCKED IN. THE HEADMASTER, 'JACK' EVANS, WAS STRAIGHT OUT OF CENTRAL CASTING.

AGED TEN, LOOKING THE IMAGE OF MY SON.

FIVE YEARS LATER, LOOKING THE IMAGE OF MY DAUGHTER . . .

WITH RAY AND MUM, EARLY
SEVENTIES. MUM WAS GUTTED
SHE'D FORGOTTEN HER BINOCULARS.

MUM AND DAD, ALL SMILES,
SHORTLY AFTER MOVING TO
THE ISLE OF WIGHT.

THE ABBOTSFIELD SCHOOL JAZZ ORCHESTRA.
MR BEAN IS AT THE FAR RIGHT, ON BARITONE SAX.

TALKING TO ROY CASTLE
ON HIS KIDS' TV SHOW
*ROY CASTLE BEATS
TIME* – HE OF COURSE
LEFT IT UP TO ME . . .

MOODY JAZZ DRUMMER
CIRCA '73, WITH MOODY
JAZZ HAIR.

THE CHRISTMAS OF '76, REALLY
MAKING AN EFFORT TO GET INTO
THE SWING OF THINGS.

WITH DAN AT CHRISTMAS
- THE ANTLERS WERE HIS
IDEA, HONEST.

BY THE TIME WE HAD
OUR SECOND CHILD, ELLA,
CHRISTMAS PHOTOS WERE
A LOT MORE RELAXED.

THE *COMIC STRIP* TOUR.
ARNOLD BROWN OFTEN
FELL SPEECHLESS WHEN
I ENTERED THE ROOM.

ON THE *COMIC STRIP* TOUR WITH
ADE EDMONSON, THE PAIR OF US
NOT LOOKING REMOTELY GAY.

THE *COMIC STRIP* TOUR - VERY ROCK AND ROLL - WITH RIK PLAYING
THE STANDING ON ONE LEG GAME. ALEXEI LOOKED IMPRESSED!

THE *YOUNG ONES* TOUR HOUSE BAND.
DAMIAN PUGH, AMANDA SIMONE, ME
AND SIMON BRINT, WHO WOULD
OFTEN MAKE US LAUGH.

LOOKING GORGEOUS AS THE BANGLES ON *FRENCH & SAUNDERS.*

. . . AND SCARY AS PETERS AND LEE ON THE SAME SERIES.

. . . AND VERY GROOVY AS ABBA.

Simon and I, maybe there's an uncanny similarity I'm not seeing.

This was all very embarrassing for Nigel, but very amusing for us. Let's face it, though, we've all been there. Some time ago, I found myself, rather incongruously, presenting a Virgin Radio-sponsored sport-related award at the Planet Hollywood Restaurant just off Leicester Square. It was an afternoon affair, so a good lunchtime spread had been provided with plenty of 'refreshment'. The place was packed with sports folk all hoping to pick up something, and a number of faces from the music industry were there to present the various awards. I remember Damon Albarn presented Ruud Gullit, who played for Chelsea, with a medal and fell to his knees and began bowing as the man took to the stage. Damon was obviously a big Chelsea fan and seemed totally in awe. I don't really know one end of a football from the other and, if truth be known, I was a bit out of my depth. I didn't know who any of these football players were and decided to point this out by making a 'hilarious' joke when it was my turn to present an award. I insisted the recipient produce some form of identification, proof that the name on the award matched the one he had on, maybe, a driving licence or a utility bill. I can't help but feel this was wasted on Vladimir Stoch, the Slovakian midfielder who didn't speak a word of English.

Later that afternoon, as I was now fully 'refreshed', I found myself in the men's lav, having a slash. It was one of those annoying lavatories that has a lodger, a man who shows you how to use a tap and the correct way to dry your hands and tries to interest you in one of the twenty-six colognes he just happens to have. For this service, a pound is meant to be deposited in his dish. I didn't have a pound, but as luck would have it, I was standing next to Thomas 'Tommy' Cunningham, the drummer from Wet Wet Wet – a band so good they named them thrice. A month or so earlier, they had come into the Virgin Radio studios for a chat and Tommy had commented on my – sorry, Duane from Raw Sex's – conga-playing technique, admiring the comedy lack of it.

Standing at the urinals, I struck up a conversation with Tommy, asking him if he was presenting anything. He said he wasn't and headed for the sink and the demonstration of how to use the tap and soap. I kept up the pleasantries as we were drying our hands and, realizing I didn't have any change for the lodger, I asked him, one drummer to another like, if he could sub me a quid for the dish. He was very cool about it and lobbed in a few coins, to which I said thanks and promptly slapped him on the back, forgetting the golden rule of ablutions – never touch another man while still in the toilet area. We left the men's room and he disappeared into the crowd, only to reappear on stage, picking up an award and now going by the name of Tottenham Hotspur legend Teddy Sheringham. Well, he was a dead ringer for Thomas 'Tommy' Cunningham and a nice bloke too. He not only stood me the price of a piss, but was fine about me touching him in the toilet. My opinion of footballers was greatly enhanced that day, but at the end of it, I still see it as grown men in shorts, running up and down and swearing at each other.

8: THE NEW ROCK 'N' ROLL

Dawn and Jen remember it happening somewhere near Newcastle. Simon Brint, more precisely, pinned it down to the bleak, north-east ex-mining village of Seaham, County Durham. Alexei remembers only that Rod was wearing a fedora, but all of us remember exactly what happened.

We were on tour and heading south and after a lot of debate those who wanted to stop for a pic and a pint won the day, so the tour bus pulled into the small car park of 'the first pub we see in the next town'. We very quickly deduced it was a local pub for local people, who had all, clearly, spent the bulk of their lives down the mines working very, very long hours, very, very hard, in very, very shitty conditions. Unlike us.

Suddenly this small, hard-as-hammers pub was full of a bunch of soft southern luvvies, naively asking if the establishment provided sea salt and cracked black pepper crisps and the origin of the bottled water they didn't, as it happened, sell.

'Would tap do? I could put it in a bottle . . .'

Rik and Ade clawed back a sliver of credibility with the purchase of two pints of lager, straight glasses. Obviously, bitter would have been better, but the badge on their only hand-pump did little to entice the first-timer. Then it happened. Rod Melvin kindly offered to get the drinks in for the band and approached the bar. I'm sure Rod won't mind me saying this, but there is an attractive, slightly theatrical air about him, not least in the way he talks, and let's not forget Alexei remembers him sporting an impressive felt fedora as well. While ordering the round, he must have momentarily forgotten what Simon was drinking, so turned and across the room uttered the immortal words: 'Si, was that a dry sherry you wanted?' Our fate was sealed. We ate, drank and left, with the locals' perception of 'those perfumed ponces' from the south thoroughly endorsed.

This was the first time any of us had experienced 'being on the road' and we were loving it. It was all *soo* rock 'n' roll. On the tour bus, we would spend hours playing 'Who Can Stand On One Leg the Longest?' contests, or perhaps push the boat out with a game of cards. But it did get a little racy one Sunday night in Hull. An *NME* journalist was tagging along with us for his 'Comedy is the New Rock 'n' Roll' article, and he was struggling to find anything that would live up to the catchy title of the piece. The show usually finished by about half-ten, eleven at night, and in 1981, in Hull, on a Sunday, not a lot was happening. The bar was closing in the hotel, so I badgered the night porter for the location of a pool table we could use, figuring there would be a good chance an alcoholic drink wouldn't be far away. Arnold, Alexei, Nigel and Pete went out of their way to be counted out of any attempts to 'find the party' and disappeared off to bed. Rik and his girlfriend, Lise Mayer, simply didn't fancy the thought of a fruitless hunt for a good time in Hull – in fact, they had serious doubts as to whether a 'good time in Hull' was physically possible, so they bailed out too.

The porter eventually confessed that there was a place called the Coffee Club, which owned a pool table, and if you were lucky a drink could be had. Thankfully Ade and the girls still had a bit of get up and go left in them, so we got up and went, with the journo in tow, to the Coffee Club. There was a lot of leather being worn – Jen was in a long leather trench coat affair, Dawn was in her leather jacket and stetson phase, and the journalist was in what all rock journos had to wear, the regulation-issue tatty leather biker jacket. I remember a lot of squeaking going on in the cramped cab that ferried us to the outskirts of Hell. Sorry Hull, but it could easily have been.

Through the steamed-up windows you couldn't help but notice the scenery becoming increasingly bleak. Jennifer commented on the amount of corrugated iron sheeting that replaced the conventional sash windows in the houses we passed. Dawn drew our attention to the complete lack of people. We finally arrived at four terraced houses in the middle of absolutely nowhere. The cab driver pointed to the house, which had what looked like a reinforced front door, and told us we'd arrived. We so hadn't. Someone rang the bell and we arranged ourselves in front of the door, trying to look cool.

'We looked like people from London, we looked like wankers,' recalled Dawn.

Only as it creaked open did we notice that the reinforced door had a little slidey peephole set in it. Everyone knows that, nine times out of ten, places with little slidey peepholes are not good, but it was too late. Jennifer had already cleared her throat and piped up with a very clear and eloquent, 'Hello, we've come to enjoy your coffee.' I glanced at the journo and noticed he wasn't writing any of this rock 'n' roll nectar down.

The Coffee Club in Hull was like being in the certificate 18 video-game of the TV show *Shameless* – the essence of the show flashed up in your face, relentlessly. It did have a pool table as well as a few chairs and a small serving hatch through which Ade, the journo and I purchased a rum or whisky coffee, while the girls plumped for the china teapot of white wine. It sounds like I'm making this up, but I'm not. Thirty years ago, this is how it was: pure prohibition.

We all took great delight in watching Dawn being pursued by a thick-set man in a string vest and sweat pants, with an impressive array of tattoos, all of them on his face. Dawn's Achilles' heel is that she's always been a good listener. During the cab journey back to sanity, she told us part of her new friend's chat-up technique involved stating that he would kill for her, and that he'd done it before and he would gladly do it again – for her, not the blonde one (Jen), but her. I never saw the piece the journo wrote, but the title of his article certainly quickly became something of a cliché; comedy was for a brief moment widely known as the new rock 'n' roll.

While we were out on tour, Rik and Lise decided they didn't want to go back to the flat they were sharing in Hackney. Simon overheard this and mentioned he knew a woman who owned a large townhouse in Islington and was looking for tenants. My relationship with the nursey girlfriend in south London had ran out of gas during my absence so I had nowhere to go.

Happily, within a week or so of returning from the Comic Strip tour, I had migrated north to Islington and a room in Rik and Lise's rented house just off Liverpool Road. Let the mayhem commence.

* * *

Touring together meant we all got to know each other fairly well. Rik and I found we had a mutual love of Jimi Hendrix, early ZZ Top, Bilko and lager, which made living together a joy. Not long after we'd moved in, the love of lager was augmented with a flood of Scotch whisky when Lise returned from Edinburgh. She had been on the judging panel of the Perrier Awards and given twelve bottles of Glenmorangie for her troubles. Lise loved ten-year-old single malt whisky so much she could, sometimes, easily get through a whole glass over a long weekend. Robbie Coltrane would often visit and help us with the Glenmorangie. The way we saw it, the whisky was already ten years old and you don't want to be drinking that stuff after its sell-by date. That was our excuse and we were sticking to it.

Whenever Robbie stayed, I'd make sure I could crash at my new girlfriend's flat in Hampstead, freeing up my bedroom for his use. He would do the most charming thing that I later discovered was something of a Scottish tradition. On my return, there would always be a pile of loose change on the bedside table, a small thank you for 'providing a place to rest one's head'. Luckily for me, Robbie's small 'thank yous' grew bigger and bigger as his career went from strength to strength.

If Rik didn't have to be anywhere and I wasn't doing

anything, often the daily routine would begin by midday with a bowl of breakfast cereal followed by the first of the brandy miniatures. These were perfect for drinking while out and about, as they were pretty much invisible to the man in the street, and with the miniature, as its name suggests, being so small, it didn't feel like you were caning it.

Life was good, the sun shone and, for a time, I was driving a very impressive Jaguar V12 – metallic green and pepper-pot wheels with a complete FSH. No, I didn't have a clue either when I read the ad in the paper, but it transpired that 'pepper-pot wheels' was the term for the wheel trim – a lot of holes, like a pepper pot – hence the name and a nightmare to clean. The 'FSH' turned out to be the 'Full Service History'. I later discovered from my time with Jools Holland that this was a vital document. Jools very rarely purchased a car without one, and he purchased the odd car. And I mean really odd: funny little fifties vans and nutty American cars. The sixties red-and-white Corvette Stingray Convertible springs to mind, a huge beast of a car with a steering wheel the size of a plastic hula-hoop. With the roof up, you were afforded some privacy, but as luck would have it, it was always a lovely day whenever I went anywhere in it with him, so the roof was always down and packed away. He was safely behind the darkest, blackest Aviator shades I'd ever seen, so it was left to me to make the unavoidable eye contact with every single person we rumbled past, because, perversely, you never went fast in the Corvette. Just from people's gaze, I could tell they were inwardly shouting, 'Wankers!' – never more so than when Jools would attempt a left-hand turn at traffic lights. He's not a big man, never will be, and the monster he was driving didn't have the luxury of power steering, meaning that from a standing start he would fight with the wheel to negotiate the sharp left turn. It was then that people would actually stop what they were doing and just watch.

But back to our typical routine and the Jaguar V12, which had the widest, fattest, biggest cream leather seats I'd ever seen and was the most comfortable, ostentatious, 'twelve to the gallon' car in the world, and we loved it. Rik and I would climb in, decide who it was going to be that day on the sound system – there would be Chuck Berry, ZZ maybe, or a bit of Jimi – whack the eight speakers up to full volume and cruise up and down Islington's Upper Street, eyeing all the girlies, with Rik screaming his head off to the songs. When we'd heard all our favourite tracks on the C90 compilation tape, we'd head home, park up, and stroll the twenty yards to the pub on the corner of Liverpool Road and Ellington Street.

Two pints, either side of a cheese-and-pickle roll, is all we'd need to set us up nicely for the afternoon's agenda, a rummage round the crazy furniture shops on Holloway Road. When Rik and Lise handed over three months' rent in advance on the house in Ellington Street it was unfurnished, so we had a whale of a time filling it up with junk. I remember, once, carrying a really scratchy, synthetic, angular, light-green, Art Deco-esque three-piece suite back to the house. It was horrible, and I think that's why Rik bought it. This was a temporary home before he and Lise committed to the big purchase, their own place, so nothing they bought was going any further than Ellington Street. Watching him in the shops must have been where I first got the bug for the 'pissed purchase', also known as being responsible for driving a credit card whilst under the influence.

For a long time afterwards, I could never kick-start the Christmas shopping without an hour or so's hard work at the coal face in the Groucho Club. The compulsion to 'purchase when pissed' lasted right up until the late nineties when, one afternoon, I accidentally bought two overcoats. I purchased a very sharp one on Regent Street, and then a shit one nearby. With one in a bag and one on my back, I then sauntered round to David Clulow's brand new optician's shop on Old Compton Street where, gamely, I had my eyes tested and purchased a pair of glasses. The overcoats were fine; I lost the sharp one, but wear the shit one to this day. It was the glasses that were the problem. I hadn't thought it through; they only really worked when I was the worse for wear, as pissed as I was when I bought them. So I have the dubious honour of being the proud owner of an authentic pair of beer goggles.

Late afternoon would find us sitting on the scratchy, shit sofa in front of several episodes of *The Phil Silvers Show* before heading off to the Royal Mail pub on Upper Street for some serious pool, and then on to Simon Brint's flat a few doors up the road to continue recording what were to become 'The Gin Tapes'. We were all big fans of Viv Stanshall and the Bonzo Dog Doo-Dah Band. Their 'Sir Henry at Rawlinson End' creation was the inspiration for the drunken madness Simon deftly committed to tape, three floors up in his cosy one-bedroomed Islington flat/ studio. These tapes would, of course, be torture to listen to now, but in the heat of the moment they were hilarious masterpieces, the funniest things we'd ever heard.

It wasn't long before Rik and Lise, along with their old friend Ben Elton, set about writing *The Young Ones*, the TV show that every student in the country had been waiting for. At last they had a fairly mainstream programme to call their own, full of belching, farting carnage and some of the best 'real' music around at the time. Each show featured a number performed by the likes of Motörhead, Dr Feelgood, Nine Below Zero and Madness, usually in the front room of the house where Rick, Vyvyan, Neil and the other one who's name no one remembers, but who was played expertly by Chris Ryan, lived. Someone told me the band's appearance came about because, back then, there was more money to be had out of the BBC entertainment budget if there was a song in your show. Suddenly you were Light Entertainment and not Comedy. I'm sure I'm not alone, and I mean this in the nicest possible way, but I can't think why else Rik would put up with the focus of attention being taken away from him for a whole three minutes.

Simon Brint was doing a lot of music stuff, radio ads, jingles and, most notably, all the music for *The Comic Strip Presents* . . . series of films on Channel Four. I was chipping in with the odd idea and taking care of all the percussion side of things. Paul Jackson, who was producing *The Young Ones*, approached us to do a cover of Dylan's 'Subterranean Home Sick Blues' for the second series. A whole host of people were roped in to belt the number out on the pavement outside *The Young Ones* house – what a lovely, surreal, sunny day in a suburb of Bristol that was. The band went by the name of Ken Bishop's Nice Twelve. This was the name of (the fictitious) Ken's original band, most of whom were killed in tragic, mysterious circumstances and the band was abridged to just Ken and his stepson Duane, who were to carry on with a degree of success as Raw Sex.

Jools, Chris Difford of Squeeze and Stewart Copeland of the Police, amongst others, all agreed to act the giddy goat in Bristol, and Stewart did it for no money. When asked where the cheque for £120 should be sent, he modestly admitted to Lise that he was independently wealthy and didn't need it. He had arrived in Bristol behind the wheel of a Range Rover that looked one-and-a-half times bigger than all the other big Range Rovers in the street, and told us he had been stopped by the police for speeding on the M4. He was chuffed that he got off without a ticket, putting it down to the Police badge he was wearing. I wonder if it works for Sting and Andy Summers. Or anyone who wears one of the band's badges for that matter.

My abiding memory of the whole thing was playing 'Pass the Matchbox' in the lounge of the hotel that the crew were using as their base. Simon Brint will be the first to tell you he hasn't got the smallest nose in the world and watching him with a matchbox wedged on it, carefully trying to pass it to an excitable Stewart, a man with an equally prodigious proboscis, was a beautiful thing to behold. My appearance in the video of the song can best be described as coquettish with a hint of whimsy.

* * *

As I mentioned at the beginning of the book, life with Rik and Lise was never ordinary. You never quite knew who was going to turn up on the doorstep. It was while I was living on Ellington Street that I began my long-standing friendship with one of the visitors, one Julian Holland. Rik had made a bunch of appearances on the first series of Channel 4's ground-breaking live music show, *The Tube*, which Jools and Paula Yates were hosting. Rik and Jools had got on well, so much so that plans were quickly put in motion for the pair of them to do some work together. Before that could happen, on the back of the phenomenal success of *The Young Ones* TV show, there was a Young Ones tour to get through.

Rik was keen that there should be some live music in the show, as the trio on the Comic Strip tour had worked so well. Unfortunately, Rod 'Fedora' Melvin was unable to commit to a big long tour as, I think, he and his wife had just had a child. So rather than do what you are supposed to do, which is advertise and then audition a bunch of keyboard players, being careful to pick the one best suited to the job at hand, Simon and I looked to the first person we knew. All the pianists I knew were too 'jazz', but Simon knew of a guy who was with the Regents when they had their top ten hit, '7teen'. Rik knew the track and loved it – well, he knew the first line, 'Seventeen, and not yet a woman', which he would sing, repeatedly. Everyone liked the idea of the keyboard player who'd had some chart success, and it also implied a degree of competence – 'If he's had a top ten, he must be good . . .'

I'm not sure if we even auditioned Damian Pugh. He just turned up on the first day of rehearsals at the Irish Club, 82 Eaton Square, Belgravia. He was an amazing man with a curly mop of hair, always in a two-piece suit and forever rolling fags. Damian was one of the nicest blokes you could ever wish to meet, but don't go looking for common sense or any leadership skills. It was only after we had embarked on the tour that he confessed to suffering from what he casually called 'keyboard blindness' (an inability to comprehend the keys on the piano) – most notably with his left hand. But he was always a joy to be with. Once, when we'd finished breakfast at a greasy spoon, Damian went to the counter to pay, then turned to shout over to our table, 'Hey! Simon, what was that called, what I've just eaten?' I wonder what he's doing today – and if it's safe!

The Irish Club, despite its imposing address, was a pretty down-to-earth place, moved to hiring out its abandoned function rooms to the likes of us for revenue. There was a cosy bar on the left as you went in, where a handful of old regulars would sit nursing their pints, every now and again taking it in turns to get up and lose another ten-pence piece in the fruit machine. Because it was a members' club, the machine could pay out a lot more than a pub fruit machine – this one boasted a £50 jackpot.

It wasn't long before the majority of the band's lunch break would be spent in the Irish Club bar rather than huddled round the cellophane-covered platters of assorted sandwiches and cakes laid on for us in the rehearsal space. It was to be short-lived, however, as one lunchtime, as we were leaving, Damian casually popped a ten-pence piece into the fruit machine and immediately won the £50 jackpot. The whole bloody lot came spewing out of the machine in assorted coinage all over the floor. The regulars, who had spent months feeding the machine and whose money it all was, were seething. What made everything worse was the painfully slow speed at which the machine paid out its jackpot – it went on for ever. Each ker-chung was a little stab in the ribs for all the old guys in the bar, who all knew they'd have to wait for at least another three months for the chance of a fifty-quid jackpot and a little bit of excitement in their lives.

The delightful singer and actress Amanda Simmons was recruited to belt out a few numbers in the show and, as we were without Dawn and Jen, she proved to be a welcome feminine presence on the tour. She also possessed the most incorrigible giggle. One of the high points of the show was Amanda and the band's rollicking version of 'These Boots Are Made for Walking'. Listening back to a tape of the show one time, you could actually hear Rik's howl of appreciation from the side of the stage as we moved through the number's key change.

The first leg of the tour was to be all universities or colleges, as they were deemed solid audiences. Phil McIntyre, who was putting the show on, wasn't going to take any chances with half-sold venues. He'd been in the business too long and knew exactly what he was doing. Then again . . . As we pulled into Sheffield around lunchtime, the first thing we noticed was the abundance of posters advertising forthcoming attractions, from Def Leppard to Victoria Wood. Try as we might, no one could spot a poster for 'Straight From TV! – *The Young Ones*! Live On Stage!'

'Not to worry,' someone said. 'This happens if the show gets sold out enough in advance, so there is no need to waste money putting posters up.'

The bus pulled into Sheffield University and the tour manager, Phil Harper, known affectionately as 'Herpes', went in to announce our arrival and double check we were in the right place. It was a rather sheepish Herpes who emerged from the stage door of the theatre complex. Very calmly, and matter of factly, he announced that there had been some sort of cock-up and we were exactly one month early. Of course, that's why there were no posters announcing our imminent arrival – they were all going up in the next week. This wasn't a good start. Was tomorrow's gig going to be one month away, too? Initially, no one got off the bus. It was all far too embarrassing, the thought of students pointing and laughing at us, accusing us of being a bit keen.

There was a general feeling of, 'Well, we've come this far, can't we just do the show anyway?' And so it was that Rik, Ade and Nigel were despatched to local radio stations to let everyone know the Young Ones were in town and playing that night. Not the best of starts to a nationwide tour, but it kept us on our toes. The guys managed to drum up some trade as the show that evening was packed, but it also went on all night – it was about four-and-a-half hours long. No one had factored in the laughs and the outrageous milking that was occurring on stage. The audiences were going berserk for Rik, Vyvyan and Neil. I think they had completely underestimated the reception they'd get when they bounced on stage; of course, it was no bad thing, it just meant everything took an age.

A few days later we arrived at the Nottingham Playhouse during what looked like a riot taking place outside the theatre. 1,500 tickets had been sold for the gig and it was sold out, but there were about 500 people, mainly students, milling around and getting restless, trying to get a ticket. As soon as I mentioned, as a joke, that it was getting a bit hairy outside and it was only a matter of time before the rioting started, people's true colours started to surface. Colours that, funnily enough, weren't too dissimilar to their stage alter egos. Ade was fairly OK about it and thought it all quite amusing, but it was beautiful to watch as Rik and Nigel contemplated what might kick off: visions of marauding students running riot and dragging people out of dressing rooms and carrying them aloft to be pulled to pieces in the street.

The tour took us back to Hull, to a better hotel this time which, thankfully, meant we had no need to call on the dubious pleasures the Coffee Club had to offer. Rik was keen to check it out as he'd passed when we were last there with the Comic Strip tour, and having heard all about it from those that did attend, he was itching to see it for himself. But this time round, Hull was to provide a different distraction, but equally bleak.

The routine was very similar in each town: get to the hotel for midday and drop our stuff off, then head over to the venue to sound check for an hour or so, then try and kill the four hours till show time without resorting to the pub. About six doors up from the hotel, I'd spotted a massage parlour sign and, having never experienced the delights on offer at such an establishment, suggested to Ade we should check it out, as I didn't want to go on my own. He confessed to never having stepped inside a massage parlour either, but thought it might be handy as he was suffering with a niggling back complaint. At four o'clock in the afternoon on another wet Sunday in Hull, Ade and I walked down from the hotel and up a narrow flight of stairs to, according to the sign in the window, 'Hull's premier massage salon oasis'.

The place was, as expected, deceptively small with

bamboo as a theme throughout. In the reception, four low-level bamboo armchairs faced each other around a bamboo and smoked glass coffee table, on which were scattered a few magazines, a couple of health and wellbeing-related publications and *Tit-Bits*. A woman, in her early twenties and looking the part, welcomed us in and, very matter of factly, asked for seven pounds from each of us. Then we were shown into a room where we could take all our clothes off and get into a white robe. We emerged from the changing-room and were instructed to sit down and make ourselves comfortable. The lady asked if we wanted a drink and, not waiting for the answer, disappeared. Time passed immeasurably slowly but, just as we were getting the feeling we should abort the mission, another much younger woman appeared at the top of the stairs. Great, our only means of escape blocked, we were trapped. She opened a door to a very small room just big enough for the padded masseur's table and invited one of us to come with her.

'Go on, Rowly.'

Quick as a flash, Ade had kindly offered me up to the woman who was beginning to look younger by the minute. She really didn't look like she had the wherewithal to sort out the muscles in a drummer's back.

I slipped the robe off and quickly wrapped a small towel round myself and lay on the table. She started lightly rubbing the back of my legs which was fine. It was early doors and she probably needed to warm up – two minutes earlier she had been in her nylon parka jacket having just arrived out of the rain. I feel the need to remind you here that I had never had a massage before in my life, so had little if nothing with which to compare what this, quite possibly sixteen-year-old girl was doing. As she started to work her way up my body, the small talk began. She wanted to know how my day was going and had deduced from my accent that I was from out of town, so asked what I was doing in Hull. I told her I was a drummer playing in the show just up the road and mentioned *The Young Ones*. She'd never heard of them, which immediately made me look like a nutter. Maybe she wasn't sixteen after all, maybe she was fifty and I was crap at pinning an age on anyone, but I don't think so. Surely, at her age, she must have at least heard of *The Young Ones*? She didn't watch telly, she said, she didn't have time. She picked up on the fact I was a musician, though, and was quick to point out she played the clarinet and it wasn't expensive. I was a bit confused. That'll be why she didn't watch any telly then: if she wasn't playing the clarinet, she was hard at it, putting the hours in as a professional masseuse.

Making very little impression on my back – at best I could feel a light stroking sensation – she reiterated the statement that she 'played the clarinet'. I then mentioned the incredible coincidence – my dad also played the clarinet! This slightly threw her but again she stated quite clearly and a little slower this time, that: She. Played. The. Clarinet. Trying to appear knowledgeable, I asked whether she played the 'A sharp' or 'B flat' clarinet, as my dad played both. I think I'd lost her by this point, and the clarinet as a topic of conversation dried up, as did her effort to massage my back. By now, this massage felt like nothing more than her standing in the same room as me. Rather curtly, she told me to get up as she had finished and promptly left the small room.

Once I was dressed I sat in the reception waiting for Ade and flicked through *Tit-Bits*. We walked back to the hotel, each gingerly trying to ascertain what the other had experienced at 'Hull's premier massage salon oasis'. Very little, by all accounts. I honestly didn't make the connection when the massage lady started talking about playing the clarinet, and the fact that it didn't cost much. It was only later that night, when we were all back in the bar of the hotel and I mentioned it to a couple of the roadies, that the penny dropped. Never been a lucky place for me, Hull.

I didn't see much of Rik after gigs as Lise was on tour with us. She and Rik must have been working on the second series of *The Young Ones*. She also had the unenviable job of standing at the side of the stage when Rik was performing, and jotting down anything he said that was unscripted. If it got a laugh, it would be woven into the next night's routine. Nigel was never one for letting rip after a show, and Simon would invariably fall asleep an hour or two into a serious drinking session. Damian would like a drink, but I think he too had a tolerance problem and would wisely peel off to bed before doing himself a mischief. Not so Ade and I.

The early eighties saw the arrival of the 'wine in a box' phenomenon, and there would always be at least three on the rider each night. Twenty-four cans of lager, six litres of table wine and a bottle of Scotch. The beauty of the box of wine is that it keeps fresh and you have no way of telling how much is left. It was perfect for the display of food and booze laid on at every venue. These boxes would travel with us until they were empty. No more opened bottles of wine left to waste – you can see the sense.

If I knew the hotel had a pool table, I'd always smuggle a couple of boxes back to the hotel as we could set them up in the corner, under a coat, and help ourselves. Nobody wanted to trouble the night porter and end up paying through the nose for a drink. And when I say 'nobody', I'm pretty much exclusively referring to me and Ade. The signal for bed would be when the wine boxes were empty, but not before we'd played the 'Who Can Fall Down the Big Sweeping Stairs in the Hotel Without Letting Go of Their Wine Box' game. It needs little explanation, as I think the title pretty much says it all. The things one can achieve when, tipsy . . . One hotel we stayed at was covered in scaffolding. Ade and I were in adjacent rooms so after our pool and wine box antics, and before going to bed, I got naked and climbed out along the poles to his room and knocked on his window. I was sure I'd scare the life out of him. He pulled open the curtains and wasn't fazed at all even though we were four floors up. His reaction was simply, 'I didn't think you'd do that, Rowly, but you did, well done, now *please* go to bed.'

* * *

We'd grown into a cosy band of travelling performers, so it was a sad day when we had to return to London and get on with our 'day jobs'. In Rik and Ade's case, that was writing a film for the next series of *The Comic Strip Presents* . . .

I had a drumming gig at the Institute of Contemporary Arts in The Mall, London – it sounded a bit 'poncy', but a couple of weeks' work in the centre of town, no matter what it constituted, was not to be sniffed at. *Slow Fade* was a multi-media, arty theatre production set in eighteenth-century Russia, from what I could gather. The stage was covered in a ton of leaves, there were back-projection screens everywhere and there was a motley selection of instrumentalists on stage. It all felt a bit experimental, but turned out to be quite incredible. The man who put it all together was Mike Figgis, the film director who went on to make *Stormy Monday*, *Internal Affairs* and *Leaving Las Vegas*, to name but a few. *Slow Fade* became Mike's first film for Channel 4, entitled *The House*. Some of the sound-track, Mike tells me, was lifted from the live show, where I can be heard playing my 'experimental arty' heart out.

This regular evening gig left the days free, and it wasn't long before, with nothing better to do, I was tagging along with Rik and Ade for the usual two-hour pub lunch and pool session at the Royal Mail in Upper Street. They had started putting together an idea for a *The Comic Strip Presents . . .* film, based on their Dangerous Brothers characters. Rik and Ade, very magnanimously, offered to pay me £100 to come up with ten ideas/gags they deemed usable in their script.

Later that afternoon, having exceeded their offer and come up with, amongst other things, a good name for Peter Cook's psychopathic contract-killer character – Mr Jolly – and what was eventually to be the title – *Mr Jolly Lives Next Door* – they offered to take me on as a fully fledged co-writer. This was in lieu of the hundred pounds, but I was completely chuffed to bits so didn't think about it for a second.

A big mistake as, to this day, I don't think I've seen a penny out of the bastard film. I even appear in it as three different characters: a put-upon barman, a double for Peter

Cook and part of Raw Sex, the house band in the Neon Tepee, the girly drinking club Richie and Eddie visit. Added to that, Simon and I did all the bloody music, so I ended up having quite an involvement in the whole venture.

At one point, it looked like it wasn't going to go ahead. For reasons best known to themselves, Rik and Ade had talked Stephen Frears, of all people, into directing it, but then he suddenly got a 'proper directing gig' and it didn't look like he was going to be available. Rik put his foot down and came out with: 'If he doesn't direct it, it's not happening.' It was classic Rik, but it was touch and go for a few days. As it turned out, I think, Stephen just couldn't do the last week, but Rik and Ade knew exactly what they were doing and, seamlessly, took over the director's seat for the end of filming.

While filming *Mr Jolly*, Rik celebrated his twenty-ninth birthday, so I turned up with the biggest cream cake I could find. Instead of decorating it with twenty-nine candles, I swung by my pyrotechnic supplier: a borderline-legal newsagents and toy shop in north London. On location, during the break for lunch, I produced the cake and lit as many of the twenty-nine 'candles' as I could before the whole thing went up. Everyone got a bit of the cake that day, but not necessarily to eat. Rik and Ade loved it, but I don't think wardrobe or Stephen were too happy.

* * *

I really enjoyed touring – it was the nearest you got to having regular work mates, people you saw day in, day out and could strike up some kind of friendship with. People you could be outrageous with, cheat death with . . .

In 1984, Nigel Planer, as his alter ego Neil, released 'Hole In My Shoe', originally a hit for the Sixties band Traffic. It reached number two in the UK charts, so, not one to miss an opportunity, he put a tour together on the back of it. The 'Bad Karma In The UK' tour was not on the same scale as the Young Ones tour but due to the people involved it was infinitely more dangerous. Nigel had two hours to fill so he not only recruited Raw Sex to help out, but also four comedian actors known collectively as the 'Wow Show': Mark Arden, Steve Frost, Paul Mark Elliot and Lee Cornes. They were all consummate professionals but they really knew how to let rip, and to party. For the first time I was surrounded by people who could match me drink for drink! For so long it had been a case of popping out for a drink with friends and sixteen hours later being the only one at the bar. Now, with the Wow Show on board, we could really put some hours in. This culminated in a misunderstanding during a three-week run at St Mary's Hall in Edinburgh during the festival. We were all in the pub opposite the theatre, it was dusk but for some reason I had got it into my head that it was dawn and the sun was just coming up. The light was exactly the same – and pubs were open all hours during the festival, hence my confusion. I was convinced we must have been doing an extra show – possibly for charity – at nine o'clock in the morning.

Not so much later a tour bus was ferrying us round the country. It was more a minibus that at times struggled to contain the Wow Show's enthusiasm. The chap Phil McIntyre, the tour promoter, had allocated to drive and look after us, was a nervy man to say the least. Nigel would sit with him at the front trying his best to distance himself from the refreshingly childish mayhem that regularly flared up at the back of the bus. On a journey back to London from Bristol, Mark Arden and I managed to climb out of a rear sliding window and clamber onto the roof rack that ran the length of the vehicle. Mark and I lay there for a while, on our backs staring at the stars with the wind in our . . . everything. It really was the most exhilarating experience. We then inched our way to the front of the bus. Hurtling down the M4, in the fast lane, at seventy miles an hour, two heads slowly appeared at the top of the windscreen, we smiled and waved at Nigel and the driver who, understandably, went *absolutely* ballistic. The poor driver was a wreck and unable to carry on so it was left to Steve 'I've only had a few pints' Frost to drive us the rest of the way home.

9: THE BUNKER SHOW

It wasn't long after we returned from the Young Ones tour that I got a call out of the blue. It was Paul Jackson, the guy who had produced *The Young Ones* TV series. He was about to make Ruby Wax's first chat show, *Don't Miss Wax*, and wondered if I fancied doing the warm-up in the studio. I reminded Paul that I was a drummer and was in fact at that very moment learning the drum pad for the West End musical, *The Secret Diary of Adrian Mole*. I was 'depping' for two weeks while the original drummer had a holiday. I couldn't understand why this guy would take time off and was so keen to get away from such a good opportunity. Soon all would become clear.

Before agreeing to try my hand as a 'warm-up', though, I just needed to get a few things straight with Paul. I'd seen loads of warm-ups at shows I'd gone along to at the BBC with Rik – they were all aspiring comedians able to fall back on their material in front of 300 people. I spelled it out to Paul that I didn't have a joke in my body, that I'd not done any stand-up and that I didn't even tell jokes to friends. He said he didn't want to use a comic as he didn't want someone rattling off a bunch of gags that were nothing to do with what was happening in the studio that evening. He went on to say that whenever he'd been out with Rik and me for a drink, I was always able to see the funny side of things and that was what he wanted to try out on Ruby's new show. A bloke making friends with the audience and seeing the funny side of things. No pressure there, then . . .

I said yes to Paul and forgot about it, as Ruby's show was a few weeks away – unlike *The Secret Diary Of Adrian Mole*, the musical, which was just round the corner. I turned up at the stage door of Wyndham's Theatre, just off Leicester Square, with only a thick pad of drum charts and my stick bag. Part of the reason I'd said yes to the gig was that the kit was already in place in the pit so I wasn't schlepping gear in and out. I actually thought this might be quite cushy. As it happened, initially, it was one of the scariest things I've ever done.

There were only three musicians in the orchestra pit: a musical director at a stack of keyboards to my left and a guitarist surrounded by four or five guitars on my right. I was sitting in the middle, facing out to the audience behind a huge kit, six rack toms, far too many cymbals and a whole bunch of nutty percussion equipment bolted here, there and everywhere. Between the drums and the keyboards was a thick baffle-board to minimize spill and create a little bit of separation between the instruments. This meant I couldn't actually see the musical director. There was a small square hole cut out of the board, through which at the beginning of each number his finger would appear to count me in. Most numbers had a four- to eight-bar drum fill at the top, which gave all the kids on stage time to get into position before launching into a song. The guitarist made little attempt at eye-contact as his nose was buried in a well-thumbed copy of *The Hitchhiker's Guide to the Galaxy*. He would only look away from it for a split second before he began playing. While the last chord was still ringing in his guitar, he would have placed it back on the stand and be back into his book. The show had been running for months, and it was obvious everyone working on it was more than familiar with their job requirement.

Such was the fear and panic surging through my body on the first show, I belted through all the numbers, which resulted in the curtains coming down twenty minutes early. The cast loved it – after all, they got home early. When I got home, all I did was sit there and think, 'Shit, I've got to do that again tomorrow!'

The second show was a little better and by the fifth or sixth performance I'd be sat there staring at the audience, the only people I could see, with a coffee mug in my hand surreptitiously getting through a litre-and-a-half bottle of screw-top Soave per show. This was battery farming for drummers, it was madness. I was a chicken, trussed up in a small space, no communication with anyone, doing the same thing over and over again.

From the age of thirteen, all I had wanted to do was play the drums, and in a matter of days working in the pit at Wyndham's Theatre, on the Charing Cross Road, all the affection and love I had for playing was rinsed out of my body. By the end of the two weeks I despised the kit and didn't want to have anything to do with it. So I was ready, thanks to Paul Jackson and Ruby Wax, for the birth of the accidental comedian.

The show was recorded at the Drill Hall in Cheney Street just off Tottenham Court Road, where twenty years later I'd be holding forth on the Radio Two show, *Jammin'*. The two experiences couldn't be more different. With *Jammin'*, I knew exactly what was going on and what I was doing – it was my show and I was in charge. With Ruby's show, I can safely say I had absolutely no idea what the hell I was doing. And do you know, I think it showed.

The warm-up's job is simple: keep everyone focused when there is a lull in the proceedings. Scenery might have to be shifted about, a camera might go down or the talent, in this case Ruby, might need some attention or something doing to her, and in Ruby's case we could all think of a few things we'd like to do to her. In all these situations, the warm-up bounces on and keeps the 'party' going. That's why stand-ups do it – it's really handy to have at least fifteen minutes of material up your sleeve. There is only so much improvised, free-association winging it you can do, and I did pretty much all of it during the thirteen-week run of shows. I also had the perfect, last resort get-out clause, if something didn't work; I'd hold my hands up and say, 'Look, there's been the most horrendous mistake. I'm actually a professional jazz drummer – I can't think what's happened . . .'

Stuffed for anything to say I would resort to actually buying jokes from people in the audience, asking how much they thought their effort was worth and then throwing it open to the audience for their opinion. If I was lucky, I could soak up five or ten minutes doing that, but never more than once per show. You really could never relax. What didn't help was that Ruby was a naturally incredibly funny person, with a razor-sharp wit. Away with the fairies, yes, but thoroughly entertaining. Each week I faced an audience with absolutely no material and it seemed to work – that quickly became an intoxicating drug. But it's a very dangerous way to get a very quick fix.

* * *

I have to admit to being in the right place at the right time down at the Drill Hall working on *Don't Miss Wax*. One night, after the show, a lady approached me and asked if I wanted to appear on a new programme ITV was putting out through the night on Fridays and Saturdays. It was to be called *Night Network*. The lady was Jill Sinclair, the producer of this brand new show, and at first I trotted out the usual, 'But I'm a drummer, and a jazz one at that . . .' I didn't feel I should let on that my 'warm-up' technique she had just witnessed was based on nothing more than thin air and half-a-dozen sharpeners. But, to my eternal thanks, she persisted and a meeting was arranged at the very grand LWT to talk about some ideas and how I could be involved.

Unfortunately, the ideas they were knocking around didn't really do anything for me. One involved sitting there introducing cartoon clips and, to be honest, when it comes to animation, beyond *Boss Cat*, *Road Runner* and *The Flintstones*, my interest wanes. I fancied having a chat with people, chewing the cud, having a laugh but they informed me that they already had a chat show called *Pillow Talk* featuring Emma Freud interviewing people while they were actually in bed together. The show caused a stir one week when Jeffrey Archer was a guest and maintained he was naked under the sheets. We all felt for Emma on that occasion, as I'm sure Jeffrey did.

I was a big fan of Roy Plomley's *Desert Island Discs* on

Radio Four and thought a TV version of that would be worth doing. Instead of records, we would play music videos. In order to create some distance from the radio show, I thought a nuclear bunker would be a good 'location' to be stranded. The idea for *The Bunker Show* was simple: the three-minute warning has gone off, so what eight videos will you take into the Bunker and spend the next three years of your life with? A guest and I would be in the Bunker with a VHS machine, a couple of folding deckchairs, a big wall of canned food and – crucially – loads of booze. During the show, I'd swig from a huge litre bottle of Scotch, not *actual* Scotch, I think we settled on flat ginger beer as the best substitute. It completely fooled Mel Brooks when he was on the show. He was appearing on any show that would have him to promote his 1987 film *Spaceballs*, the sci-fi spoof he'd written, directed and, judging by the amount of times he shoehorned a reference to the bloody film into our conversation, probably financed himself.

We recorded two shows a day at 11 a.m. and 3 p.m. Mel's was the morning recording, as I remember committing one of the cardinal sins in TV: turning up at the studio after your guest has arrived. I was very hung-over and, thinking about it, probably already stank of booze, which must have got Mel assuming the Scotch was real. Whenever I put the bottle up to my mouth, he would look over to his 'people', off camera, and shrug in disbelief. At one point, I said, 'Mel, if you think I'm pissed, you should see the bloke who's going to edit this – he's off his tits in the pub next door.' Mel used to be a jazz drummer, so we ended the show swapping fours on anything that made a noise. I think he went away happy, if not a little confused. I saw him the following week on *The Des O'Connor Show* in much more sedate surroundings.

Gary Glitter, ring any bells? He appeared on *The Bunker Show* and was very entertaining, if a little odd. He pretty much hijacked the show to make a desperate plea to his estranged girlfriend – he was clutching a large framed picture of the poor girl – to have him back. We were none the wiser back then, but yep, you're right, she didn't look *that* old.

We were all looking forward to Spike Milligan appearing on the show. He said he'd only turn up if a very specific bottle of red wine was provided for him which, naturally, cost a fortune. The producers grudgingly went along with the request, and I looked forward to trying a bottle of wine that, I think, came in at more than what I was being paid to do the show. As it turned out, Spike was very strange – 'impenetrable' is the word I'd use, or maybe 'nightmare'. He insisted on telling me the ancient Chinese chicken joke and was barely able to contain his laughter as he delivered the punch line, '. . . this chicken's rubbery'. You could hear the feigned laughter from the studio floor, the producers obviously not wishing to upset Spike. He also left with the bottle of wine intact, the bastard.

There was one guest on *The Bunker Show* whom everyone was dreading, but turned out to be an absolute delight. Between us, we were able to push the boundaries of decency on British television that little bit further. Ian Brown, the guy with whom I wrote the television series *Set of Six*, once told me he'd got a call from Freddie Starr's people asking if he would be up for working on Freddie's new show. Before Ian could reply, the guy on the other end of the phone pitched in with, '. . . before you answer, you don't have to worry, he's off the tablets'. I'd been a big fan of Freddie's since the early seventies when he appeared on the impressionist show, *Who Do You Do?* and *Russ Abbot's Mad House.* That was back in the day when Saturday night TV was a real treat – being about twelve probably helped. On *The Bunker Show*, Freddie arrived and, before you knew it, was changed into his then trademark shorts, wellingtons and Hitler gear – fair enough. One of the videos he'd picked was Robert Palmer's 'Addicted to Love', which featured a backing band made up entirely of gorgeous women in skin-tight, slightly transparent black dresses, all with identical make-up and all swaying in time to the music.

'So Freddie, I've an idea I know the answer, but here goes anyway. Why this particular vid?'

'Well, Rowland, it's going to be lonely in the bunker, and I think the girls will be able to help in a way the Elvis tapes I've brought with me won't, if you get my drift . . .'

What we did next wasn't clever and certainly wasn't grown up, but we got away with it and that was the main thing. We played the 'Addicted to Love' video and when we came back to the bunker, liquid soap – a fairly new invention then – had been squirted everywhere and was gently dripping off everything as the cameras found Freddie and me in the folding chairs. Freddie had subtly loosened the first two buttons on his army shorts and was reclining in what I can only describe as a 'spent' manner.

'That was Robert Palmer and "Addicted to Love". Feel better for that, Freddie?'

'Thank you, Rowland, yes. And it's not a bad song either, as it happens.'

10: DR SCROTE AND
THE LAST RESORT

'You were an idiot, but always in a very pleasant way. You weren't an idiot *to* people, you were kinda an idiot to yourself, and you appeared to be indestructible, of course,' recalls Jonathan Ross.

My agent didn't ring me very often, but in late 1988 I got a call asking if I could go in and see some people at a production company called Channel X. They had offices in Wardour Street, right in the heart of Soho, which was a good sign. In the late eighties, any media company worth its salt had to be within walking distance of the Groucho Club, and this lot were in the next street! Their office was at the top of about five flights of stairs, never a good thing as, unless you can lay claim to an Olympic medal, you arrive red-faced with breathing difficulties and covered in a light sheen of visible sweat. Not good for a first impression, but that was exactly how Alan Marke and Jonathan Ross found me when I was introduced to them in the cramped reception area.

I was ushered through to Jonathan's office, which was how I'd imagine a Japanese toy-shop owner's lock-up to look: wall-to-wall plastic toy shit. Jonnie had seen me mucking about with Jools and was interested in getting me to do something on *The Last Resort with Jonathan Ross*, his chat show. They were looking for fresh ingredients for the third series. The first had been well received – Jonnie admits it was more by luck than judgement – but they were aware the second hadn't built on the first, and here they were about to launch into another series. They wanted some fresh blood. Jonathan had spotted a funny guy on *Saturday Live*, Patrick Marber, and called him in for a chat, but to no avail. Such was their fondness for him, he later surfaced on *Saturday Zoo* doing the weirdest three-minute puppet shows. He'd created a magical world inside a shoe box with his array of paper and string 'puppets' all wedged on the fingers of one hand – a barely recognizable Michael Jackson puppet featured heavily, as I remember – while he held the shoe box with the other.

Jonnie and Alan had been in the States and heard a funny character on the radio called Dr Science. He was a chap who answered all your science questions like, 'Where does gravity come from?', to which Dr Science would reply: 'It's all made in a small factory in Idaho that's run by a sweet old couple called Jack and Martha.' Not riveting stuff – maybe you had to be there. Anyway, they thought I might be good as an English version of this, each week answering a few of the viewers' questions in a hilarious, well-rehearsed manner.

I didn't really see it, and anyway it sounded too much like work, having to learn a load of information – something I wasn't good at, at the best of times. But the doctor aspect of the idea appealed – as soon as you mention someone is a doctor, there is the assumption that he knows what he's doing and can be relied on. A doctor who's a bit out of control felt more comfortable. Playing an unpredictable character no one could second guess was more up my street, and I really liked the idea of scaring people. Jonnie's show went out live. What could be better?

The doctor's eventual name was a nod to Viv Stanshall and his comic narration of 'Sir Henry at Rawlinson End'. In it there's a character called Old Scrotum, the butler. My brother Richard had all the Bonzo albums, and 'Sir Henry' was a track on their 1972 album, *Let's Make Up and Be Friendly*. I must have been about thirteen or fourteen when I first heard it, and we would sit together laughing our heads off. Viv Stanshall's voice was strangely hypnotic. I could listen to it for hours. He could say anything and it sounded fantastic, and let's face it, he steals the show on Mike Oldfield's *Tubular Bells* album.

Dr Scrote's first appearance on *The Last Resort with Jonathan Ross* set the tone perfectly. Dressed in country tweeds with a fag on the go and a large vodka and tonic, here was a doctor who felt the wind had gone out of his sails as far as conventional medicine was concerned and was keen to follow in the footsteps of daytime TV doctors – money for old rope. That, and the impending medical tribunal, meant Dr Scrote felt, perversely, that live television was the perfect place to lie low for a while.

'It got to the end of series three where you were about the most popular thing on the show, you bastard,' says Jonathan.

The doctor was introduced and ambled on with a large Dr Johnson leather bag with the words 'Dr Scrote's Bag-O-Fun' written on the side. It was a 'fun for all the family' game he'd devised where you had to work out which organ the good doctor had removed from which celebrity pictured on a set of cards. The bag contained a huge ox tongue, which was matched up with the picture card of Ben Elton, who at the time had the nickname of 'Motor Mouth'. There was also a massive liver that went with the Oliver Reed card, obviously. A large pair of bloodied bull's eyes went nicely with the photo of George Michael sporting a huge pair of Aviator dark glasses – you get the idea. All the organs had been liberally covered in blood, which made the whole thing really quite disgusting.

There's a thing all channels have called the 'duty log'. This is a list or recording of all the complaints a programme receives. After Dr Scrote's first appearance, Jonnie's show received more complaints than the whole of his first series put together. Result! One woman rang in to say she thought it was disgusting, and from now on she would not be watching television on a Friday night. Apparently, if you receive more than fifteen complaints, steps are taken, knuckles are rapped, people are told off. It never failed to amaze me that the people in charge took the handful of nutters who phoned in so seriously. Fifteen people thought it was disgraceful, one-and-a-half million people thought it was fine, so who do they pander to? The transparent nutters!

The producers at *The Last Resort* were refreshingly relaxed about the ideas I came up with for Scrote. I'd think of something over the weekend, come in on Monday with a vague idea and by Wednesday a props list would be put together ready for rehearsals all day Friday and the live show that same night. To keep it 'super fresh', Jonathan would avoid finding out what I was up to until it was too late and we were live on TV. With the 'Bag-O-Fun', he genuinely didn't know what I was going to produce from the bag, and how disgusting it was going to be, and I got the impression he was miffed when his immaculate suit got splattered with blood, something that wouldn't have happened if we'd rehearsed it. Why he was upset, God only knows – the man had a different suit for every day of the year and I'd only messed up his Friday 12 June one.

As my brother Ray was a doctor, I would ring him on Friday afternoon and jot down a few pertinent medical words and terms I could drop into the conversation with Jonathan to get people thinking, 'Hang on, he's not a real doctor, is he?'

This vaguely anarchic approach to television didn't always go according to plan. Sandra Bernhard was on one week, and I appeared with a reflex hammer, tapping everyone's knees and elbows. We'd forgotten to tell any of the guests this was going to happen. So when I lunged at her with my little hammer and whacked her on the knee, she went ballistic and started beating the shit out of me – not planned and quite painful, but great fun to watch. Catching up with Jonathan after all these years, he was happy to play down both his and my aptitude back then: 'That was our downfall, we didn't know how to write structured gags. I'd say the wrong thing out loud and try and get away with it, and you'd do the wrong thing out loud and try and get away with it. We did both look great back then though.'

* * *

To the Groucho Club for lunch with Katie Lander and Heather Hampson, the two executives I had to curry favour with each week on *The Last Resort*. It's Katie and Mike Bolland's child I haven't quite got the hang of in the picture taken at Jonnie and Jane's wedding. At the Groucho, the ladies are drinking tap water and ordering two starters each. Not wanting to follow their lead, I order a bottle of house white and steak. 'White, with steak?' they chorus. The way I see it, we either all have red-stained teeth or none of us do. And talk about a result – when the bill came, it was all spirited away onto corporate entertaining. I must go out with people who make TV shows more often – I think there are still one or two left.

Katie steers me towards the time David Frost appeared on the show. The theme was a village fête, and Dr Scrote was in charge of the first-aid tent. It was Vic Reeves's first TV appearance; he was going by the name of Cylus Proud-harvest and had with him a length of wood he'd nailed some prunes to and a flute he'd made out of a cucumber. You either got it or you didn't. A few in the studio were per-plexed, including one of the stagehands, who came out with a classic comment after the show: 'That bloke was fuckin' rubbish. If he hadn't had that fuckin' cucumber flute, he would have died on his arse . . .'

What a game old stick David Frost turned out to be. I had an inflatable sex doll I'd bandaged 'strategically', as I knew my mum would be watching, and was using it as a training dummy, the type you see people demonstrating mouth-to-mouth resuscitation on. My only problem? 'Oral Nora' – that's what it said on the box – was in need of some air herself. I offered the doll up to David for assistance, maintaining that I'd tried my best, but was feeling a little dizzy. Totally unfazed, he took the doll and began blowing her up. It was a beautiful moment. The only man to interview every world leader was standing there, slowly turning red, blowing up a sex doll for Dr Scrote.

There was a very refreshing unpredictability to the show, so it came as a bit of a surprise when recently Jonnie admitted to learning all his links and gags for the show off by heart. Apparently he'd be up all Thursday night writing out, over and over again, everything he was to say the next day. I had absolutely no idea this was his routine. He remembers, 'Ian Brown's script was perfectly fine for what it was, but it wasn't quite right for me. There were jokes in it I often didn't even understand, they were clever *Week Ending* jokes, Radio 4-style gags that were no good for me whatsoever.' Jonnie never used an autocue so I just assumed he was just chatting away. 'And you made it harder because when you came on and were getting laughs making stuff up, it made me feel worse.' And then, just as he had me feeling bad about myself, he came out with, 'I was furious you were so good, furious. It was horrible, it was really fucking irritating you were so good. In fact, I'm glad to finally get the chance to clear the air!'

By the third series, Jonnie and Alan were keen to take the show out of the studio, and the first outing took us as far as the London Palladium. It transpired we had the run of the place; this included the trapdoor in the floor of the famous revolving stage. Realizing this would be a once-in-a-lifetime opportunity, I let it be known that Scrote would have to be doing something involving the trapdoor for the show. Quite what that would be I hadn't, as yet, worked out. Again, I have to take my hat off to Jonnie and the producers of *The Last Resort* for trusting me and whatever I was going to bring to the show.

On this occasion, Dr Scrote ended up dressed as Widow Twankey and on cue was to appear via the trapdoor in a huge puff of smoke. What the doctor hadn't accounted for was the sheer volume of the panto dress he was wearing, so he became wedged in the trapdoor. Jonnie gamely tried to free him, but it was no good; the more he pulled, the tighter the doctor became jammed. Eventually Jonnie left him there, staring out into the audience, while he returned to his desk to carry on with the show. The doctor just had time to utter the words, 'You know why they call me Widow Twankey? 'Cos me husband's DEAD!' This was a line I'd heard Mark Arden use in a show I'd done with him a few years earlier, and I shouldn't have, but it was too good an opportunity to miss. Apologies, Mark. Jonathan's fairly sure this show was Lily Savage's first TV appearance; she was on first and butter wouldn't melt in his/her mouth.

Harry Dean Stanton was the next guest, and the first thing he said when he spotted my cross-dressed torso poking out of the stage in front of him was, 'What the fuck's going on with that guy?' The mistake had been made, but Jonathan simply carried on regardless. In the late eighties, the 'F' word wasn't an option on television, and dropping it into the first sentence, third word, of a live interview really was not good. Funny, but not good.

Harry's contribution was cited by the powers that be as another reason for the show to be pre-recorded, but to Jonnie and Alan's credit, they were having none of it. *The Last Resort* was a live show, and that was its unique selling point. It's a sad indictment of the media today that seemingly everything Jonnie does has to be pre-recorded.

I must have recorded *Riveron*, my Thames-based chat show (about which, more later), earlier that week. Jonnie had kindly agreed to be a guest, and the only female guest we could get to bob about in the Thames with me was Transvision Vamp's Wendy James. Jonnie was very pleased to meet her. While rehearsing at the Palladium in the afternoon – while I was actually wedged in the trapdoor – I mentioned to Jonnie that on the back of the *Riveron* show, I was now 'seeing' the world's most attractive woman, Wendy. He didn't believe me, or didn't want to believe me.

'What, you've actually shagged her?'

'Yes, mate.'

'No! But she's gorgeous. And you've had sex with her?'

'This morning.'

'Nooo! I don't believe you, this is too much. I'm insanely jealous. You're having me on.'

We both had microphones on, and our voices were reverberating round the theatre. I couldn't bear it any longer, so I suggested he turn round and take a look in the stalls. Sure enough, Wendy was sitting there, and she'd heard everything single thing we'd said. A very cool customer, she was flattered by these comments. She just sat there and lit up another fag. Smoking in the stalls of the Palladium? Positively encouraged then, but an arrestable offence now.

The 'Show From Your Home' was one episode of *The Last Resort* that was truly surreal. A family in Poulton-le-Fylde just outside Blackpool had won the chance to have the show broadcast, live, from their home. We all piled up there on the Thursday and made a beeline for the Blackpool Pleasure Beach Funfair. Katie and Heather were having kittens watching the majority of the following day's line-up, the worse for wear, risking life and limb on really dodgy rides. Typical telly execs; they weren't remotely worried about our welfare; all they were concerned about was the fact that if something went horribly wrong at the funfair, *they* wouldn't have a show . . .

As it happened, they did have a show – and a truly bizarre one. The *Coronation Street* actor Chris Quinten was a guest. He wasted no time showing off with a backward summersault on one of the family beds, only to dislocate his knee really quite badly, live on television. After the interview, he could be seen clearly in shot, in the background, clutching his knee and doing that dazed middle-distance staring thing people do when they are 'speed-analysing' the horrendous mistake they've just made. I'm sure if you look back at the tape you'll see poor Christopher mouthing the words: 'What the fuck have I just done?' On crutches, he gallantly hobbled on for the end-of-show 'goodbye' wave, but was uncharacteristically absent from the after-show knees up.

La Toya Jackson was another guest on the 'Show From Your Home'. She arrived minutes before we began broadcasting, straight from an airport, apparently, and made it clear she was dying for the lav. With about two minutes before show-time, she emerged from the small family bathroom that contained the house's only toilet, made a few adjustments to her trouser suit and presented herself for the interview. Now, I'm not saying it was her, but *somebody* proceeded to stink the whole place out. It got everywhere:

in your clothes, your hair, the furniture. She didn't bat an eyelid and, when it came her turn to go on, sauntered into the through-lounge and took her position. She perched on the arm of the velour family settee and spontaneously draped an arm on Gran's shoulder. Gran was sitting slightly below her, knitting away furiously, trying to ignore the stench.

Jonnie, ever the professional, welcomed her on to the show, quickly asked after her welfare, then went straight to the 'How is Michael doing?' line of enquiry. Jonnie didn't once bring up the cloying pong in the interview – he must have had a cold that day, thank God. After the show, he confessed to smelling something but naturally assumed, in the cramped confines of the living room, it was one of the camera crew. Let's face it, it usually is.

Dr Scrote had the run of the kitchen. I was pointing out some of the hidden dangers to the mother of the house, who was a bag of nerves to start with. Unbeknownst to her, we had rigged up the kitchen with electrical sparks going off all over the place and live mice in her bread bin. There was a great visual gag with a wine glass simply placed in front of the microwave oven. I invited Mum to push the button that opened the door, and as it sprang open, the wine glass, as if in slow motion, was pushed off the counter and smashed on the floor at her feet. At one point, I picked up her china teapot and smashed it on the edge of the sink and drew her attention to the very dangerous, sharp edges a shattered pot can produce.

The poor woman was now visibly shaking. I ended by inserting my arm in the eye-level grill, which, of course, was on. My arm instantly caught fire and I stood there with the flames licking up my arm and calmly asked Mum if she could help me out with a damp tea towel, and then threw back to Jonathan. Mum was now a complete wreck. Job done.

As soon as the cameras were off me, I belted into the garden where two stunt organizers ripped my shirt off and quickly removed the asbestos sleeve I was wearing. You just wouldn't be able to do that today. Then again maybe you just wouldn't want to . . .

*   *   *

I didn't really get to know Jonnie during my first series of *The Last Resort*. Whenever he wasn't required in the studio, he'd disappear off to his dressing room, which, like his office in Wardour Street, resembled an Aladdin's cave of gadgets. I remember going into his dressing room once and he was transfixed by the grey plastic toy he was clutching. It turned out to be something called a Nintendo Game Boy, and 'one of the first in the country, Rowly!' Jonnie was playing Tetris and seemed proud of the fact he had been doing so for the past hour. I think it was about six or eight months before anyone else in the country even knew what a Game Boy was.

A year or so later, it was a similar deal, but this time it was laser-disc films. Jonnie had one of the first machines that played LP-type laser-discs. But because it was sooo new, there were only about four films released on this format, and naturally Jonnie had all of them, and naturally we watched all of them. His obsession with acquiring the latest version of whatever, as long as it involved a battery or a plug, proved quite handy for me. After enjoyable evenings being wined and dined at the Ross household, guests would often find themselves the proud owner of something that had been superseded by a smaller, faster, lighter, sexier version of pretty much the same thing. Come to think of it, such was Jonathan's generosity, during *The Last Resort* days, I was also amassing an impressive rail of vaguely barmy jackets, the trousers always being a touch on the tight side for me, which I put down to my hereditary child-bearing hips . . .

There was a period towards the end of the Friday night series and throughout the *Saturday Zoo* and *One Hour with Jonathan Ross* shows that Jonnie and Jane's crazy house in Hampstead became the party place to be. They simply loved having people round, and after the *Zoo* shows pretty much everyone involved would descend on their townhouse for raucous merriment till the early hours. I don't remember either of them ever saying anything along the lines of, 'OK guys, that's enough, sod off!' Some nights I'd be there with, maybe, John Thomson and/or Simon Day, having the time of our lives. We'd go to find Jonnie to ask him how to turn on the latest bit of equipment he'd just taken delivery of, only to discover he and Jane had slunk off and gone to bed, leaving us to it.

There were about eight or nine of us there one time, and Jonathan being Jonathan, he was keen to acquaint us with the latest 'new thing' – Japanese takeaway. I think it was two mopeds, laden with food, that turned up in the end. This was the only time I ever saw Jonnie baulk at the cost of something, but then he had just ordered a takeaway that came to just over £400.

I think, judging by the size of it, Jonnie was the first

person in Europe to acquire a satellite dish. Their town-house off Haverstock Hill in Hampstead had a first-floor patio area big enough for a table and six chairs – we'd spend many a lovely summer Sunday out there. The patio ambience changed slightly when they erected on it an eight-foot dish so big it had its own electric motor for manoeuvrability. If it had worked, it would have been great. Everyone was invited for the Frank Bruno versus Mike Tyson Vegas fight in February 1989. Within fifteen minutes of the event starting, we were all in cabs over to Alan Marke's place – he had cable that actually worked. Alan remembers that evening being only slightly marred by Wendy's band turning up mob-handed and, like locusts, cleaning out the fridge of food and booze.

Saturday Zoo was an ambitious yet chaotic stab at Saturday night entertainment, boasting stand-up, sketches, music and guests. It was a great idea that sadly wasn't given enough time to settle in. If it had, I reckon it would still be on TV today, just like *Saturday Night Live* in the States, which has been going for an age with a constantly evolving regular cast. The regulars in the *Zoo* were pretty impressive: Steve Coogan, Rebecca Front, Graham Fellows as John Shuttleworth, Mark Thomas, Simon Day, John Thomson and Patrick Marber.

Talk about a fickle business. Next door to the green room a bunch of suits would sit hunched over banks of screens and computers constantly analysing how many people were watching the show. If the figures dipped after or during your spot, that was it, you were nowhere to be seen the following week. I was brought in as a comedy foil for Jonnie, having hung up the Scrote stethoscope. True, the show was a bit all over the place, but you really did get an hour-and-a-half of live entertainment every Saturday night. One show had Christopher Walken reading from a kid's storybook with more than a whiff of his *True Romance* character Vincenzo Coccotti, or was it *Pulp Fiction*'s Captain Koons? It was Walken giving us the full, unhinged menace, while reading all things Flopsy, Mopsy and Cottontail.

Lenny Kravitz performing 'Are You Gonna Go My Way?' was also a joy to witness close up in rehearsals. He was on the same show as Kylie Minogue who spent the whole day stuck like a limpet to his back, as I remember. They behaved as if they were either an item or were just about to become an item. Or maybe they had been an item and were just incredibly close mates. It was difficult to tell and I didn't like to look too closely for fear of being accused of staring.

For me, each week *Saturday Zoo* really was a blank canvas. A lot of what went on was dependent on who was on that week. As soon as we heard that Naomi Campbell was the 'What the hell are we going to do with her?' guest, it didn't take long, holed up in the King and Queen pub on Cleveland Street directly opposite the Channel X office, to come up with a foil for her, fashion designer 'Jean-Claude Van Plop', pronounced 'plow-up'.

Wardrobe ran up a 'fan-testical' three-piece suit for me as Jean-Claude which, although quite garish, looked perfectly fine from the front. The 'gag', and I use the term loosely, was that when I turned round, there was no back to the suit. My bare arse would provide the punchline with the lovely Naomi giving it a hearty slap as we turned on our heels and walked upstage to the back curtain.

Naomi arrived just in time for the dress rehearsal, and I warmed to her immediately when, after being introduced to Jean-Claude, a runner asked her if there was anything she wanted. She took one look at what I was wearing and said, 'I better have a very large vodka and grapefruit.' This threw the work-experience lad, who had been programmed to provide teas or coffees from the canteen and the odd off-menu herbal concoction for Jonathan. Up close Naomi really is an Amazonian thing of beauty.

The director, Ian Hamilton, and the producer, Kenton Allen, weren't too happy about people drinking, especially during the dress run, which is fair enough. But I thought, 'If Naomi can stamp her foot hard enough and pull off a large vodka and grapefruit, we're laughing.' She did – which meant I could, too. Result! I got the distinct impression that, A) this wasn't her first of the day, and B) she was now knocking them back in an attempt to distance herself from what was about to happen, as there had been no rehearsal and she had no idea what was going on.

I was matching her drink for drink because, A) I was standing next to supermodel Naomi Campbell, and B) my arse was hanging out the back of my suit – oh, and there *really* had been no rehearsal. I knew roughly what was going to happen – walk on, spout some fashion-related non-sense, turn round to walk off and expose myself. Simple. We'd each polished off at least three massive V&Gs by the time that 'fashion's latest collaboration' Naomi and 'Jean-Claude' took to the stage – she a pissed but beautiful giggling mess of stupidly long ebony arms and legs, me attempting my best Belgian John Inman impression, just trying to hold it together with my nether regions on display to the nation. I'm sure the vodka didn't do much for our timing, but provided more than enough Dutch courage to sell the 'arse/tackle' punchline to the sketch. It went down very well; it's amazing what you can get away with when a famous face and an infamous arse come together.

The minute we left the studio Naomi was escorted out of the back of the building and into a waiting limousine to be whisked off, probably for more drinks, this time with the Aga Khan, possibly in Paris but probably on board a massive yacht. She may have just gone back to her hotel, of course, for a glass of milk and a prawn sandwich – we'll never know. Either way she disappeared so I never got to reciprocate her 'nice arse' comment.

Soon after that I realized that, as long as you got 'your order' in by Wednesday, anything on the costume and props front was possible, and the world was my oyster. Or rather, my mollusc. The highlight of the series, for me, was the week I was to persuade Jonathan that what he needed was some sort of animal sidekick. Everyone knew Phillip Schofield's television career was in the doldrums until he teamed up with Gordon the Gopher. If Jonathan could find the right, cuddly, lovable foil, his career would know no bounds, and I had a few ideas I was keen to run by him during the show.

'No pressure, Jonathan. Let's just see which one you hit it off with.'

First up was an ill-conceived inchworm called Alan. A long foam and felt tube of a costume had been made with a small aperture for my face, but I was unable to move without assistance as my arms and legs were tightly bound inside the impressive-looking worm-cosy. I just lay on the

floor next to Jonnie, complaining about the acute claustrophobia and breathing difficulties I was experiencing,
eventually insisting I be cut out of the bloody thing, immediately, before I have a seizure.

Later in the show, I wheeled myself on in a wooden con-
traption that bore an uncanny resemblance to a giant
mollusc – it was Alan the Mollusc. No opening for my face
this time; instead a small hatch hinged open to reveal the
top of my head. Jonnie couldn't help but notice that, due to
the heat, I was completely naked inside the wooden shell.
Manoeuvrability was, again, the sticking point with this
'fun-loving and loyal sidekick'. On squeaky casters, I made
a painfully slow exit as Jonnie introduced that week's music
guest.

One of America's funniest comedians, Steven Wright,
was the last guest, and while he sat with Jonathan at the
desk doing the interview, I descended from above on a
Kirby wire dressed as 'Hamish The Friendly House Fly'.
As had happened with Sandra Bernhard and Dr Scrote on
The Last Resort, no one had mentioned to Steven what
I was going to be doing: arriving over his shoulder and
perching on the table right next to him. This completely
freaked the poor guy out. He was a wary man at the best of
times, and it looked like he was about to have some sort
of panic attack. Ignoring him, I carried on as best I could,
shouting, 'Here you go, kids will love this: fly anywhere you
want, shag in mid flight, and I live on dogshit. You can't top
it mate!'

Having managed to squeeze a laugh even out of
Steven Wright, I signalled to the Kirby Wire operator to
have me hover above the table and then land on Jonathan's

shoulders. 'I tell you what, I'm sold,' he said. 'I think we've found our mascot. Can I ask you a personal question? Is it as painful as it looks?'

'Yep!' I replied. Possibly my finest hour, or rather forty-five seconds, on *Saturday Zoo*.

Jonnie and I got to know each other a lot better during the *Zoo* series, and became quite close for a while. So much so that in 1990, Jonathan and Jane hired a villa in the south of France for a two-week holiday and invited me along. It quickly emerged that the villa wasn't a run-of-the-mill villa, three or four bedrooms, bit of a pool, maybe a view of the sea if you squint. Jonnie, never one to do things by halves, had hired Château Dior in the Côte d'Azur Alps. It was Christian Dior's place, the one he'd lovingly restored in the fifties. Value today: £12 million.

What with it boasting fourteen sumptuous bedrooms, I wasn't to be the only guest. The place ended up more like a hotel, with a succession of Jonnie and Jane's friends checking in and out throughout the fortnight. Pianist Steve Nieve had been invited out there, so we decided to travel together as a car hire was necessary at the other end. Steve fronted *The Last Resort* house band and had just done all the music for *Set of Six* so was, easily, my new best friend. On the plane Steve mentioned he was looking forward to driving in the south of France, 'as long as we get a convertible'. This was music to my ears: I could relax, maybe even have a drink – I was travelling with my own chauffeur! We landed at Nice airport at about seven o'clock in the evening and I shuffled off the plane the wrong side of about sixteen bottles of vodka, excited at the prospect of getting up to Dior's place in the mountains.

At the car hire, Steve did all the talking. I gave him my driving licence, so I could be included as a named driver, and headed for the small cafe-bar in the airport. I was halfway through ordering a nifty sharpener for the road when I heard, rather unnervingly, my name being called out.

It was Jonathan's mother, Maureen. I'd got to know her quite well as, like me, she seemed to have the constitution of an ox and was often the last to leave a drink and a dance around at Jonnie's place. She too was on her way to the château and was looking for a cab to get her there. I was having none of it. 'Relax, Maureen,' I slurred, 'my man Steve will chauffeur the pair of us up into the hills, in a convertible no less. Do you have a head scarf? We're in the south of France, for Christ's sake.'

I finished my beer and Maureen, excited at the way her evening was unfolding, downed a dry white wine in one. Refreshed, we went in search of 'our man'. We found Steve, easy to spot in his trademark shades, and headed off to pick up the car. He knew Maureen and was happy to have her aboard, as a touch of nifty map-reading was going to make or break our journey to Château Dior, and I got the impression he had little faith in my ability as navigator. It had cost an arm and a leg, but he'd managed to secure the convertible, which was a result. But things took a turn for the worse when we got out into the car park.

We pushed open the tinted double doors and were immediately hit by the warm evening air and the sun setting over the hills in the distance. It was dusk and, unfortunately for us, getting duskier by the minute. Steve operates on only the one setting – chilled. 'You'll have to drive, Doctor' – he'd never used my name the whole time I'd known him – 'I can't really see in this light.' With that, he threw his bag into the boot, ambled round to the passenger seat and climbed in. Maureen had already installed herself in the back seat and was loving it. Young Steven has some sort of medical problem with his eyes, hence the dark glasses that never leave his face. It's not just the bright light he has trouble with, he's really, really not good with night driving, so never does it. His offer to do the driving tomorrow, 'once the sun was up', didn't help the situation I found myself in, that of designated driver, open brackets, completely pissed, close brackets.

I tried to sober up as quickly as possible which, as we all know, is physically impossible – why do we even attempt it? The only thing I had going for me was the lack of a roof: I had all the fresh air I could handle. By the time we had pulled out of the airport compound and on to the public road, Steve had already tuned the radio into a groovy jazz station and Maureen had begun talking. She stopped, momentarily, an hour-and-ten later just as we pulled on to the gravel drive of Château Dior. We had stopped several times for directions. The journey had been one of the most frightening of my life – sober it would have been a stretch. You get up into the Alps and it quickly becomes clear that you are attempting to drive on 'local roads for local people'.

I wasn't alone when it came to perilous journeys to Dior's place. Vic Reeves and Bob Mortimer arrived on two huge motorbikes with hilarious tales of how, at over a hundred miles an hour, each of them had taken it in turns cheating death. Even Jonathan and Jane very nearly didn't make it. In typical fashion, Jonnie had bought Jane a red

Mazda MX-5 sports car about ten minutes before setting off on holiday. Eager to try it out, he wasted no time jumping behind the wheel – Jane hadn't passed her test – and heading for the south of France.

He now recalls, 'I had no idea how to drive the car – at the time I had a beaten up old Vauxhall Astra. We spent hours driving through the night with either no lights or full beam. We were really pissing everyone off. And, man, it was cold. I couldn't fit in the bloody thing with the roof on, so we did the whole journey with the bloody top down.'

I'd never really 'done' holidays as an adult. I remember checking my passport before heading off to Iceland for *Set of Six* and discovering it was about eight or nine years out of date. Please feel free to punch me full in the face when I say this, but I suppose I was in the very fortunate position of not needing a break from what I was up to. Touring was pretty much going on holiday: a sight-seeing trip round the country with a gig at the end of the day – perfect. At the château, there were a lot of people who knew how to holiday – doing absolutely nothing and loving it. Paul Morley and his then wife Claudia were guests. They seemed quite good at doing nothing, Paul especially. He sat in the shade on the spectacular veranda one sunny afternoon and he must have spent about two-and-a-half hours playing with Jonnie's brand new, 'state of the art' Nintendo Tetris. Every time I walked past him, you'd hear a small, polite, audible 'shit' as the machine had beaten him yet again.

That evening, I witnessed Jonathan enlightening Paul to the fact that by pressing the 'A' and 'B' buttons on the console, the falling shapes could be rotated left or right, thus making it easier for them to slot together. Paul had spent the best part of an afternoon playing the thing, and his score had barely got beyond double figures. That's holidays for you.

Things were slowing down nicely on my first holiday in ten years when someone noticed that a lot of the houses on the opposite side of the valley were exploding. A forest fire had appeared over the hill and was devouring everything in its path. All the villas in the region had large gas or oil containers and these were igniting with spectacular effect. A few people got a bit panicky, convinced the encroaching fire was going to kill us all. This moved the indifferent amongst us to crack open the more expensive booze the place possessed. By the time the fire brigade turned up to reassure us that everything was safe on 'our side of the valley', I had already managed to climb on to the roof of the château with a glass and a bottle of house champagne for a better view.

Alan Marke was there and remembers me dressed in a dinner suit for some reason. 'As soon as they spotted the pissed bloke dolled up to the nines on the roof, they completely forgot about the fires raging less than half a mile away and went into overdrive to rescue you,' Alan remembers. 'Our almost complete lack of French didn't help matters. We couldn't explain that you had a habit of doing this sort of thing all the time and that you were fine where you were.'

The Rosses and the Rivrons also holidayed together in Florida one year – a logistical nightmare, but a truly fantastic period of our lives. Jonathan seemed completely unaware that he would regularly stray beyond the bounds of generous into a place I don't think I've seen anyone else inhabit. And with his love of America, and given that he is never a man to do anything by halves, it's surely only a matter of time before we hear of Jonathan's cash purchase of a new home when the media have finally hounded him out of the country: Disney's Magic Kingdom Castle, Florida. I really wouldn't put it past him.

11: MESSING ABOUT ON THE RIVER

The pop singer Wendy James was very hip at the time. She was getting some notoriety with her band Transvision Vamp in the late 1980s and was adored by both girls and boys. As potential girlfriend fodder, on paper, she didn't tick many of my boxes; but in the flesh, bobbing about in the East India Deep Water Dock – Christ on a bike!

The Bunker Show on ITV was being well received, as I could often be found drinking with the producers, Dave Morley or Jill Sinclair, in the bar at LWT, something you don't see when your show is going down the pan. Then, 'You drink alone, my friend.'

The LWT studios are situated on the South Bank next to the National Theatre and command, from the third-floor bar, panoramic views over the Thames. We were there one night in 1989 and I happened to mention something along the lines of, 'Look at that fabulous view of the Thames. What a waste, it doesn't even look like boats are using it these days. We should have a chat show in the Thames, but not on pontoons or in boats. I could be bobbing around in the water, and the guests could swim out and chat to me.'

This was said the wrong side of much vodka and slightly in jest, but the producer stared out over the shimmering water, with St Paul's Cathedral and the city illuminated in the background, turned to me and, downing the last drop of his pint, said: 'That's a great idea, let's do it. My round!'

Four days later and I was being fitted for a wet suit. I really hadn't thought this through.

It has to be said that, when consulted, the river police weren't very keen on the idea – something to do with very strong currents and the fact that, on average, they pull out of the murky water one-and-a-quarter human bodies a month. They let us ponder this for a moment and offered to show us some photos of the last few months' 'catch'. We hastily thanked them, made our excuses and left. Their last words to us were, 'A river-based chat show is not ideal.'

The broadcast pilot was called *Riveron* – see what I did there? – and recorded in November after dark. I remember the weather was chilly; in fact, it was sleeting to snow. We heeded the police advice in the end and used the East India Deep Water Dock to double for the Thames, so rather than risk the odd torso floating past, we had boats cruising up and down as background action – it really did look like the Thames! As token set-dressing for the show, tethered by weights and wires, were a floating television set and a few standard lamps. Slightly alarming was the fact that these props were all 'juiced up' and glowing. Now even I know water and electricity don't mix, but everyone seemed to think it would be fine, citing, 'It's only a bit dangerous if you're in the bath with a toaster.' We'd all come too far by now to turn back, so I listened to what they said and went with the flow.

In an attempt to look as 'normal' as possible, I wore a formal dinner jacket, complete with bow tie, over a wet suit. My hand-held microphone also had its own wet suit of sorts: a condom. The wet suit was a new experience for me, especially the advice for when I got too cold, which was almost immediately: 'Just piss yourself and you'll be fine, that'll keep you warm.'

Talking of piss, that was the other concern, brought to my attention by the alarming number of St John's Ambulance members milling around a turn-of-the-century ambulance that had been parked as near as possible to the action. As the East India Dock was home to thousands of rats, all of them incontinent, the slightest drop of water ingested could be a problem. At best we were looking at a bunch of painful injections; at worst, the injections plus a full-on pumping of the stomach. This was news to me, as it certainly wasn't mentioned in the letter sent out to potential guests.

Do you want to be a guest on a ground-breaking chat show? Can you swim? The invitation was simple and to the point, but still did a good job of scaring off just about every female approached. As mentioned earlier, I'd managed to talk Jonathan into appearing as a favour, and I think he enjoyed it, certainly more than Mark Shaw, lead singer with the then popular band, Then Jericho. He'd overdone the eyeliner at home and underestimated just how wet we would all get. Waterproof eyeliner really was the order of the day on *Riveron*. Not for Mark, though. Within minutes, he was not so much the young, androgynous pop singer as the very poor Alice Cooper lookey-likey. However, Tony Blackburn, ever eager to please, embraced the concept of the show by arriving on a jet ski.

The one woman who had agreed to appear on the pilot was going to be late as she had only just arrived back from

New York, which was not a problem as it gave me the opportunity to get out of the water for the first time in about three hours. She was our only female guest so she could show up when she wanted, as long as she did show up. While I was on dry land getting a hot drink, Wendy James walked into my life and didn't mince her words: 'Hi, I'm Wendy. You must be Rowland. You stink of piss. Nice.'

She was the last guest, and we made an odd couple bobbing about in the freezing water talking nonsense, and an even odder couple when we were back on dry land. She was classic rock-star chic with a fag on the go, all lace, crucifixes, shredded Levi's and shagged biker boots; she looked about sixteen. I was classic 'bloke beyond my years', trousers by Paul Smith, shirt by Pink, Crombie by Austin Reed. I thanked her for being the only woman who consented to be on the show, quietly marvelled at her beauty and headed for the car to take me straight to the Zanzibar club in Holborn. It's thirsty work, all this bobbing about. While I was rounding up some drinking partners, Wendy approached me and rather sheepishly inquired, 'You play the drums don't you? We're doing that kids' show *Going Live* tomorrow – only we don't have a drummer. Do you fancy sitting in?'

'Of course,' I replied. 'Do *you* fancy a drink?'

'Of course,' she replied. The die was cast.

The next day I showed up at the BBC studios in Wood Lane, played drums for Transvision Vamp and immediately pissed off the rest of the band as Phillip Schofield wanted to know all about 'Dr Martin' from *The Last Resort with Jonathan Ross*. It was felt 'Dr Scrote' didn't sit comfortably at 10.30 a.m. on a Saturday morning kids' show – they had a point. I spent the rest of the day and the next eighteen months of my life with beautiful, bonkers Wendy wondering what the hell was going on, but never stopping long enough to let anyone tell me.

Riveron went down well. Tragically, not long afterwards the pleasure boat *Marchioness* sank after being hit by the dredger *Bowbelle*. Fifty-one people died in the Thames and it was, quite rightly, deemed insensitive to carry on with *Riveron*.

Over twenty years later, people still ask me about the hazy memory they have of a mad show featuring me and a bunch of people in the Thames. You would never be able to make it today, and I'll be eternally grateful to the people who give me the chance to make it then, if only I knew their names and where they lived.

* * *

Set of Six or should that be 'S.O.S.' . . . ?

Dr Scrote was proving to be the perfect appendage to Jonathan's role as host of *The Last Resort*. As and when the show required a touch of lunacy and madness, the good doctor could be wheeled on to provide five or six minutes of nutty escapism. It worked because Scrote was never on long enough to become boring. I always thought that it was much better to do a blinding five or ten minutes than an OK but padded half hour.

So there was a mix of flattery and trepidation when news filtered through that Seamus Cassidy, the commissioning editor for Channel 4, wanted to do something more with Dr Scrote. He thought there was a series in the character, but I had my doubts as I really didn't think it could be sustained.

Seamus suggested a sketch-based show featuring Scrote amongst other unrelated characters. I really wasn't happy about playing a bunch of different people, mainly because I didn't think I could. It was amazing how quickly the pair of us managed to talk the whole thing down the pan . . .

I went away to think about this incredible opportunity slipping out of my hands, and what better way to do that than by dragging Ian Brown, house scriptwriter for Jonathan on *The Last Resort*, out to lunch at the Gay Hussar, the Hungarian restaurant on Greek Street? After wading through a plate of the house speciality goulash and polishing off three or four bottles of incredibly deep red wine, we'd cracked the Scrote conundrum. Ian remembers the plan being sketched out on one of the Gay Hussar's heavy, white-linen napkins that we were forced to pay through the nose to keep. And it was a good job we paid up: I could just imagine going back to Seamus, hammered, and shouting, 'We've worked out how we can do it! But the Gay Hussar won't let us have it, and anyway the bastards have probably laundered the fucker by now!'

We carefully folded up the napkin, paid the waiter through gritted teeth and retired to celebrate at the Sunset Strip Club in Dean Street. We didn't stay long. On arrival, Ian had fallen down the dangerously steep stairs to the club and his ankle was fast ballooning up to comical proportions, while I had been told the girls wouldn't come out and take their clothes off until I'd got rid of the big white napkin I was clutching. No amount of explaining that it was the blueprint to my future and not a tawdry tissue to clear up any excitable indiscretions in the back row would cut any ice with the manager. So we hobbled back to the *Last*

Resort office in Wardour Street and typed up 'the linen' into a two-page treatment for Seamus.

The idea was simple and born out of the fact I couldn't act. Dr Scrote would be one of sextuplets, all identical brothers and all played by me. Rather than attempt to act, I'd just put on a different costume in order to be a 'different' person. As well as Dr Martin, there was David Scrote, the photographer, Ronnie Scrote, the compulsive grass, Terry Scrote, the boxer, Giles Scrote, the farmer, and Tarquin Shirley Stanstead Scrote, the MP and eventual tramp.

Each week we'd catch up with one of the brothers, fifteen years after they'd all gone their separate ways after their joint eighteenth birthday party. It was to be shot as a spoof fly-on-the-wall sociological documentary looking at the way different environments affect people – the camera was to catch up with the brothers and look at to what degree the career paths they chose had changed them. Being Scrotes, all of the brothers' lives were unravelling so the camera was there to witness it all, and with Tony Bilbow's laconic voiceover the shows came across as both funny and painfully sad. So much so that when Steve Nieve, who provided all the music for the series, saw it he commented: 'You can't put these out, they're too sad.'

Ian and I wrote the series during the summer of 1988, we made them in 1989 and they went out in 1990, a period in my life where things were galloping along in a fairly out-of-control manner – not that dissimilar to the family Scrote, in fact.

I didn't really have anywhere to live as I'd kicked myself out of the flat I'd bought with my ex-girlfriend and was away touring with Dawn and Jenny most of the time anyway. The few nights I was in town I spent with Wendy at the flat the record company had secured for Transvision Vamp in Kensington Church Street. It was a spacious two-storey apartment that was left to disintegrate slowly as a result of the twenty-four-hour open house policy the band maintained.

The people at Channel X, who were making *Set of Six*, were keen to know where I was from day to day and suggested I should get an address where things like cabs and scripts could be sent, happy in the knowledge I'd receive them. A short-term one-bedroom business flat was secured for me in a mansion block at the top of Kensington Church Street, a stone's throw from Wendy's Animal House. It was reminiscent of the 'pad' Peter Wyngarde, playing the flamboyant playboy investigator, inhabited in the early 1970s TV series *Jason King*. The producers could really keep tabs on me, and I was given one of the original mobile phones for a while, the one you wore on your shoulder, with the handset that was attached by a curly wire to the huge battery pack. It didn't last long in my possession, as they soon realized it was far too valuable to lose.

The boxer, Terry 'The Tornado' Scrote, renamed 'Terry Scrote' after his first professional fight, was an accidental excursion into the world of method acting. I was unfit and marginally fat, and didn't want to look like a sometime comic pretending to be a boxer, so Channel X hooked me up with Nigel 'The Dark Destroyer' Benn's trainer, Bryan Lynch. He ran a gym above a pub in East Ham.

I stopped the booze completely and lived on nothing but grilled chicken and peas. For six weeks, I'd get a cab from Soho around four in the afternoon to Canning Town and train for three hours, then get the Underground back to the Jason King flat in Notting Hill. I was so fired up on endorphins from the training, most nights I'd don a sweatsuit and then go running round Holland Park for an hour or so. It all paid off. I dropped two stone, pretty much learnt how to box and, at least, looked for all the world like a lightweight boxer.

I was the spitting image of a lightweight boxer one day while filming in the Lonsdale boxing apparel shop in Beak Street, London. Being fully togged up in the gear can be a tad debilitating – once the gum shield's gone in and the gloves have been taped on to your fists, that's it, you're buggered, you can't really do anything, apart from hit someone, that is.

I was waiting outside the shop in the street ready to make my entrance when a middle-aged woman approached and asked me for my autograph. She offered up a small writing pad and a pen. I explained as best I could, what with the gum shield, that I was unable to sign the note pad as I was sporting a huge pair of red boxing gloves making it impossible to hold the pen. She looked a little confused and dejected and, to be honest, not the full shilling. This was confirmed when I suggested that if I spelt it out, she could write my name in her note pad – which she did. She visibly perked up as a result and went on her way.

Under the slim pretence of research, Jonathan, myself and Gerald Scarfe – he was going to direct three of the shows – got ourselves invited to sit ringside at the Dark Destroyer's showdown against Michel Watson, in a huge tent in Finsbury Park. Benn was the hot favourite. If he beat Watson, he was guaranteed a multi-million-dollar Las

Vegas showdown with Michael Nunn, and we were on his team! What could possibly go wrong?

Watson knocking the shit out of him in the sixth round was enough. We were seated on front-row benches just inches from the ringside and were getting showered with the fighters' sweat and, towards the end, sadly, a lot of the Dark Destroyer's sequins from his very showy shorts. This was a huge upset: Benn was supposed to win.

After the fight, defiantly sporting our 'Dark Destroyer' baseball caps, we were shown to a limo and whisked off to Nigel's favourite Greek restaurant somewhere in the heart of East London where the 'victory' party for the poor chap was to be held. The place was festooned with banners and balloons celebrating his win. Trouble was, he hadn't. To say the atmosphere was muted would be an understatement. Everyone put on a brave face, but we thought it best to leave when, inevitably, the crying started.

What a fantastic gentleman Gerald Scarfe is. As soon as his name was mentioned as a potential director, he was in. Nothing seemed to phase the man. Not even our first meeting. Katie Lander, one of the producers, and I went to see him at his imposing townhouse in Cheyne Walk, Chelsea. He made us a cup of tea and showed us upstairs to a magnificent living room with two huge windows looking out over the Thames. The view was nothing compared to the carpet though – it was one shade off pure white. I'd never seen the like before, it was spotless. How on earth could a family, especially Gerald with his pen and inks and his wife Jane Asher, with all her cakes, live on a carpet like this and it remain so virginally white? By not inviting people round and offering tea.

Katie hadn't even taken a sip of the drink before she managed to decant it on to the carpet; the whole mug of boiling hot tea fanned out from where she had attempted to sit down and quickly soaked itself into the beautiful white wool. Gerald, unphased, took it in his stride and produced a hankie to soak up any excess. He seemed fine with it, but Katie and I were gutted. We attempted to carry on the meeting as best we could, but whatever Katie and I said paled into insignificance compared to Gerald's huge white living room carpet and the brown stain that seemed to be turning increasingly dark. The next time I saw Gerald, I asked after the carpet, but he, ever the gentleman, had completely forgotten about it.

The character Terry Scrote lived with Uncle Bertram, a middle-aged man with a fondness for budgerigars and boys. The brief for Uncle Bertram simply read, 'middle-aged paedophile type'. Gerald and Ian had set up a small room in the Channel X office to see the actors auditioning for the part. While they were sorting themselves out, a chap came into the room and Gerald looked round at the man standing there and said, 'Sorry, would you mind waiting outside? We're not quite ready for the auditions yet. The audition's for a typical middle-aged paedophile.'

'No, no,' came the reply, 'I'm John Hubbard, the casting agent . . .' Nice one, Gerald.

Ronnie Scrote, the compulsive grass, was under a witness protection scheme and, after some very cheap plastic surgery to change his features, was to be relocated to another country, in sunny South America, he thought. He ended up in freezing-cold Iceland. We spent nine days filming there, at a time of the year when it never gets dark, during which I was slowly losing the plot. The prosthetics I had to wear for the plastic surgery scars took three hours every morning to put on, so the make-up artist, David Myers, and I would have to be up four hours before everyone else. I don't think Dave and I slept for the first three or four days. I'm sure as one half of the much acclaimed 'Hairy Bikers' Dave now gets all the sleep he wants.

Our contact in Reykjavik was eager to introduce me to the delights and dangers of potato poteen (pronounced 'pochine'). The country was under strict licensing laws in the late eighties, and booze was prohibitively expensive so even Ulrich, a mild-mannered tourist board employee and our guide, would have some 'hooch' on the go somewhere in his house.

I was at Ulrich's house on our last night in Iceland, with a few of his friends all fiercely knocking back poteen and diet coke. Ulrich made sure I was mixing the lethal potion and coke 'sensibly', as he knew of two or three friends that had gone blind knocking the stuff back neat. While he recounted the tale and carefully measured out my next drink, a chap who had been happily sitting at Ulrich's dining-room table keeled over and fell to the floor, lifeless. I don't mind having a drink with drunks, but I draw the line at dead people.

Ulrich seemed unconcerned. 'Just leave him,' he said, pointing out that as his mate Sigurveig was around eighteen stone, we'd never be able to move him, not in the state we were in anyway. That was fair enough, but 'Dead Bloke' really didn't look like he was breathing. When, eventually, I did leave about three hours later, poor old 'Siggy' was in exactly the same position, having not done the usual curling up into a foetal position in readiness to sleep it off. Ulrich kindly forced a plastic bottle of poteen under my arm to take back to London. Ian Brown remembers that being the sum total of my hand luggage for the flight home. He also remembers having to strap me into three seats at the back of the plane, for mine and everyone else's safety.

'Despite all the stress, you were never less than professional, even in the darkest hour,' recalls Ian.

As co-creator of the show, Ian had found himself in the unenviable position of being my mediator and minder. He wasn't only fielding calls from the crew and producers as to my whereabouts, but during the trip he also had Wendy ringing from London asking after me and, in tears, threatening to jump on the next plane to Reykjavik. As we know, this would have been madness, as Iceland already had the crazy woman slot filled in the shape of Björk.

I very nearly didn't make it to the airport. Having escorted my bottle of poteen back to the hotel, I immediately passed out on the bed. Ian shook me awake, threw my things into a holdall and kindly dragged it down to the coach for me. I washed my face, tried to throw up, couldn't, and made my way to the waiting bus. Suddenly I could see the method in Sigurveig's madness. The poteen's fine as long as you make no attempt to move or look at things.

I stumbled out of the hotel, still clutching the death juice, and boarded the huge coach that was at least helping to block out some of the bastard perpetual daylight. As I made my way down the coach, I became confused. I could see the crew and Ian seated and ready to go, but through the windows. Some of them spotted me, put their thumbs up, smiled and waved. Suddenly the coach I was on let off the big air brake sound and began moving. I was on a coach that had parked directly adjacent to ours. It was half-full of old people who were, apparently, heading off to see the geysers for the day. I managed to get the driver to pull in only after he was already one hundred yards up the main road, made my apologies, got off the bus and headed back to the hotel. How they laughed . . .

It wasn't just the poteen that had got to me. I'd painted myself into a corner of responsibility of which I'd had very little experience. This wasn't the five-minute blinder, arsing about with 'no strings attached' in someone else's show: this was my show. I'd also sold Seamus the idea that I'd improvise all the dialogue as I didn't want to learn a ton of lines. Spontaneity would be the thing . . .

This situation had prompted another of 'gentlemen' Gerald's classic lines. We were setting up to film the concluding 'big fight night' at a venue in south London. There was a huge audience, pro boxers, cameras on cranes, the works. Mike the cameraman sidled up to Gerald and me and said, 'So, Gerald, where do you want the camera?'

Gerald turned to him and, very matter of factly, said, 'I don't know, I've no idea what Rowland's going to do.' I didn't realize at the time, but Gerald was ready to 'walk', and it was only 'cup-o-tea' Katie, the spilly producer, and her way with words that talked him round.

Another person about to 'walk' around this time was Ms James. I hadn't seen that much of her, as I was away filming, and unlike Dawn and Jenny's tour, where she could just turn up and tag along, filming *Set of Six* was a different kettle of fish and distractions were not to be encouraged. Anyway, Transvision Vamp were taking off big time and she had disappeared off to Hong Kong to promote their album. This didn't stop the communication, however, it just made it that little bit more expensive . . .

We'd set photographer David 'Top Shot' Scrote's flat in Bexhill-on-Sea on the south coast. We were intrigued by the fact that the town boasted the highest proportion of OAPs in the country. So we all piled down to Hastings and checked into the Royal Victoria Hotel on the sea front. It was like stepping back in time, and then getting a cab a bit further. I'm sure it's a lovely hotel now – please God, somebody must have given it a lick of paint over the last twenty years – but in 1988 it felt like the place had slipped off the radar.

Every day I'd leave the hotel to head off for filming and every day I'd return to be met by the old boy on the desk: 'Arr, Mr Rivron, a lady rang for you today, from Hong Kong she said, but it was a really clear line, so I don't know if she was fibbing or not?' This went on for a few days, and then the old boy offered up a number that had been left for me to ring.

Without thinking I went to my room and tried it. It was a hotel in Hong Kong all right, and after about fifteen minutes we established there was no Ms James staying in the hotel. Cheers, that only set me back about twenty-five quid. The next day I returned to be given a fresh twenty-four digit number to try. This number proved more fruitful as I was, eventually, put through to Wendy's room. The pair of us regressed to sixteen-year-olds as we slowly dismantled our relationship, adamant that no one was to blame and, anyway, 'It's got to be for the best.' All interspersed with silent pauses that seemed to go on for an eternity.

When it came time to check out of the Royal Victoria, I came down from my room to find Heather Hampton, one of the producers, settling the bill and remonstrating with the receptionist about a mistake with a phone bill.

'But he only made two calls. How can it be £156?'

The young receptionist scrutinized the sheet of paper and came back with, 'Well, madam, they were both to Hong Kong, and one of them appears to be for one hour and six minutes.'

If you haven't seen the Scrote brothers in action, I recommend you cut along to the iTunes store where you can pick up the lot of them for about eight quid. Bargain.

12: THE GROUCHO

The Groucho was meant to be a club for literary types but they quickly realized a lot of them didn't have that much money, so the membership was quietly broadened out to 'literary and media'. Suddenly the place was packed and I could own up to having 'a local'.

Tony Mackintosh opened the place in 1985 and in his own words: 'It was for people working in the media – we were to offer the same facilities and courtesies that you got from traditional clubs, but in a contemporary setting in terms of rules, services, atmosphere and design.'

And he pretty much stuck to that. Before the Groucho Club in Dean Street, Tony was responsible for the Zanzibar Club in Great Queen Street. I knew it well because of its proximity to the Blitz Club, barely a hundred yards up the road. The 'Zanz' was a long narrow place – I think it boasted one of the longest bars in town – with a small stage and mini grand piano at the far end. I'd often play a set on the cramped stage before heading up the street to the Blitz for the later gig with Biddie and Eve. The stage was adjacent to the door for the toilets, and as everyone 'used' the lavs in those days, it was perfect for keeping an eye on who was coming and going. It was at the Zanzibar one night that I bumped into comedian and actor Andy de la Tour in the men's toilets, tending to a flesh wound on his bald head. He maintained he'd just been shot by something. I was able to put him straight, as I'd just let a banger off on my head that must have travelled the length of the bar and clipped him. It was at the Zanzibar that Keith Allen threw a bar stool at the wall of bottles behind the bar and promptly went to prison for a short while. Things happened at the Zanz that didn't occur elsewhere. There's a lovely photograph taken by celebrated snapper Nobby Clark of John Kelly, a dear friend who was the then editor of *The Economist* magazine, asleep at one of the tables, in a sharp suit and slightly on fire. He took it in good spirit and I'm fairly sure I offered to replace all smoke-damaged items of clothing. At one point an article appeared in the gutter press concerning Wendy James and me having a drink-sodden argument in the club. It was a belter, as she wasn't one for mincing her words. It carried on into the street where a few paparazzi were loitering and culminated, uncharacteristically, in her punching me full in the face. It had been sold to the paper by one of the female night managers who admitted to using the money to buy a new pair of breasts. For a while I claimed part ownership of those breasts, as I felt I'd inadvertently paid for them. My suggestion that I should at least be granted visiting rights fell on deaf ears.

In 1984 the Zanzibar changed hands, and slowly those with the wherewithal and good enough livers surfaced at the Groucho Club. My first visit was shortly after it opened in 1985. I was a non-member and as drinks could only be purchased by members I was 'forced' to put them on a member's tab. I charged them to Stephen Fry's tab, who, apart from calling me 'a little oik' when he found out, was very good about it. I quickly secured membership of my own that I'm sure, over the years, has been abused in the same way I shamelessly abused Stephen's. I've never bought a packet of fags in my life, but would regularly see, when I could be bothered to look, 'cigarettes' on my bar bill. Hold on. Thinking about it, Stephen used to be a veritable chimney back in the day . . . The 'big oik'.

When it comes to the game of poker that changed my life for ever, I have to put it down to beginner's luck. I was completely out of my depth, especially with the guys who played poker regularly upstairs in the Gennaro room at the Groucho Club. Keith Allen was there, Stephen Fry, Liam Carson (the manager) and myself. I don't remember anything about the game (to be honest I didn't really understand it) but somehow at the end I found myself with a cheque begrudgingly signed by Stephen and honorary membership to the club. Liam wasn't in a position to pay the money he owed me but did have access to the list of club members' details and saw to it that a magical 'H' was typed next to my name on the register. That was it – I was a member for life.

Liam was able to work his magic again one summer in the early nineties when I had everything in storage and nowhere to live. It must have been shortly after I'd run off with Wendy, and then quickly realized the error of my ways and run back again. As a result I was homeless. The club had about a dozen bedrooms designed for out-of-town members or those who couldn't get it together to go home. As a result, the rates were quite reasonable, very reasonable if you were block booking, as Liam now suggested I do.

So I spent the summer of 1991 living at the Groucho

Club with all its many advantages and massive disadvantages. Having the bar as your new front room started out as very advantageous – I must have saved a fortune on cabs – but it eventually topped the list of massive disadvantages. As I was staying there, my tab was always open, mostly to outrageous abuse by whoever I'd made friends with that night. On the plus side, I was able to walk to work, well at least every Saturday morning. *Loose Ends*, Radio 4's arts and entertainment programme hosted by the delightful Ned 'Twinky' Sherrin, went out live from Broadcasting House on Portland Place, and for a couple of years I was one of their pool of contributors. I'd head off during the week with a producer armed with a tape recorder to report on the opening of a new 'whatever' and come Saturday be sitting round the table with the other guests. I would introduce the piece to Ned and, of course, the listening public. One week there couldn't have been a new 'whatever' to report on, so I was given Britt Ekland's autobiography and told I was going to be interviewing her on the show the following week. Try as I might, I could not make any headway with her tome, which I rather shamelessly admitted to her live on air. At one point, I even went so far as to come out with, 'So Britt, tell us about yourself.' Not the most conventional of interviewing techniques, but one that put me on a map of sorts – Britt and I became a feature on one of the many in-house BBC radio educational courses. We were the stars of 'how not to conduct an interview', something that, to this day, I am very proud of.

In the pub after the show – it was a tradition that Ned would treat all the guests who were inclined to a plate of finger food and a pint – I made my apologies to him over a sausage roll for the debacle with Britt, who was happily tucking into her second large dry white. But Ned wouldn't have any of it and thought the whole thing very amusing: 'We should provide you with some more books you have no intention of reading and guests to confuse.'

It only took me about twelve minutes to get from the Groucho Club to the BBC – even quicker if I'd been to bed the night before. And that was the problem. Living at the club meant you never had to break the continuity of going home, because you already were home. Sitting at the bar, it was not so much a case of the classic, 'What are all these people doing in my dressing room?' It was more, 'What are all these people doing in my house?' And there was always somewhere to get lost within the 'Bermuda Triangle' of the Groucho Club, Jerry's Bar further down Dean Street and the evil Fedenzes in New Burlington Street, off Regent Street. I'd spend all my time wherever fun was happening. I didn't stay in on a Friday night and say, 'Oh great, Jonathan's on.' I didn't have that timetable sensibility. If there's a polite way of putting it, I was not entirely in control. Where's the halfway house between in and out of control? That's where I was. I wasn't an alcoholic. I was just desperate to enjoy myself – at any cost to myself and those around me.

The celebrated drunk Jeffrey Bernard lived in a flat the other side of Berwick Street market from the Groucho and soon became a regular, slumped on one of the dusty old red velvet sofas that cluttered the bar. He'd often be there, on his own with a large one, at ten in the morning with the sun streaming in through the wooden blinds. It was an honour to sit with him and listen to his vitriolic ramblings about people I didn't know from Adam. The poor bloke pissed himself once and didn't give a toss. It must have been after he'd had his leg removed, as I remember helping Mary Lou, one of the managers, to put him into his wheelchair; I then helped one of the waiters to spirit away the two-seater sofa he was sitting on, leaving it on the back fire escape to dry out. Then as Jeff was leaving, he realized his address book had gone missing, and that it must be down the back of the sofa he was sitting on. I didn't go and retrieve it, some brave waiter had to.

It was while I was living there that I became infatuated by one of the receptionists. She was gorgeous, with a permanent smile and the most incredible body. I had become friends/drinking partners with artist Marc Quinn, and he'd invited me to the 'Absurdist Ball', a bunch of arty types trying to out-absurd each other in an old warehouse near the Tower of London. I nagged Monica, the aforementioned receptionist, into coming with us, and she did! Game or what!?

The next date was to be a more formal affair. I invited her to Two Brydges, a very private Georgian townhouse club off St Martin's Lane. She finished work at five-thirty, and we strolled through Soho and made our way up the narrow alleyway, Brydges Place, that gave the club its name. We were five steps from the door when a pigeon, or it could have been a seagull, dropped its load all down one side of Monica. From the state she was in, hair, face, arm, dress, leg, it could quite easily have been an albatross loitering on the scaffolding we had walked under. I saw this as a good sign – first the absurdists, and then the 'shit hitting the friend'. Monica didn't hold it against me – she was later to become my wife. As you can tell, the Groucho has had a major effect on my life, culminating in me marrying into it.

Even when I found somewhere to live, a squalid room in Islington, I'd head straight for the club once I was up. It was the beginning of the nineties, and 'Young British Artist' Marc was doing pretty much the same thing, heading straight for the club from his room round the back of Waterloo. We'd sit in the corner steadily getting hammered, but in an incredibly content way – there was a lot of laughing. Marc was working on his first acclaimed piece of art, called *Self*. It was a frozen sculpture of his head made from ten pints of his own blood. Charles Saatchi bought it for £13,000 – it later went for £1.5 million. I remember sitting with him one afternoon when he suddenly announced he had to go and meet a man about a sack full of coconuts that had fallen off the back of a lorry. Apparently, coconut milk freezes at the same temperature as human blood and Marc was keen to try a pain-free version of *Self* before he committed himself. He asked me to ride gunshot, but I declined as I had more pressing business to attend to: falling in love with the receptionist.

How times have changed. Marc requested a smoking seat on the flight. It was a Friday, about two in the afternoon. Marc and I were settling in for a drink after our two-hour liquid lunch when I produced my passport – I must have needed it for something I was doing that morning. This was the sign Marc was looking for, as within minutes we were in a cab over to Exton Street, Waterloo, to pick up his passport. The cab then ferried us to Heathrow – this was pre-Heathrow Express and even the Underground was yet to go that far west. We were on our way to

Paris, aiming to get there in time for drinks at the launch of the Paris Art Fair. We very nearly missed the flight. Marc was breaking in a newish pair of brogues and because he was an artist never wore socks, so was unable to run for the plane. I went on ahead and stalled them until Marc hobbled on board, and we sheepishly installed ourselves in the last row, the bloody smoking row. It was a hellish journey, as the plane was full and 'no way' was anyone going to swap their seat with one with the smokers 'behind the bike sheds'. I sat there as every one of the little ashtrays in the fold-down armrests very quickly began to overflow with no one doing anything about it. Everyone seemed to be manically chain-smoking, no doubt worried the plane was going to crash and burn. As it was, the back row was already alight.

We arrived in Paris and headed for the opening party where we quickly caught up with all the beautiful people and Jay Jopling, Marc's art dealer. Jay remembers the pair of us flinging the doors open and declaring, 'Les Anglais sont arrivés!' and me helping Marc in as his brogues were now killing him. It was only seven o'clock in the evening and, already, we were fully paid-up members of the Paris Art Fair, as we wandered round Marc's exhibits. He'd made some busts out of bread dough over chicken wire, which he'd baked and glazed . . . Funny, you don't hear much about those pieces these days. We shared a bed in a small hotel that Marc claimed was once a brothel. I didn't believe him until I saw the erotically painted walls and mottled glass ceilings. If I was in any doubt, then being introduced to the man who ran the place nailed it. Honestly, you could not make this up: he had one eye and a deep scar from the empty socket to his Adam's apple. We only stayed the three nights.

One of the chaps who ran Two Brydges was Alfredo Fernandini, a delightful Peruvian and friend to everyone. He introduced me to a cocktail from his home town that would have huge ramifications. It was the deadly but moreish Pisco sour. Alfie would often turn up at the Groucho after he'd locked up at Two Brydges, so we wouldn't see him till about one in the morning. One night he arrived with a bottle of Pisco and insisted we all fall in love with it. We quickly formed a queue. It's not a long drink, the Pisco sour, so it's easy to knock back the first two or three while you're still getting your bearings. By then, of course, it's too late, Madam Pisco has you in her clutches, she loves you, and you LOVE her. The effect is similar to Peru's other major export, cocaine; it also reminds me of the effect tequila slammers have. When I was touring with the Jools Holland Rhythm and Blues Orchestra, there would always be a bottle of tequila on the rider. It was salted back to the hotel where it became known as 'Debating Juice'. We'd sit around drinking the stuff, neat, and getting really animated and opinionated, pissed but incredibly focused.

That is exactly what happened the night I was introduced to the Pisco sour. It was Friday night, lock-in night at the club. Come two o'clock the bar was officially closed, and once the last punter was safely off the premises, the fun could begin. A lot of the waiters cycled to work. They would bring their bikes in, and we would see who could cycle from the back of the brasserie, through the bar, to the reception area, the fastest being rewarded with booze. This looked great fun, the wrong side of half a dozen Piscos, so

I asked if I could have a go. As a lot of the bikes were of the mountain variety, I suggested the start point should be at the back of the upstairs restaurant. Then it would be down the wide sweeping stairs – or mountain – to the bar and out into reception. There were no takers, so I took it upon myself to show them what I meant. One more quick Pisco sour to get me focused, and I was off up the stairs with a state-of-the-art mountain bike over my shoulder.

As I came hurtling down the stairs, I made the classic mistake of gripping the front brake and not the back. In hindsight, I would have survived much better if I'd deployed no brakes at all, as the bar stools would have slowed me down. Three steps from the bottom of the stairs, I flew over the handle bars and slid the length of the bar along the carpet on one side of my face. I stood up, acknowledged the applause and retired to a dark corner to assess the damage. My left ear had suffered the bulk of the damage. It was a shiny, sticky mess from the carpet burns. I couldn't move a few of the fingers on my left hand either, and we quickly deduced that the frame of the bike had buckled out of line.

Two days later, on Sunday, I drove down to the Isle of Wight to visit my parents. Luckily, Raymond the doctor-brother was there, too. He took one look at the condition I was in and drove me to the nearest hospital, where an x-ray revealed I'd broken a few bones in my hand. Two hours later and I was back at my parents' place with a plaster cast from the tip of my fingers to my elbow and some nifty ointment for the still-weeping left ear. I tried to talk them out of doing the full plaster cast thing at the hospital, suggesting a little bit of strapping would do the trick as, wouldn't you know it, I was due to be playing with Jools and the band at the Brecon Jazz Festival that week. But I was overruled. It was to be a cast for no less than four weeks.

I phoned Jools that night with the news, and he didn't seem too perturbed, but then again the only reason I was playing in the band was because Gilson Lavis, his original drummer, had suffered a coronary whilst on stage. A few broken bones at the bottom of the stairs at the Groucho Club was nothing compared to a heart attack during the encore.

The Pisco sour knife was twisted a little further when I learnt that poor Gilson, who had been coaxed out of convalescence to do the festival, had his drum kit nicked after the show. News of the waiter's mountain bike wasn't good either; it had to be replaced and 'luckily' I was able to buy a new frame for a mere £300.

* * *

I made some very good friends through the Groucho. One of them was the Blur bassist, Alex James. Between tours, Alex would sit in the club twiddling his thumbs. Often he would sip a drink on the menu at the Groucho called 'The Rivron'. It was Pimms No. 2 (a little bit fiercer than No. 1), with a double Stolly floated on the top. That was about 18 quid. You only needed two or three. One night, Alex and I were sitting at the bar, not looking at each other but chatting and staring straight ahead, drinking. Completely unannounced, he threw up over the bar, fainted and fell over backwards off his stool. We figured he'd gotten the wrong side of a few too many Rivrons. Be warned – a Rivron can do that to you.

There was a guy called Dave who used to sit outside the

club begging. Over time people got to know him – he'd spend Christmas with various club members. He was becoming as much part of the club as the brass engraving of the duck in the doorway by which he sat. Inebriated, Alex and I got it into our heads that Dave warranted an official title. Alex lived in a beautiful old townhouse off Seven Dials. We went there and spent, easily, a whole day and a whole night trying to come up with an appropriate title for the guy. By the end of our marathon session, we had cracked it. He was going to be called . . . Outside Dave. That took twenty-four hours and the whole contents of Alex's fridge.

Another time, a producer from the *Good Stuff* television show phoned me in the Groucho and said, 'You're supposed to be outside Broadcasting House to interview Lee Evans in the limo.'

'Fuck,' I thought, 'I haven't been to bed for four days and I'm wearing the same clothes. I whiff a bit.' So Alex and I legged it over to Moss Bros and bought new clothes off the peg. Alex decided he wanted to look like a 1978 private jet pilot. In his wide-lapelled grey suit, big kipper tie and Aviator glasses he really looked the part, especially swaying back into the club, fag on the go and not a care in the world. I bought a new shirt and jacket – but according to Lee still reeked to high heaven, cooped up as we were for two and a half hours in the back of an already stinky limo.

The longer you spent at the club, the greater your chances of being in the right place at the right time. Keith Allen and Alex had cobbled together a song for the 1998 World Cup and asked if I'd fancy popping some drums on it. I was more than happy to oblige. In typical Keith fashion, he went against the grain. He thought, 'Let's do a football song that's not about football, but about cups of tea and Indian food.'

They were in the studio the next day. I was doing something for *Good Stuff* that morning over in Greenwich and remember having to get a limo bike, sharpish, over to the Townhouse Studios in Shepherd's Bush, where they were all waiting, to record the drums. I'd come straight from filming, so arrived dressed in a pinstripe suit, shirt and tie, glowing in tan makeup. Quite a good image for a session drummer, I thought. After a bit of multi-tracking, the drums were down and suddenly the song made sense. Apart from the drums, Keith's voice and a bit of bass, there wasn't that much to it. Keith got his daughter, thirteen-year-old Lily Allen, and some of her mates to come in and do a chorus, and that was that. The song was christened 'Vindaloo' and I was, briefly, in a band called Fat Les. Of course. it was just a bit of fun – I didn't expect it to sell many copies.

I was at Disneyland in Florida doing a Virgin in-flight film when the song came out, and I didn't even give it a second thought. Then after a few days I got call saying, 'It's number two!' I couldn't believe it.

This meant that, incredibly, we had to do *Top of the Pops*. To me, this was the fulfilment of another childhood fantasy, not dissimilar to cropping up on *Blue Peter*. At *Blue Peter*, I had been in awe. Unfortunately, this time I was still in awe but also pissed. *Top of the Pops* was recorded at Elstree, home of the *EastEnders* set, so for the song we yomped around Albert Square with, amongst other people, Michael Barrymore, who was very friendly to us. We may even have popped into the Queen Vic for a pint.

Fat Les was tremendous fun but totally chaotic. It was

like setting off a Mexican firecracker – you just have to light it and get out of the way. But what was beautiful about that band was there didn't seem to be anything approaching a game plan. The format was turn up, get pissed and maybe do something. Maybe.

The follow-up single was a bit of nonsense Keith had thought up, called 'Naughty Woman'. He was obviously beginning to take this pop business seriously as we had to talk him into singing it in the nutty Jamaican accent he used when he first ran it by us in the snooker room at the club. We were definitely going up in the world as this was to be recorded at George Martin's Air Studios, a huge converted church in Hampstead: a very silly song in a very serious place. Alex kept going on about how the insulated sound-proof doors alone cost about a million quid. Joe Strummer showed up one day to put some guitar on the track – it just kept getting more and more bizarre. I warmed to Joe. I was reminded of my time with Rik, as when he opened his guitar case a few brandy miniatures fell out.

At one point, Joe was having trouble getting his guitar to perform, and the engineer suggested it maybe needed a new nine-volt battery. Joe had no idea what he was on about. Batteries? The engineer unscrewed the metal plate on the back of his guitar and replaced the battery. All the while, Joe was dumbfounded; he honestly hadn't ever needed to replace one. As with Jeffrey Bernard, it was a bit of an honour to be arsing about with the great man.

* * *

For a while it was the biggest conundrum floating round the club. Just who *was* the owner of the very sexy ladies' knickers found, by the cleaners, knocking about on the floor of the brasserie restaurant? It took a few days to filter through to me, but as soon as I'd heard all the facts, I knew it could only be one person and that I was, in fact, something of an accessory to the 'crime'.

A few days previous to me learning about 'the dreadful business with the ladies' pants', as one of the more mature female manageresses called it, I was in the company of a bunch of about ten people having a late dinner in the brasserie. It must have been something to do with *The Tube* because, amongst others, Jools and Paula Yates were there, as well as director Geoff Wonfor, and I think, Muriel Gray, the Scottish broadcaster who regularly hosted the show with effortless, refreshing professionalism in Paula's absences. There was no lying on a bed with a pop star for an innuendo-filled chat with Muriel. Her line of enquiry would involve mundane things like the artist's music, career, influences and performance.

Paula was there with her new man, Michael Hutchence, whom I had recently interviewed on the Virgin drive-time radio show. As he didn't know many of the people at the table, and as we'd had a laugh, he insisted I sit next to him. The tables positioned around the edge of the brasserie all had big squishy banquettes against the wall and chairs on the opposite side of the table. It was on one of these banquettes that I found myself sitting with Michael, while Paula went round and said hello to pretty much everyone in the room. By the time she returned to our table, the food had arrived and we were all tucking in, so Paula just slid herself along the banquette next to me, the nearest she could get to Michael without asking people to move. So there I was, enjoying a starter, sandwiched between the two love birds who, clearly, only had eyes for each other. This was more than borne out when my main course pasta-based dish arrived and Michael, who didn't do mains, asked me to swap places with Paula, who hadn't bothered to order anything. I duly obliged and, as I set about my plate of food, noticed that Paula had hitched herself on to Michael's lap with her elbows on the table, facing, innocently, into the room. Then Michael began asking all sorts of questions slightly out of context: 'How's the pasta? How long you been coming here? What's it like here during the day?'

He was really trying to keep a healthy conversation going. Initially, I have to admit, I didn't notice what Paula was 'having' for her main course, and when I did, she flashed me a broad grin and said, 'Keep talking, Rowly. Michael wants to know all about you.'

'I'm sure he does. As long as he doesn't want to know me as well as he's obviously getting to know you, Paula,' I remarked, and got on with the meal as best I could.

I'm not sure who finished first, them or me – it was quite a large portion as I remember . . .

Michael and Paula subsequently invited Mon and I to a few parties at their place in Clapham, an ordinary terraced townhouse anonymous but for the ten-foot-high wooden fencing hastily erected due to the hassle they were getting from the press. Inside the place was a bohemian tinderbox, full of little kids, famous singers – I was once sandwiched between Julian Lennon and Nick Cave at dinner; I looked enormous – and enough flickering tealight and candles to reduce the place to a heap of smouldering charcoal in seconds.

Monica was heavily pregnant with our second child, Ella, at the time, and Michael was convinced that if Paula sat for a while with her hands on her bump, she too would get pregnant, it was pre Tiger Lily and they were desperate for a child. I couldn't help feeling that a few more nights 'bonketing' at the Groucho Club would, possibly, generate more fruitful results.

* * *

The club has changed considerably over the years. Gone are the white-knuckle drinkers and scoundrels, the very people that made the place THE club to be a member of. It's been bought and sold a few times and whenever that happens to a place, a little bit of its original charm is chipped off as the incoming owners invariably put their stamp on the venture. Maybe all the people who used it as their local in the late eighties have grown up, sobered up or given up and dropped dead. Twenty-five years ago, you weren't constantly reminded that 'cigarettes kill' and that it's best to 'drink responsibly', which of course means 'don't get drunk'. Today the club is very grown up. So at the end of May 2010 I wasn't expecting much when I called in with Mon and a couple of friends for a late-night snifter after going to the theatre.

I'd been cajoled into going to see Jason Donavon's last performance in *Priscilla Queen of the Desert* at the Cambridge Theatre. One of Monica's best friends, Charlotte, was openly obsessed with him; she'd seen the show about ten times and was keen for us to catch him before he left the production.

I'd first met Jason about twenty years ago in the Warwick Castle pub in Portobello Road, during the time I was with Wendy. It was her and Transvision Vamp's local drinking hole, a place to hang out as, amongst others, the Clash were regulars and everyone in Notting Hill seemed to be obsessed with Joe Strummer. Jason's musical background, at the time, produced by Stock, Aitken and Waterman and duetting with the very young Australian soap sensation, Kylie Minogue, didn't sit too comfortably with the regulars at the Warwick, and it wasn't long before the caustic but gentle ribbing kicked in. Sadly, but predictably, this fairly quickly gave way to tactless, drunken verbal abuse – not ideal. Jason had pitched up on his own and initially seemed to be dealing with the barrage remarkably well. To this day I don't know what possessed me – maybe the fact I'd been in the pub since lunchtime – but I stepped in and asked Jason if he wanted to go for a bite to eat round the corner, an opportunity maybe for a little respite from his new best 'friends'. That and the fact I was a big fan of a nice plated meal of an evening – I could never grasp Wendy and her band's eating habits: a diet of Dime Bars and fags from what I could gather. We strolled round the corner to a lovely restaurant and sat downstairs at an intimate table for two. Back then, if you were in a gaff that had on display caged wine cellars, you knew you were in a posh eatery. So there we were, two men, one ten years the junior of the other, having a candlelit dinner, the younger new to the town and the other a seasoned old hand. A few years later, the *Face* magazine – often referred to as the 'eighties fashion Bible' – published allegations that Jason was gay. Now, I'd hate to think our evening played any part in fuelling the flames of the wholly inaccurate accusations made against Jason. JESUS! Cannot two, incredibly attractive heterosexual men go out for a candlelit meal together in what, as it happens, I have since found out to be a slightly gay restaurant?

Our paths crossed occasionally over the years and we had faintly kept in touch, which pretty much took the form of me ringing him whenever my kids wanted to go and see *Chitty Chitty Bang Bang* at the Palladium, where he was holding down the role of Caractacus Potts. We went three times in all due to the fact that our youngest, Ned, would always fall asleep after the interval. So for his sake, we would return because as he once said, 'I like it 'cos it hasn't got the glass', meaning it wasn't on television.

I did the 'keeping in touch' again to find out if we could swing by after the *Priscilla* show and say hello – it would be a fantastic surprise for his number one fan Charlotte. He asked us to pop in half-an-hour before the show and he would say 'hi' then, which was perfect. Mon and I arranged to meet Charlotte and her boyfriend Simon before kick-off outside the theatre with no mention of what was to happen. I'm sure she won't mind me saying this, but Charlotte, bless her, is a bit nervy at the best of times. She used to babysit for us and was unable to enter Ned's room as it housed two large terrapins in a tank. She doesn't do lifts, stairs with no back to them are a problem, she refuses to use metal stairs with little holes and stairwells are avoided as she can't bear the 'looky down' bit in the middle.

We all met at seven as arranged and rather than head into the theatre, Mon and I set off for the stage door. 'Where you going, what you doing?' Charlotte was suitably fazed, and then she saw the stage door and the penny dropped. 'No, no, I can't!' She was now visibly shaking. 'I can't do this!'

But it was too late. We were at the stage door and being ushered up to Jason's dressing room. Simon drily commented that Charlotte was doing surprisingly well with the stairs, but to be fair she was holding the banister, tightly, with both hands. I knocked on the door and it was immediately swung open by the great man himself, barely concealing his modesty with what looked like nothing more than a hand towel. Charlotte was now a complete bag of nerves, but I'm sure she wouldn't have wanted it any other way.

With the truly amazing show behind us, we all took the short walk to the Groucho Club for the small snifter I mentioned earlier. The place was very quiet for a Saturday night, just a few pockets of people here and there, barely visible in the incredibly low lighting the club favours on the stroke of ten o'clock. A number of times I've been sitting at the bar, potted, and convinced I was going blind when all that was happening was the lights were gently dimming 50 per cent.

The evening had been a huge success, so I took the initiative and ordered Pisco sours all round and began holding forth to Simon and Charlotte about how the place had changed and that you don't see the characters, the famous faces, here any more, just men in suits and 'kids' with far too much money. Simon let me finish before calmly drawing my attention to Kate Hudson sitting in the corner with friends: 'Rowland, she's just over there, talking to Matt Bellamy, the singer from the band Muse.' I squinted into the darkness, clocked who he was talking about but was none the wiser; I had no idea who they were. Shit! The place was still where the characters and famous faces hung out – I was just too old to recognize them. As I was taking all this in, Simon piped up again, '. . . and isn't that Hurricane Higgins sitting behind you?'

That's more like it, I thought, I actually know who he is. But this wasn't the hell-raising Alex Higgins I'd grown up with on the Embassy World Championships and BBC2's *Pot Black* snooker programme. (As a kid, in the early seventies, my brothers and I would actually watch it on our black-and-white set trying to predict the colours of the balls.) No, this was a small frail man tragically ravaged by throat cancer. It was as a nod to the great man that I called the boxing Scrote in *Set of Six* Terry 'The Tornado'.

Higgins was with a couple of people, but there seemed to be an air of reverential silence around him, obviously not helped by his difficulty with speech. It all looked like a very sad situation, so, getting the right side of my third Pisco sour, I ambled over.

'Mr Higgins, Alex, fancy a game of snooker?'

He shot up out of his seat, and I shook his hand and introduced myself. He in return put his thumbs up and before I had chance to tell him where the snooker table was, he was off. What was I thinking? This was Hurricane Higgins – he knew exactly where the bloody snooker table was!

I'd be lying if I said I beat him. He quite predictably thrashed me, but I did pot the odd one or two balls. Throughout the game he would communicate with me by scribbling what he wanted to say on William Hill betting slips he'd produce from his jacket or small paper drink napkins. As he potted the first red, I couldn't help dragging up the one and only joke I've ever sold. It was to *Not the Nine O'Clock News* for the princely sum of £25 back in the eighties. As soon as the red went down I said, à la the umpire keeping score, 'One'. Alex sped round the table, eyes transfixed on the balls in front of him, and lined himself up for the blue, which he potted effortlessly. I then said, '. . . another one.' You see, I still think that's quite funny – not Alex, it was clear he was taking the game a little more seriously than I was.

One of the betting slips reads '*HES VERY IMPATIENT IS OUR ROWLAND RIVRON HIS GAME IS A GREAT LAUGH MY GAME IS MORE DIFFICULT. NOT HECKLERS PLAYERS AND PEOPLE TALKING OR MOVING IN MY EYELINE. DISTURBS THE FLOW.*' I think I got off lightly. In the 1986 UK championships he headbutted the referee, and at one point threatened to have fellow player and compatriot Dennis Taylor shot.

It really was an honour to actually play a frame with one of the world's best loved snooker players. I think he enjoyed it – he gave me a big hug after potting the last four balls in a row – and if my bar bill is anything to go by, I think we all did.

A few weeks later, while on summer holiday with Mon and the kids, I heard the news that Alex Higgins had died. After a couple of days, I got a call from my agent's office asking if a journalist from the *Irish Daily Mirror* could give me a call. A few minutes later, a woman phoned and asked for a quote as, according to her, I was the last person to play a frame of snooker with the great Alex 'Hurricane' Higgins.

13: THE VICAR OF TROLL

'I remember you were probably the biggest drinker I knew who wasn't Jeffrey Bernard,' says the Reverend Richard Coles.

To St Paul's Church, Knightsbridge, for an audience with its curate, Richard Coles, chaplain to the Royal Academy of Music and former member of the pop combo the Communards. The impressive church runs adjacent to the Berkeley Hotel, the hostel of choice when world leaders are in town. The local, everything-you-need, one-stop-shop is Harvey Nicks. When it comes to tending your flock, it looks like Richard has landed butter-side up.

Knightsbridge also boasts some of the oldest and finest pubs in London, but rather than run the gauntlet of the parish locals, Richard suggests we go back to his place. There's a faint whiff of a double-take and a wry smile as we both acknowledge what has just tripped off the gay Reverend's tongue. But that's pretty much what I did do every weekend between 1989 and 1990 when plain old 'Richard Coles' had a house in Islington, at Number One Moon Street, the sort of address I always thought sat better with a CBBC kids' show than the deranged madness I witnessed there on a weekly basis.

Richard had very much an open-house policy back then

which, thinking about it, is where he finds himself today. Being a fully paid-up member of the church, his door is always open, but little gets nicked, unlike during the crazy days of Moon Street.

With the job as reverend comes a small basement flat tucked away round the back of the church, where we head for a cup of tea and a fag (a cigarette that is) . . . for Richard, not me.

I first bumped into Richard while working on LWT's *Night Network*, the groundbreaking show that went out on Friday and Saturday from midnight through to about 6 a.m. We immediately hit it off. I felt I'd found a kindred spirit as we shared an irreverent approach to life. Neither of us would ever let work get in the way of a good time. Often, going out for a good time with him took several days, during which I was reconnected with the gay fraternity. Richard's circle of friends were an eclectic mix, to say the least. A lot of the women were in fact men.

This was before twenty-four-hour TV – hence the rather grand 'groundbreaking' tag for *Night Network*. Others on the roster included the aforementioned celebrated broadcaster Emma Freud, DJ and sometime pop star Mick Brown, and DJ and wannabe urban hero Tim Westwood who – Richard is quick to point out – is the son of the Bishop of Peterborough. Tim's credentials as Mr Hip Hop know no bounds – in Britain that is. Listening to Timothy's accent (from somewhere just south of Snoop Dogg) on his many radio and TV appearances, it's almost a shame he didn't follow his father into the pulpit.

Richard's job on *Night Network* was to review films for the show, something he'd never done before. But that didn't matter; he was an intelligent and articulate pop star, and there weren't many of them about at the end of the eighties.

We were first introduced to each other dressed as tramps. Jill, the series producer, got a bunch of us to go and busk in front of various London landmarks for a promotional video, myself on snare drum and Richard on a little battery-powered Bontempi keyboard. I remember Paul McCartney – current worth £800 million – doing a similar thing once, busking for loose change outside a train station for 'a merry jape', and I thought then how tactless it was.

But back then we didn't think twice about doing stuff like that. We were on television, which had the knack of blinding you to any moral questions that might be floating around and clouding the issue. How we went from dressing as tramps to virtually living like tramps neither of us is quite sure, but it wasn't long before I found myself, every weekend, wandering through Troll, a labyrinth of dark corridors and rooms with sticky floors, deafening music and the occasional bean bag.

While everyone has no doubt heard of the gay club Heaven, in the arches off Villiers Street round the back of Charing Cross Station, I'm fairly sure not too many people are familiar with the 'club that exists within the club'. During the week this most secret of places was known as Sound Shaft. But come the weekend it became Troll and was run by a friend of Richard's, a big, imposing chap called Tim Stabler – Stabler by name but, refreshingly, not by nature.

'Tim was the only person I knew who's ever been diagnosed with trench foot because he didn't take his shoes off for about three weeks,' says Richard.

It was alleged that Tim would regularly jack up an ounce of speed a night, but he was a big man so you'd never really know. He was fond of a kimono and threw himself into fan-dancing, as I remember. He sported a big, impressive moustache and a bridge that often popped out, which he would superglue back in while still dancing. He never liked to leave a party. Nobody could confirm it, but before his Troll days, Tim had allegedly spent time 'up north' show-jumping with Princess Anne and was at one time a regular on the pro equestrian scene. When not in delicate Japanese silks, wielding huge hand-painted paper fans and off his tits, Tim could easily have passed for one of the horsey set.

The inhabitants of Troll were known as 'a day-glo, fun-loving crowd', which all sounds harmless enough. I remember them more as a bunch of hysterical queens on ecstasy, and that was no bad thing either. The music was always very good and incredibly, incredibly, loud. Around this time, I still owned up to being a jazz drummer, and this was the first time I'd witnessed white-knuckle club culture. The loudest music I'd heard up until then was probably when I got a good seat, near the front, at Ronnie Scott's during a Buddy Rich Big Band residency. A lot of the music in my life back then could be catalogued as listening for pleasure: the Cedar Walton Jazz Quartet, Bill Evans Trio, Betty Carter. Acoustic jazz, basically.

I prided myself on the fact that whenever I gigged it was always very quietly; I was never a noisy drummer. For a time, I was known as the quietest drummer in London, an accolade that saw me corner the market in gigs that required just the presence of a few musos – a small band – to facilitate the extension of a drinking licence. One such venue was the popular eatery Langan's Brasserie, just off Piccadilly. Nowadays people are positively encouraged to drink twenty-four hours a day, but this was the late seventies, when drinking in public after eleven o'clock was frowned upon, unless, for some inexplicable reason, there was a band present.

Some nights, if Peter Langan, whose name shone in neon above the door, was in and drinking, just being in the same building with our instruments did the trick. We'd go as far as setting up then actually get paid to get pissed with Peter, having not lifted a finger to play a note all night.

The music I experienced at Troll could never be classed as 'listening for pleasure'. This was music employed in the same way doctors employ defibrillators – to bring people back from the dead, or at least keep them alive. I had visions of the happy, shiny people dancing around me, all off their faces on the horse tranquillizer Ketamine, PCP and ecstasy, clutching their hearts and dropping stone dead as soon as the music was switched off, which is, perhaps, why it never was. This was, however, something completely new to me – and I loved it. The music, that is. I didn't much care for the horse tranquillizer.

'You're the only person I know who lived like you did and consistently earned a living . . . You never had that thing, you know, where you were circling the drain. You always looked like you were going to survive, no matter what,' says Richard.

Not everyone dancing at Troll was an hysterical queen. Heck, some nights I was there. What I mean is, there was a smattering of what were affectionately referred to as 'fag hags', women who liked to hang out with gay men. Someone told me Judy Garland was a classic fag hag, but I had trouble picturing her in regulation hot pants and singlet sweating cobs dancing in an oversized bird cage suspended from the ceiling. I did witness some of the most attractive women I have ever seen, dancing virtually naked and really letting themselves go, safe in the knowledge that they weren't going to get hassled by a bunch of leery, hetero oiks.

Now, I'm not putting my hand up to being an oik. I am, however, hetero and, yes, there may have been the smallest amount of harmless leering on my part. For that, I apologize. Right now. Twenty years later. Sorry. In my defence, though, thinking about it, there couldn't have been that much leering as the place didn't sell alcohol and everyone knows that for 'leering' read 'lager' – it's a booze-fuelled pastime is leering. The 'bar' in Troll was run by a lovely bunch of National Front gay skinheads and only sold water, admittedly at spirit prices. It was always a 'dry' event – but for the six quid miniature bottles of water and the bevy of gorgeous, salty, fag-hag cob-sweaters in cages.

Only at Troll would I witness a guy, an incredible vogue dancer as I remember, slip away for a few minutes, have sex with one of the unhappily married men who would cruise the arches and return with just enough money to buy . . . some water.

Occasionally, after thirty-six hours of dancing, a double-decker bus would be 'procured' and all those with enough stamina or an inability to come back down to earth would pile on and take off to the New Forest or somewhere similar for the day. This would all start off with the best of intentions, but quickly go pear-shaped. Trees would be set on fire, things happened in bushes and cars would be stolen to drive back into town for 'fresh supplies'. Then there would be the tears and the tantrums, as people slowly realized what the hell was going on. The amazing thing was, no one was ever arrested – asked to move on, obviously, but never detained.

Regardless of what anyone got up to, the weekend would always come to a rest at Richard's in Islington. The handful of people who had travelled down from Leicester would eke out the last few hours of the fifty-six-hour bender at Moon Street before heading north and back to reality, often clutching the odd gold disk they'd removed from a wall, seemingly with Richard's blessing.

'We did talk about serious things sometimes. You said one thing that I've never forgotten and I've used since – you said comedy is about reassurance . . . least that's what I think you said, you may have said "insurance" . . .' recalls Richard.

I realized things were getting seriously out of hand when, one day, Richard produced a crumpled cheque from his back pocket and casually mentioned we should swing by a bank at some point and 'by the way, what time do they open?' – he had no idea. He really wasn't looking too chipper, so I offered to bank it for him, until I noticed it was for £40,000. For a moment, he genuinely had no idea where it had come from. But after a while, we were pretty sure it was probably the money from the sale of a flat he'd forgotten he owned in Kilburn. I think it was an investment made for him by his accountants The flat only came to light after he received a stern letter from a solicitor saying a lot of people were being stung by wasps from a nest that had built up, over time, in the empty premises belonging to one Richard

Coles. Apparently, the heating had been left on for a few years, presenting the perfect environment for wasps to thrive.

For me the mayhem at Troll only lasted a year, but to be honest, it was enough. I peeled off and left the survivors to it. Dr Scrote was getting into his stride, so I threw myself down that path. This meant, sadly, I didn't get to party with them all in Ibiza, where, apparently, Richard bought a speedboat and promptly ran over Shirley-Shirley-Party-Girlie, one of the boys from Leicester – or to enjoy the strips of acid one of the girls had smuggled on to the island in her front toilet. Probably a good thing, thinking about it. Richard eventually found God, which I'm sure saved his life – a turn of phrase people use all too often, but in this case was much nearer the truth. In fact, I've never seen Richard looking happier.

'You know I cremated Ned Sherrin and Clement Freud . . . so when the time comes, Rowland . . .'

14: PLAYING WITH JOOLS

To Julian Holland's townhouse, which he shares with Christabel, his wife, and quite possibly a few of his kids. I'd not been to the house before, but his initial directions reassured me that not much had changed from the time we were in and out of each other's pockets all those years ago: 'Head for Buckingham Palace and turn left.' I did as he said, and there he was, wearing far too many layers as usual, on the doorstep of his beautiful five-storey, terraced town-house with immaculate window boxes that retained just the faintest whiff of Christmas decoration. It was late January, but then nothing ever happened too quickly with Jools. He beckoned me in and put the kettle on. He couldn't entertain my suggestion of a pie and a pint, and that came as no sur-prise as I'd never known him take an alcoholic drink during the day – I suppose it works for some people . . .

With a small plate of digestives and two mugs of Tetley's (tea, not bitter), we made our way through a labyrinth of corridors to a drawing room at the back of a house Sherlock Holmes would have been happy with. My inten-tion was to digitally record our conversation as I'd done with most of the other people I'd tracked down. In a restaurant or pub an upturned glass made for the perfect 'stand' for the small digital machine. Jools offered a pile of books to rest the tape machine on. The top one happened to be Terry Thomas's 1959 autobiography, *Filling the Gap*. A good omen, I thought.

Before we started turning the clock back, Jools reminded me of an incident I must have mentioned to him during our touring days. He felt it should be included in this book, as he thought it set the tone perfectly for the person with whom he was to become good friends.

I was four years old and we were living at 43 Greys Road on the RAF camp in Uxbridge. I hadn't started school and would spend endless sunny days playing in the small back garden. Garages were being built at the back of our house, and every day I would sit on the low brick wall at the end of our garden and watch the builders working and ask them all those annoying questions four-year-olds do (why is a spade called a spade? Why is mud sticky?). Every day at the same time, they would stop for lunch. Today it would be a stroll to the nearest cafe or shop for a takeaway tea and a filled roll. In 1962, the workmen all had packed lunches and would down tools, find the nearest comfy seating and tuck into big doorstep cheese sandwiches. We'll never know if I really wanted one of those giant sarnies or just fancied the idea of one. Either way, I ended up swapping my Dad's gold wristwatch for half a workman's sandwich. Dad must have left it in the kitchen on the sideboard; it was, obviously, the first thing I spotted when looking for something to swap that wasn't one of my prized beaten-up Dinky toys.

Mum and Dad searched the house, top to bottom, and eventually asked me if I'd seen Daddy's watch. When I innocently admitted what I'd done, it was too late. Mum and

Dad tried to locate the workman with the shiny gold watch, but to no avail – he'd long gone. In my defence, I *was* only four . . .

The first time I made my presence felt with Jools was 5 November 1984. Rik Mayall had made a few appearances on the first two series of *The Tube* and was currently Jools' new best friend. So Jools invited Rik and his girlfriend Lise to a fireworks party he was throwing at his flat above a hairdresser's called Sid's in Blackheath. The fireworks were to be ignited on a small second-floor patio at the back of the building, not actually in the flat – that would come later, after I had got to know Jools a lot better and he was able to trust me. As I was living with Rik and Lise in Ellington Street, they kindly invited me to head south of the river with them. I think they were a bit scared – well, Rik certainly was – of south London, and they wanted to go as mob-handed as possible.

Jools and his friends were all very pleasant, and a lovely, if somewhat pedestrian, time was being had by all. We were the only people from north of the river, and I couldn't put my finger on it, but for some reason I felt ever so slightly aware of that. The patio roof-garden wasn't very big, and this was reflected in the size and excitement of the fireworks on display. That, and Jools' generous hospitality, moved me to suggest that some 'close-hand' pyrotechnics might be the order of the day. I produced a Brocks Firework Banger from my breast pocket and asked Jools if I could borrow a lighter. Making sure there was nobody standing to my left – I'd done this before – I lit the banger and placed it, carefully, on my head. This trick was always enhanced if Rik was present – as soon as he saw I'd whipped the banger out, he would become hysterical, insisting we were all going to die. After some impressive loud fizzing and billowing white smoke, the banger exploded and flew from my head. Jools and his friends were suitably impressed, and I felt the north-south 'ice' finally cracking. Jools remembers, 'Immediately, like a deranged Spiderman, you were up the drainpipe and on to the slippery roof.'

The success of the close-hand firework display and its inherent danger prompted one of the guests to produce a very large rocket. They were convinced it would be fine to launch it from the patio. In a moment of rare, lucid vigilance, I intervened and explained that the rocket was far too big for the patio, and one would have trouble standing a safe distance from the launch. I did, however, tell him that all was not lost and that it could be launched from the chimney pot of the roof next door. With the rocket between my teeth, I scaled the drainpipe and inched across the tiled roof. As I did this, Jools tells me, the mood amongst the assembled partygoers changed from happy-go-lucky enjoyment to, 'Oh my God, please get him down, he's going to kill himself!' Jools maintains women were sobbing, and if they were, then I apologize profusely. It was never my intention to upset anyone.

Jools had never met me before and thought it rude to say anything as he assumed I knew exactly what I was doing. Rik was insisting that everyone be quiet and not interrupt, for fear of putting me off. I hooked the rocket on to the rim of the chimney pot, lit it and made a hasty retreat, sliding down the roof and jumping on to the patio roof-garden. The rocket skewed into the sky and was a huge success, although it was greeted with a muted cheer, as, I think, everyone was more relieved they hadn't witnessed someone falling three storeys to a certain death.

The next time I bumped into Jools was in Plymouth, at Lenny Henry's charity gig in aid of sickle cell anaemia research. Jools was there with his 'big band', which amounted to him on piano and Gilson Lavis on drums. I was Raw Sex-ing, with Simon Brint on piano and me on conga drums – the similarity was uncanny. Two fine pianists and two giants of the drums, on the same stage. After the gig we exchanged pleasantries and went our separate ways. The following day word filtered through that, on their journey home on the M5, Jools and Gilson drove headlong into a car travelling the wrong way up the motorway.

John Lay, Jools' manager, was driving the car and suffered the worst injuries, his face impaled on the steering wheel. Gilson was in the passenger seat and lost a few teeth, broke his nose and completely buggered his arm and shoulder, breaking all sorts of bones. Jools and Christabel, his girlfriend, were in the back. Both of her legs were broken, but Jools emerged from the carnage a little shaken but essentially unscathed. In hospital, Gilson commented that when he regained consciousness in the wreckage he could see Jools on the hard shoulder talking with someone and thought, 'Typical, he's only giving a bloody interview.'

The accident happened in March. Jools had a bunch of tour dates booked throughout the summer, and it quickly became clear that as the months passed, Gilson wouldn't be well enough to play. Jools had been auditioning some of the top session drummers of the time to sit in for Gilson, but to no effect. They were all great players, but it wasn't working. Jools says, 'There's a certain touch in drumming that, for instance, Ringo Starr has, Charlie Watts has, Earl Palmer, the great drummer who played on "Tutti Frutti", has – a certain feel of swing and danceability.'

Rik mentioned to Jools that I had roots in jazz drumming and that he should, 'Give Rowly a go.' Jools could see no harm in giving Rowly a go, either. We had got on well at his fireworks party when I'd scared his friends half to death and nearly killed myself, and we had had our mutual appreciation society event in Plymouth: 'Also, he was such an agreeable fellow, Rowland, I thought it might be quite fun to have him along on tour. He came over to my place, and what was really impressive was, without thinking or being told what to do, he was playing the music exactly right – too quietly, but dead right.' Playing too quietly became the eternal problem with Jools and me, not so much on the tour that summer, but when I returned a few years later, two days after Gilson had had a heart attack. By that time the band had mushroomed to 'The Jools Holland Rhythm and Blues Orchestra' and it was a nightmare – the quietest drummer in London driving the loudest band in town. For the time being however, it wasn't just a drummer he needed. John Lay had to have his face reconstructed and spent months with a terribly painful-looking external metal frame holding his head together. He really was a scary thing to behold, and there was no way he could commit to doing the driving, or anything else, on the tour.

Jools says, 'We needed someone who was a tour manager and could also book dates as we went along, and for some reason we ended up with, the late, great Malcolm Hardee . . .' Malcolm ran the Tunnel Palladium, a comedy club located at the southern approach to the Blackwall

Tunnel in Greenwich. The Tunnel, as it was called, was a fierce gig – heckling was positively encouraged, things being thrown at the stage the norm. Raw Sex played there a couple of times with a very funny man called Lee Cornes, whose alter ego Dickie Valentino, a failed but crushingly optimistic gag- and tunesmith, perfectly complemented our alter egos, Ken and Duane Bishop. One particularly tough night at the Tunnel, 'Dickie' turned to 'Ken and Duane', and slipping out of character said, 'That's it, I'm getting off, they've started throwing coins, it's too dangerous.' Another time, comedienne Hattie Hayridge was doing her set when a huge plastic bread delivery basket came flying through the air. It just missed her by about six inches and smashed against the back wall of the stage.

This was Malcolm's domain, his natural home – he was the only person who could hold his own in front of the baying crowd. Very often he would do just that and perform a variety of tricks with his knob, abseiling it down his leg, pissing into a pint pot and drinking it, or giving his classic impression of French President Charles de Gaulle, using his own spectacles placed on top of his genitals with his testicles representing the politician's cheeks. He was doing this years before the Australian show, *Puppetry of the Penis*, was somehow let into this country to perform.

Let's not forget that Malcolm is the man responsible for 'The Greatest Show On Legs' and their legendary 'balloon dance': three naked men passing balloons to each other that, initially, cover their modesty. Air escapes from one of the balloons, and it deflates, but then another balloon is produced from someone's mouth and inflated just in time. It was a very impressive and funny routine that has been often copied but never bettered. An appearance on OTT, Chris Tarrant's adult version of Tiswas, resulted in them, briefly, being 'the act' to have at your event. They were hired to perform at Freddie Mercury's birthday party, but were cancelled minutes before show-time as, apparently, there were too many photographers at the bash and the organizers didn't want naked men dancing on stage for fear the event would be reported in the national press as 'too gay'. Elton 'Joan' and Freddie kissing? That was fine, but men in the buff with balloons? Sorry, just too, too gay. Malcolm was so pissed off that he and his mate Martin Soan stole Freddie's birthday cake. I now refer you to Malcolm's own autobiography, I Stole Freddie Mercury's Birthday Cake, for the full and hilarious account.

I remember drinking heartily with Malcolm at the Gilded Balloon, Karen Koren's comedy venue in Edinburgh, during the Festival one year. He'd spilt the majority of his fresh pint on the floor, so grabbed one of the small towels on the bar and proceeded to mop up the beer and return it to his glass. When he'd rescued all he could, he carried on drinking as if nothing had happened. He finished the last drop of the filthy liquid, studied the glass with its layer of dirt and grime, turned to me and said, 'I wish I hadn't done that.' But he had – he was Malcolm Hardee. During the same drinking session, he sold his wife's coat to a passer-by. No sooner had Mrs Hardee entrusted him with his plastic fashion mac, than a Japanese tourist approached Malcolm and asked where he had bought the coat, to which he replied, 'Fuck knows, but you can have this one for fifteen quid.' The Japanese lady hastily produced the £15 and scurried off with Malcolm's wife's coat. Mrs Hardee wasn't best pleased with her husband's cavalier attitude to part of her autumn wardrobe.

At his funeral in 2005, the flowers on the casket spelt out the words 'Knob out', one of Malcolm's catchphrases, and after the service they were thrown into the Thames, the same river that had so tragically taken his life. (He was returning in a dinghy from the Wibbley Wobbley pub he ran in a converted barge at Greenland Dock to the houseboat where he lived, and fell in.) Unfortunately, a little further down river some important dignitaries from the European Commission had gathered at the great gates of Greenwich Park. They were assessing its suitability for the equestrian event at the 2012 Olympics. As they looked out over the river, the words 'Knob out' in flowers floated by. An apocryphal tale, surely? No. A friend of Jools, a Greenwich councillor, was escorting the dignitaries that day and witnessed the whole thing. Even from beyond the grave, Malcolm was able to make his penis felt – sorry, his presence felt.

These few tales should help indicate the kind of man that Jools thought had all the right qualifications to oversee a nationwide tour.

Jools had purchased a second-hand 7 Series BMW to get us round the country and remembers it as the sort of car that was popular in Thamesmead, the sort of car one might see waiting outside Belmarsh Prison to meet a recently liberated villain. On a sunny Saturday in July, we all convened at Jools' studio, Helicon Mountain in Greenwich, ready to embark on the long hot summer tour of '87. I arrived as Malcolm was adjusting the driving seat and making himself comfortable behind the wheel of a shiny new BMW. Then, just as we were about to set off, Malcolm let it be known that he was actually banned from driving, but he was happy to use someone else's licence if they'd lend it to him. Jools didn't want to have anything to do with it, and advised Keith Wilkinson, the bass player, and myself not to get drawn in. Jools ordered Malcolm out of the car and got behind the wheel himself. Before we'd even begun, Malcolm's duties as our tour manager were being thrown into doubt.

Christabel was travelling with us. As her legs were in plaster from her toes to her thighs, she could only travel comfortably in the front passenger seat, so Malcolm was ordered to sit in the back between Keith and myself. We put him in the middle because Keith and I maintained that, as two-thirds of the show, we should at least have what little legroom there was. Malcolm wasn't happy about this arrangement, but then he wasn't happy about most things.

We eventually set off. It wasn't ideal, but we were on our way – sadly, not for long. At the end of the road, Malcolm ordered Jools to pull over to the side of the road. We'd travelled one hundred yards, and already Malcolm wanted to get out of the car. He approached a skip we'd passed and began rummaging through it. We all sat in silence, unable to hazard a guess as to what the hell he was doing. Walking back towards the car, he was folding what looked like a large piece of tarpaulin.

'Malcolm, what the bloody hell are you doing?' Jools asked.

'It's a tent. I'm going to save a fortune on accommodation,' Malcolm explained.

His plan was to pitch it in the grounds of all the 'posh'

hotels we were staying at, with a view to trousering the money that would otherwise have been spent on his accommodation.

The Stoneycroft Hotel, Leicester, is now a very respectable three-star hotel, but in 1987 it was typical of the calibre of hotels we were using: communal phone and bathroom in the hall, limited off-street parking – far from 'posh' and incredibly cheap. Unsurprisingly, none of the hotels wanted to have anything to do with Malcolm and his knackered tent, and we were all of the opinion that it wasn't quite the right image for a tour manager, a man supposed to be responsible for our welfare and only a phone call away, not living rough in the grounds of a hotel. Malcolm clearly didn't want to part with this golden opportunity to save a small fortune, but barely two days into the tour Jools refused to drive any further with the stinking roll of tarpaulin filling the boot. The tent was eventually returned whence it came – another skip, this one in a lay-by halfway up the A1. Malcolm was OK about it; as he squeezed back into the car he casually asked Jools if it was possible to fit a tow bar on the BMW as he had a mate who owned a small caravan . . .

'I'd really like to have a photograph of the faces in the audience, during your drum solo, of expectancy, joy, confusion and fear, seeing this wild man, beaming, produce a firework and explode it on his head,' says Jools.

I was never a big fan of the drum solo; I'm much happier providing a pulse, a rhythm, a beat. There was one number in the set where Gilson had the opportunity to shine, a big drum solo, and he did it magnificently. Jools insisted that I do 'something', as the audience would half expect it.

When the time came for 'the drummer to shine', I thrashed around, made a noise and then brought the solo down to just the bass drum and high hat. I placed the sticks on the snare drum and produced a firework banger from the breast pocket of my jacket. I'd then ask the audience if anyone had a lighter I could borrow – they always obliged – and, using the first one I could catch, I'd light the firework and place it on my head. The banger going off signalled the first beat of the bar of snare-drum triplets that would launch us all back into the number. It looked, sounded and was fantastic – perfectly throwing the focus away from my inability to pull off a big, fat drum solo.

'Malcolm wanted to be dropped at a roundabout. He was off to Glastonbury, and before we'd pulled away out of sight, he had secured a lift. After that, we seemed to generally manage quite a bit better,' recalls Jools. Life in the BMW was a little less cramped with Malcolm performing in the comedy tent at Glastonbury. The Hardee 'hum', strengthened by such a hot summer and which none of us could help detecting, had momentarily left the car. There was a most disagreeable side-effect to Malcolm's desire to be at one with nature and eschew such modern-day trappings as showers and soap: he stank.

Nevertheless, the car was a different place without his relentless yet entertaining contempt for life. The thing about Malcolm was that he said it as he saw it – invariably, with embarrassing consequences. He was a man with little time for pleasantries. He seemed to wallow in a perpetual state of dissatisfaction and at times he wasn't so much an accident waiting to happen, but more an accident waiting to be cleared up. But you couldn't help thinking that through

Malcolm's filthy bi-focals, life was to be enjoyed rather than endured. He only ever did things on his terms, which is why most people were left exasperated.

Another upshot of his brief departure was that we'd lost our 'litmus paper' test as far as the audiences were concerned. At each gig, Malcolm would amble on stage to introduce us and fire off the same 'joke' to test the mood of the audience: 'How do you get a nun pregnant? Fuck her.'

He was convinced, from the reaction to that one gag alone, that it was possible to gauge whether they were a good or a bad crowd. If they howled with laughter, he knew it was going to be a good one and we were going to be fine. Whereas, if the joke was met with indifference, he'd say we'd have our work cut out for us and wish us luck. Quite what the connection was between a filthy joke about a nun and the boogie-woogie music we were about to unleash on the crowd had in common, we never quite ascertained. Malcolm was convinced that base humour and boogie-woogie music complemented each other perfectly.

Without Malcolm, we all happily took on various roles. Jools held on to his job as 'pilot', Keith was appointed 'chief navigator' and Christabel was 'hotel liaison officer'. With two broken legs, it was her job to ring ahead and ensure we had a parking space as near as possible to the entrance of the hotel. I was christened 'cabin stewardess brackets male' and took it upon myself to come clean about my mild OCD history and restore my corner of the car to its former spotless glory. And it wasn't just the interior. At traffic lights, I would jump out and clean the window screen, wait for a tip from Jools and then jump back in the car, usually as it was slowly pulling away.

Malcolm's residency in the comedy tent at Glastonbury was all too quickly over, which meant that within five days we were heading back to the same roundabout we'd dropped him at. We'd all overlooked the fact that very few people take a bath or a shower at the festival, and as Malcolm wedged himself between Keith and me in the back of the car, we immediately noticed that the Hardee 'hum' had gone up two notches. As a result of the accident that had put John Lay and Gilson Lavis out of action, Jools refused to travel more than sixty-eight miles per hour. Our next gig was in Plymouth. It was one hundred miles in eighty-degree heat, with 'Malcolm in the middle'. It was hell.

The Plymouth gig was on a small stage in a really dodgy nightclub, heaving with pissed students, who, due to the weather, were in various states of undress. Far too many people had been allowed in and women were fainting all over the place.

We didn't make it on to the stage until about eleven o'clock. The nun joke had gone down a storm. But not as well as the Jools Holland Big Band. It was a belter!

The following day's gig couldn't have been more different – Dartmoor Prison. Malcolm was responsible for securing the gig. He'd spent time at Her Majesty's pleasure in Dartmoor after nicking a Rolls-Royce belonging to Tory MP Peter Walker. He knew the chaplain of the prison, who would occasionally book musical groups and arrange shows for the inmates. The Salvation Army band had been the last 'group' to perform within the 200-year-old granite walls, and securing an altogether more contemporary band was considered something of a coup for the reverend.

We drove on to Dartmoor on a really sunny afternoon,

which made the whole thing all the more surreal. I always associated remote moorland prisons with dark, overcast skies. Not that I had ever been to one – this was my first time behind bars and I was really looking forward to it, knowing we'd done nothing wrong and were going to be waving goodbye in a few hours' time. Or were we? As we drove up to the huge main gates, Malcolm became agitated and eventually admitted he wanted us all to help him smuggle a load of tobacco into the prison for some of the inmates. He didn't want to get caught with all of the snout on him, as that would result in immediate arrest and incarceration. He reasoned that if we all made out we were fierce sixty-a-day smokers, we could legitimately be carrying a certain amount of loose tobacco about our persons. I was up for giving it a go, but I'd never smoked in my life – as you know, my mum had put paid to that – so knew I couldn't pull it off. Keith flatly refused to commit a crime at such close quarters. Christabel had remained at the hotel – I can't think why – and Jools just sat with his head in his hands. If Malcolm wanted to smuggle his contraband, he would have to do it alone and risk the consequences.

Which is exactly what he did, the madman, and bloody got away with it! The grounds of Dartmoor Prison are, as you'd expect, immaculate, and reminded me of the officers' mess on the RAF camp I grew up on. Nothing was out of place, everything that could shine, shone. Everywhere you looked there were manicured flowerbeds and grass areas with not a blade out of place, like billiard-table green baize – I was in OCD heaven. Having said that, this old prison was the grimmest, bleakest, most austere, scariest place you could imagine.

And wouldn't you know it, the vicar was straight out
of an Ealing comedy. He was Arthur Lowe meets Ian
Carmichael, sporting a grey barathea jacket exposing just
enough dog collar, Bobby Charlton hair and sensible shiny
shoes. I wonder if when you apply to be a vicar, you go and
see the powers that be and they say, 'Well, you don't look
like any vicar we've seen in the Ealing comedies we've
watched. So I'm afraid you've failed this part of the exam,
but good luck trying to pass the rest of the tests with
those piercing blue eyes, rugged good looks and incredible
physique.'

The gig was to take place at four o'clock in the afternoon, in the huge gymnasium. A makeshift stage was in
place at one end with a 'backstage' area. I must admit, I was
a little thrown by the number of inmates who fetched and
carried for us and just hung out while we were setting up.
I'm ashamed to say, I couldn't help myself asking the vicar
if coats and bags would be OK left where they were. He
smiled a knowing smile and assured me nothing would
go missing as these were the trusties, a position that had
nothing to do with money, but simply inmates who could be
trusted. Yeah, right!

At five minutes to four, the inmates began filing into the
hall in total silence. They formed rows in front of the stage
and, once everyone was in, the command was given for
them all to sit down, cross-legged on the wooden floor.
Sun was streaming in through the high windows, and the
inmates were all wearing the same regulation blue prison
clothes. It was like a freaky junior school assembly, which
got weirder when the dog-handlers marched in and took up
strategic positions around the gym. Malcolm, you bastard!

We're not even getting paid for this gig! What the hell are we doing here? The vicar took to the stage and the crowd immediately began to stir. In typically understated fashion, he asked the men to 'Settle down and stop all the chitter-chatter.'

By the end of the first number, Keith had thought better of the sexy hip-thrusting playing stance he was used to, and I found it almost impossible to look out into the audience. None of us had ever played to a sea of men sitting politely, cross-legged, in dappled sunshine.

And yet despite the strained circumstances, it was a truly fantastic gig. Jools announced we were going to play our last number, 'Nut Rocker', and a few bars in, a big Rasta guy stood up and waited for a nod of approval from a few of the guards, then signalled for everyone to stand. They had obviously been told to stay cross-legged until the last number, and only when they'd been given the OK could the guys get up and dance.

It was bizarre: 600 grown men suddenly rose to their feet and danced themselves silly, surrounded by very anxious-looking guards with Alsatian dogs pulling at their leashes.

Instead of a rider, the vicar's wife had very kindly provided some plated sandwiches for the band after the gig, which we gratefully devoured. When we were packed up and ready to go, the vicar thanked us and said what an absolute success the event had been but for the one dinner plate that had gone missing. It occurred to me that it was 'obviously going to be sanded down into the shape of a pistol and used to kidnap one of the guards before a mass breakout ensued'. 'I do hope not,' replied the vicar with a faint whiff of concern.

In the meantime Malcolm managed to get shot of all the tobacco to his mates, none of our stuff went missing (as in hindsight we knew it wouldn't) and we were back at the hotel in time for dinner. Result!

15: DOWN *THE TUBE*

God knows what she was doing watching the programme in the first place; she must have been in her late sixties.

I was on the phone to my mum, catching up with all the news and lying through my teeth about how well I was doing, as you do, when she dropped into the conversation that she'd seen a 'lad' on a new television programme who reminded her of me, the way he spoke, his mannerisms, that sort of thing. The programme was Tyne Tees Television's groundbreaking music show, *The Tube*; the 'lad' was Squeeze pianist, Jools Holland. This was 1982, two years before Jools and I became acquainted. I was completely unaware of the programme and the 'lad' in question.

The odd thing was, my mum wasn't the only one who had spotted a similarity; a few people I was working with had also mentioned it. What the hell was going on? And how could this be? There was Jools, born and bred in London SE10, while I'd spent my formative years way out west in UB8. Twenty-five miles apart, the two places couldn't be more different: Greenwich with its beautiful park, Victorian foot tunnel to the Isle of Dogs, Royal Observatory and proximity to majestic Old Father Thames; and then there's Uxbridge, bloody Uxbridge, with no park that I'm aware of, the odd footbridge, absolutely no opportunity to study the night sky and one of the biggest, noisiest, most congested airports in the world, Heathrow, on its doorstep. After weeks of meticulous research, 'hometown of a Groovy Feller' is the only entry I could find that linked Greenwich with Uxbridge – Groovy Feller? All will be explained. Three years after Mum's doppelgänger moment, I was putting in my tuppence-worth on the very same programme and being gainfully employed supplying the odd humorous observation for the 'lad' Jools.

Every Thursday at eleven-thirty in the morning, Jools, his co-host on the show, Paula Yates, and I would meet under the information board at King's Cross for the three-and-a-half hour train journey to Newcastle. We would take lunch in the cramped first-class buffet car while all of England passed us by and I always thought it the most ridiculous thing, attempting to serve a full-on, plated hot meal – heavy cutlery, heavy linen – while hurtling along in a wobbly train. Things have come on leaps and bounds in the twenty-five years since. Railway journeys are so much smoother these days, and what's happened to the faintly reassuring noise it made on the tracks, sounding like, 'Du-bu-du-dumm du-bu-du-dumm'?

I got the impression the 'in-carriage' chef was always over-compensating for his minute galley kitchen on wheels by cooking huge intimidating lumps of meat (anything the Ritz could do . . .) and it didn't stop there. Way before we were told we'd all die if we didn't have our 'five-a-day', British Rail was serving at least seven in one meal. Jools and I went for the works, while Paula would be Paula, and head straight off menu, insisting someone fetch her a boiled egg, or half a grapefruit and a limp lettuce leaf.

For three-and-a-half hours, I'd sit and listen to the pair of them catching up on all the week's news and gossip, Paula taking the opportunity to pour her heart out about the latest altercation between her and 'Saint Bob', as she called Geldof. She seemed incredibly philosophical about it, almost light-hearted considering what was unravelling in her private life. For the first couple of journeys north, whenever something salacious cropped up in conversation, Paula would flash a look at Jools and then nod in my direction, as if to say, 'Is he all right, can he be trusted?' Jools would close his eyes and, wearily, nod a 'Don't worry about him, he's fine' affirmative.

The train would pull into Newcastle railway station at about half past three, and we'd jump into a cab and head over to the Tyne Tees studios in City Road. Paula and Jools always had things to do with the producers, so I'd happily wander round the different stage areas where bands were in various states of readiness for the following day's show. I'm a big fan of people-watching. I'll happily sit in a pub on my own and observe, and no, it doesn't always have to be a pub, although it does have its advantages. Ade Edmondson could never get his head round me sitting in a pub on my own – he thought it madness, couldn't entertain the idea, but I used to love it. Imagine how enhanced the people-watching becomes when the people you are watching happen to be Duran Duran or the Cure. I'd sit and be privy to those scenes we all find most absorbing in rock documentary films: the bickering, the laughs, the demands, all infinitely more interesting in my eyes than the polished end product, performing a song.

If possible, before we headed out to our hotel, the

Gosforth Park, five miles out of Newcastle, I'd try and steer
Jools into the Egypt Cottage, the pub adjacent to the studios. It always looked so inviting with its warm red glow
through dappled pub windows, and there was never time,
after the show, to pop in for a swift one. *The Tube* ended at
six-thirty and anyone who wanted to get back to London
that night was forced to leg it to the airport for the last
flight home at seven-thirty. Some weeks we'd be in the cab
and pulling away from the studio while the last band on
were barely into the first of their two numbers that finished
the show. Miles Davis was on the flight one time after what
you could loosely describe as an interview he'd given Jools
on the show. The whole of the front row of the plane had
been reserved for just him and a large box of popcorn. A
trifle odd? Narrr, by home time, we'd all got quite used to
him. After everything he had been through – let's face it,
not everyone has been comprehensively smacked over the
cranium with an NYPD standard-issue two-and-a-half-foot
truncheon (I don't think he went on many demos after that)
– Miles still looked very good.

When he arrived at the studios he didn't fancy one of the
conventional dressing rooms; they were all perfectly ade-
quate, but not for Miles. The next thing we heard was that
a table, a chair and a mirror had been delivered to Studio
Four, next door to Studio Five, where *The Tube* was filmed,
as this was now Miles Davis's dressing room: a dressing
room roughly the same size as *The Tube* studio, big enough
for three or four bands and two hundred people. But this
was all fine – after all, this was *Sketches of Spain* Miles
Davis. The only problem was that to walk from Studio
Four to Five one had to negotiate three corridors and,

quite possibly, the odd communal area. Miles stipulated that there should be no vestige of cigarette smoke on his route to the studio from his dressing room. No smoke, or people. People? Fine – hey, this was Miles Davis, widely considered one of the most influential musicians of the twentieth century. 'Everybody, get out of the way! And put that fag out!'

Miles spoke in a barely audible whisper for the whole of the interview and at one point presented Jools with an abstract picture he'd drawn of a dancer. I think it was a dancer, but it could quite easily have been a starfish.

Miles died five years later on 28 September 1991 (my birthday in fact – please, no presents – a cheque's fine, paid to 'Cash'). On the 29th, it was suggested Jools get the 'dancing starfish scribble' insured, or put in a bank. If only I'd thought to corner Miles and ask him for five seconds of his time, to knock one off for me, I'd be rich! Hindsight – makes you want to spit sometimes.

Stuart Bateup – real name – the guy who would direct me falling over flamenco dancers ten years later on *Good Stuff*, was a researcher on the programme and had written a list of questions for Jools to put to Miles. Stuart thought nothing of including this 'breezy opener': 'You're looking well. Now tell us, is it true you've been injecting yourself with monkey glands, Miles?'

My close-hand pyrotechnics were going from strength to strength: I'd progressed from the simple banger on the head and was now juggling rockets, ladies and gentlemen. I'm not sure if they sell them today, but in 1986 a twelve-pack of six-inch-long firework rockets could be purchased over the counter for a couple of quid, and they were lethal. To juggle rockets, place one between each finger of both hands and grip gently. Light the rockets and, once they've achieved 'full burn', throw into the air. It worked perfectly, late one Thursday night, pissed, at the Gosforth Park Hotel where, in front of Jools and a couple of the producers, I premiered 'Rowlando the Gypsy Prince and His Amazing Rocket Juggling!' Eight mini rockets shot into the air and I stood there, looking up into the night sky with both hands outstretched, waiting, and waiting, and waiting to begin juggling. They loved it and were keen for me to perform the trick live on the show, the next day.

As with *The Last Resort*, the people in charge at Tyne Tees were disarmingly cool about what could be attempted on *The Tube*. At the Friday morning meeting, to discuss the finer points of the show, Jools brought up the 'juggling rocket' idea and was met with stunned silence, always a good sign. It was decided the studio's Safety Officer should have a demonstration before it could be performed live on air. Now then . . . the Safety Officer. You never come across the Safety Private or Lance Corporal. The Safety Sergeant has a ring to it, but no, if you're in the business of safety, you go straight in at officer level. Talk about impressing your mum on the first day at work. 'How was your first day, dear?'

'I'm already officer material, Mum.'

Anyway, I made it clear, as we made our way to the car park, that what they were about to see wasn't nearly as effective in, quite literally, the cold light of day. I positioned the little rockets between my fingers and instructed Jools to light the touch-papers. I waited for all the rockets to get up a full head of steam, everyone stood back and I let go. To this day, I'm not entirely sure what went wrong. It would be easy to question Chinese workmanship, but I think the blame lies wholly at the feet of human error. Mine. One or two went straight up and disappeared, as planned, the others had a mind of their own. People dived for cover as the firework rockets ricocheted off the parked cars and flew in all directions, some even fizzing along the floor and disappearing under cars. The Safety Officer saw the funny side of it, despite the fact that lots of things, mainly cars, could have caught fire, but obviously banned me from doing the trick. Paula commented that she was now inclined to believe everything she'd heard about me, and that if only I'd get in shape, she'd actually find me slightly attractive. She had a way with words, and men, did Paula.

I didn't like to ask too many questions, but Thursday nights at the Gosforth were, on occasions, interesting. We'd check in and every now and again Paula needed to hide from over-eager musicians who'd got the wrong idea. She'd insist I swapped keys with her and not let on to the people on reception or to Jools. I also spent most Thursday nights out on the town in Newcastle – there was a fantastic, huge nightclub that cost the princely sum of £1.70 to get into. I rarely made it back to the hotel much before three in the morning, thereby avoiding any contact with potential, unwanted gentlemen callers to 'my' room. Paula never liked to be on her own, or go anywhere on her own. On show day at lunchtime, I'd often be singled out to go with her to the canteen at the studios. She'd usually order a cheese sandwich and just peck at the cheese, avoiding the bread completely. One time, we were sitting at a table and her lunch that day amounted to no more than a glass of milk.

She never touched alcohol but was, obviously, mad for dairy.

This may sound odd, but my abiding memory of Paula is the pair of us sitting at a table opposite each other in the Tyne Tees canteen. She had no make-up on and was wearing a V-neck jumper and jeans: she looked about sixteen and gorgeous. We were chatting, which usually took the form of Paula's 'twenty questions' about my love life, and I must have said something 'hilarious' just as she gulped down a huge mouthful of milk because suddenly milk began projectile-squirting out of both her nostrils, over me, over her, everywhere. I'd never seen anything like it. She had a fierce fit of the giggles; she couldn't stop herself laughing, only able to gesticulate with her hands that she needed something to mop up the mess. That's how I'll remember her, looking lovely, helpless with laughter and covered in milk snot.

* * *

In the years when we had cruised down Upper Street in my metallic green, pepper-pot-wheeled Jaguar V12, by far the most popular cassette, which Rik and I would play at full volume, was ZZ Top's 1979 album *Degüello*. Ten incredible songs, and apart from 'Esther Be the One' – a soft rock ballad in my book – we were 'shouty' word-perfect on every one. I never usually got excited by the acts that appeared on *The Tube*, but when word filtered through that ZZ Top were to perform I made sure I was in the right place at the right time.

Two-thirds of the band and their manager finally turned up about half-an-hour into the show. Having missed a flight from London, this wasn't as bad as it looked. Billy Gibbons and Dusty Hill, the guitarists, were going to mime to a track and seeing as they had arrived sporting regulation long coats, sunglasses, hats, beards and clutching guitars, they couldn't be more ready to walk on stage. On a dirt-cheap, whistle-stop tour of the country promoting their latest album, there was no room for drummer Frank Beard (ironically the only member of the band without a beard). It was too much hassle setting a kit up wherever they went.

The studio's sound engineer appeared and inquired about the tape with the track on they wanted to mime to. Without missing a beat, the manager produced a cassette from his top pocket and offered it to the engineer, mumbling something about how it may need a bit of rewinding. Now, even I know you can't broadcast a music track on television from a C60 cassette. It would sound awful. It sounded great in the Jag, but wouldn't cut the mustard on TV. The engineer half-heartedly inquired about the whereabouts of the quarter-inch tape he could play out. There wasn't one, and no amount of explaining the problem to ZZ's manager was going to produce one. Suddenly everyone was getting into a flap apart from Billy and Dusty, the 'Gilbert and George' of rock, who stood motionless, said nothing and looked fantastic.

After some nifty lateral thinking by one of the producers – it might have been Malcolm Gerrie – the problem was solved when a runner was dispatched to the nearest record shop (they were still called 'shops' in 1986; the word 'store' applied to a lockable cupboard where all the stationery was kept). If he couldn't purchase their latest CD, then anything by the band would do even if it was on vinyl, since this would be much nearer broadcast quality. Billy and Dusty eventually went on and mimed to a number I'd not heard before with a disturbingly electro drum track I assumed was their latest offering. More reason for Frank to sit tight at home, as there is nothing worse than watching a drummer trying to get away with miming along to what is transparently a drum machine. I was half hoping for a rendition of 'Cheap Sunglasses' or 'Dust My Broom', but it wasn't to be. They looked great though, and it was a pleasure to meet them, and yet I wasn't going to be buying their latest album. But buying *Degüello* again, this time on CD? Now you're talking.

Another tricky guest was Grace Jones. She just wouldn't come out of her dressing room and we didn't know why. Counsellors were sent to try to coax her out, but nothing would work. Queues of people lined up outside: 'Hi, you don't know me, but I'm the executive producer. Miss Jones, did anyone make it clear to you that the show actually goes out live? Could you just unlock your door, please?' Such were the joys of dealing with the rock 'n' roll lifestyle.

* * *

The Tube was picking up awards all over the place; back then, one of the more prestigious was a TV Times Award. I accompanied Jools to the bash. Leslie Ash was doing a stint sitting in for Paula who, I think, was on maternity leave. I was there as Jools' 'plus one' while Leslie's 'plus one' was her then boyfriend Rowan Atkinson. There was a pretty impressive guest list: Terry Wogan was hosting, Leonard Rossiter was there, Selina Scott and Robert Mitchum, all the greats . . .

During the dinner and copious drinks before the awards, it quickly became clear that neither Jools nor Leslie had addressed themselves to the tricky subject of the acceptance speech.

'I was sat with two funny people from opposite ends of the comedy spectrum, so I asked both Rowan and Rowland what they thought I should do,' recalls Jools.

Rowan suggested saying, 'I'd just like to say a quick thank you to . . .' and then producing a list that concertinas out with what looks like a thousand names. It's an old gag, but a good one; simple, straightforward, the sort of thing these televised awards like to see. My route to the Dorchester in London, where the event was being held, had taken me via a joke shop in Covent Garden where I had purchased something, it occurred to me, that would be perfect for receiving an award on nationwide television: 'The Funniest Glasses Ever Made' – at least, that's what it said on the box.

I explained to Jools, 'When you get out your list of people to thank, put those on as if they were your reading glasses, you can't go wrong, everyone will howl with laughter.'

I handed Jools the box, and the name alone produced a small titter amongst the people at our table. Then when he put them on, Leslie, Rowan and everyone else fell about. Jools was wearing a pair of thick-rimmed plastic glasses with a fake nose in the shape of a large penis.

Looking back Jools remembers it with mixed feelings: 'I rather ignored Rowan's advice, who was at the time at the top of his game, an acknowledged master, and instead went with Rowland's tip of the funniest glasses ever made.'

Jools and Leslie waited for their names to be announced and made their way to the stage. At the microphone, Leslie didn't want to say anything so left it to Jools, who had decided it would be funny to produce an envelope, open it and thank one person, the props fellow at the Tyne Tees studios, and then exit. He pulled out the envelope from one pocket, and out of the other pocket produced 'The Funniest Glasses Ever Made' and put them on. You could have heard a pin drop.

Geoff Wonfor was in the audience with his wife Andrea. She had devised *The Tube* and was rightly chuffed that Jools was up there picking up the award for best music show on telly. These were the people he should have been thanking. Geoff told us after the event that from where he was standing, near one of the cameramen, he could hear the director shouting to everyone, 'CUT WIDE! CUT WIDE!' as 'The Funniest Glasses Ever Made' made their presence felt. This was a live show, so the opportunity to edit out Jools' 'hilarious' prank was not an option. He thanked the Tyne Tees prop man and walked off stage to the sound of his own footsteps and with a penis for a nose.

'For some mysterious reason, "The Funniest Glasses Ever Made", on that occasion, didn't seem to have the effect Rowland and I thought they were going to have. In fact I'd say quite the opposite,' says Jools.

The people running the show flew off the handle, and at one point there was even talk of having Jools arrested. It was only the host Terry Wogan's intervention with something along the lines of, 'Cut the lad some slack, he was only having a laugh,' that eventually calmed everyone down and took the heat out of the evening. If you ever get the opportunity to purchase a pair of 'The Funniest Glasses Ever Made', jump at it and wear them with pride because, hey, what's good enough for Terry . . .

16: FEELIN' GROOVY

'Be there, or be ungroovy fuckers.' Jools Holland, Channel 4, 5.15 p.m., Friday 16 January 1987.

It was in its fifth series and, to be honest, *The Tube* was on the turn; the lunatics had taken over the asylum. Succumbing to every uncontrollable urge to chase whatever was popular, a thirteen-year-old child actor and model, Felix Howard, was recruited to co-present with Paula and Jools. Everyone knew him as the kid spying on Madonna in her 1986 pop video for 'Open Your Heart'. He danced off into the sunset with her as the music faded and instantly became the new Next Big Thing. Despite the – what word should I use? – delightful Felix, the show was floundering, and many people who were involved from the very first series saw Jools' outburst of profanity, transmitted in a live trailer at peak children's viewing time, as the nail in the coffin. In a way it allowed the programme to bow out with a bit of credibility, as a further series was never commissioned.

Felix went on to forge a successful career writing pop songs for EMI artists and become one of their A&R men, and sadly we all know what became of Paula. Jools was told to go to the naughty step, where he promptly hatched plans for our next collaboration, the title of which cocked a snook at his televisual misdemeanour – it was *The Groovy Fellers*.

Pre-production began in September of 1987 with the working title of 'Jools Holland's New Shoes', but this only confused things – people assumed they were getting some kind of fashion show exclusively about footwear. In today's digital channel quagmire, there are probably half-a-dozen shoe-related programmes floating about, but in 1987 the idea of a shoe show would have been considered a tad too niche.

'We'd enjoyed working together, and following the success of the funniest glasses ever made, I thought we were clearly on to something here,' says Jools.

The premise of the show was simple: Jools was showing a Martian (me) the many aspects of life on Earth. Tim Pope was recruited to direct – he'd done some great pop videos with the likes of the Cure, David Bowie and Soft Cell. Tim certainly impressed me a few days after we'd met. Arrangements were being made for the next get-together to discuss the show, and Tim mentioned he would be unable to do the Wednesday because that day he was going to New York, but Thursday would be fine. Excuse me? It transpired Tim had a meeting with David Bowie to talk about an up-coming video and was off to meet the great man at his recording studio in New York. This was in the days when record companies had money; Tim was flying Concorde, having lunch with David and flying straight back home.

Day One was at the remote Milecastle Inn in the shadow of Hadrian's Wall, Northumberland, on a very chilly November morning. I'm fairly sure the Border Television crew didn't quite know what to make of the programme with no script, especially as the opening scenes were shots of Jools and me meeting and walking off into the mists, Jools in a Savile Row suit and me completely naked but for a small, revolving, H-shaped aerial sticking out of my head, the one nod to being a Martian. It's amazing the amount of attention you can command when you're the only person in a pub naked – and at one with yourself.

'I knew things were going well when the first scene had Rowland arriving on earth, stark bollock naked walking on Hadrian's Wall. I would challenge anyone not to derive great pleasure from that scene, as the pair of us went out for a stroll,' says Jools.

We never got round to writing anything down, either – there wasn't a script as such. Tim may have taken some notes so as to construct a succession of beautiful scenes; there is no doubting his directorial skills, because he made it look fantastic. Jools and I, on the other hand, made it up as we went along. It says something about the faith that executive producer Paul Corley, producer John Gwyn and associate producer Elaine Kemball had in us that none of them requested anything on paper prior to filming.

Jools says, 'I remember after Lenny Henry saw one of them, he said, "I think that's absolutely amazing – you and Rowland have got to be congratulated. I was absolutely stunned when I saw it, that anybody could have got the money to do that . . ."'

After wandering around naked in Northumberland for the first few scenes – we came across some hill-walkers at one point and their particularly agitated dog that really didn't help my situation – we emerged from the London

Underground into Piccadilly Circus, now both wearing identical Norton & Sons Savile Row suits.

We needed a means of transport, as our journey was to take us round the country. An old Rolls-Royce was purchased for about two-and-a-half grand – Border Television were loath to spend any more as they knew what we wanted to do with it. The wheels and bumpers were removed and replaced with a set of old Land Rover tyres and an iron bar for a bumper; the roof was cut off and lowered nine inches; and the whole thing was hand-sprayed, badly, with cans of gold paint. We were regularly stopped by police but always managed to talk our way out of the numerous, 'Is there a problem, officer?' situations. Having said that . . .

One programme in the series looked at the concept of money, what people did with it and how they acquired it. Jools and I found ourselves lying next to a chap in a tanning salon, a bank robber who suggested robbing a bank as the quickest way to owning a vast amount of money and becoming rich beyond your wildest dreams. Just don't get caught like he did, he added – he'd just done a seven-year stretch and was obviously keen to get a healthy tan after that many years locked away with little natural light at Her Majesty's pleasure.

A small picturesque Cumbrian village, local to John Gwyn, was earmarked for the 'bank job' Jools and I were going to attempt. The plan was that we would turn up with the best 'bank-robbing' intentions, only to find we'd arrived on a sunny Wednesday afternoon – half-day closing. The customized Roller pulled up outside the bank, and we piled out of the car brandishing machine guns and hastily pulled our heads into a pair of tights, me in the left leg, Jools in the right. With only the gusset between us, we ran, as best we could, up to the doors that were firmly locked shut. Jools drew my attention to the opening times and, realizing we'd been thwarted by the half-day closing, got back in the car and drove off. So far, so Laurel and Hardy.

What we hadn't anticipated was the twitching-net-curtain, busy-body diligence of some of the locals who had watched two men get out of a nutty car, put a pair of tights over their heads and stumble around for a bit while brandishing replica guns. Unbeknownst to us, the police had been called and by the time we were ready to leave the 'bank robbery' location, roadblocks – complete with armed response units – were deployed on all routes out of the village. It's not every day you're asked to step out of the car with a high-velocity firearm pointed in your face. In an attempt to defuse the situation, we decided to remove the tights we were still wearing on our head, in the hope that the Norton & Sons Savile Row suits would do the talking for us.

'Nobody, for some reason, had told the local police what we were going to do, I can't believe our incompetence really,' remembers Jools.

The shit really hit the fan, as well as the national papers. Important people at Border TV were hauled in for questioning, letters of apology were dispatched to the Chief Constable, and Jools and I got our picture in the papers – not that you'd know it was us, as we were sporting the tights. But it was exposure none the less.

The series serves as a reminder of how times have changed in television. In the eighties, there was a distinct air of 'anything is possible, access all areas'. We were allowed into the Royal Mint in Loughton to film money being printed and also destroyed. Jools and I were allowed to incinerate four million quid in old £50 notes. The place was awash with untraceable cash, but the temptation to pocket several hundred pounds was suppressed by the armed guards patrolling the gantry above us, watching our every move. Getting away with stealing just one £50 note from the Royal Mint proved impossible. I tried maintaining I was in character – it was the Martian, not Rowland, stealing the money for the sake of the programme. But they weren't amused. I sheepishly handed back the handfuls of £50 notes I'd stuffed into my suit pockets. I got the impression this wasn't the first time this had happened. They virtually produced a laminated card saying: 'Please, sir, put the money back in the furnace.'

One chap working for the Mint really did think that he had the foolproof plan. There is always one guy who thinks he can outsmart the system, isn't there? All notes are printed on large sheets, so there are twenty-four £50 notes on one sheet. These are stored in huge piles on pallets. Realizing the counting machine only used the edge of the pile to ascertain how much was there, the enterprising man took to removing the notes in the middle of the sheets with a Stanley knife. He knew some of the piles of sheets would be stored for six months before being guillotined into individual notes, so he could toil away for weeks, removing the cash. The poor chap came unstuck when he attempted to buy a sports car from a local dealership, and there was the first mistake – a local dealership. Mistake number two was paying in cash, as when the salesman counted up the fifties, he noticed that very few notes were the perfect oblong shape. He stalled our man, called the police, and within minutes his dream of the perfectly executed crime was in badly cut tatters.

Jeffrey Archer kindly offered to appear in one programme and was immediately stitched up. He granted us an audience at his Thames-side apartment next to the MI6 building in Vauxhall, directly opposite the Tate Gallery. He lived in the top two floors of the building that commanded panoramic views down the Thames to the Houses of Parliament. Perfect, we thought, for the opening shots of the episode looking at government and power. He took one look at the Roller we arrived in and immediately rearranged our interview with him to take place, not in his penthouse apartment but outside, next to the Thames. I remember the porter for the building going ballistic at the amount of oil our car had deposited on the pristine forecourt in the short time it was parked there. A year or so before our meeting with him, Archer had sailed through the *Daily Star* libel case (following the paper's accusation that he had slept with a prostitute) where he was awarded £500,000 damages and walked away a free man. He was to become dogged by scandal over the years, so how fitting that in our show Jools introduces him as, 'Look! There's Jeffrey Archer, disposing of some nefarious thing or other into the Thames. Let's go and talk to him!' Archer hadn't heard a word of his introduction and was just standing there when we approached him, beaming from ear to ear and looking totally guilty. I honestly didn't think it would make it into the show, but hey, it was the eighties, and as Jeffrey knew only too well – you could get away with anything back then.

We were having trouble being in the right place at the right time with an episode about birth and death. A hospital was lined up with access to the maternity ward, and three or four women had very gamely agreed to have the birth of their child filmed for the purposes of the show. Trouble was, there was no real telling when any of these ladies were going to 'drop'. Then some bright spark suggested we film a caesarean as they are booked in, just like an appointment at the dentist, but with all the action taking place at the 'other end'. I can safely say it's the freakiest thing I have ever witnessed.

Again, you would never get away with it today, but Jools and I were in the very same operating theatre as a woman about to have a caesarian. What with the drugs in use, and the careful curtaining arrangement between her top half and her bottom half, we were able to chat to the lady and offer her cups of tea at one end, while she was being cut open down the other in order to let her baby out. Peering over the curtain to see how the doctor was getting on was a big mistake – I don't know about Jools, but I was nearly physically sick. So both Jools and I retreated to the nod and smile.

The words have yet to be invented which could succinctly convey what was happening to this poor woman, but I'll have a go. It looked like a huge shark's open mouth, and there was the doc rummaging around inside the gaping jaws, and all the while Mum's nattering away to Jools about Christian names, oblivious to the madness going on with her nether regions. We popped in the next day with some flowers for Mum and a hula-hoop and large Airfix model for the kid, who would be in their early twenties now.

In another episode of *The Groovy Fellers* Jools let me drive the car. One night, we found ourselves in the Blackwall Tunnel, that extraordinary Victorian feat of engineering which runs under the Thames. The authorities blocked it off, so we had the run of it. It was two in the morning. I'd been hoiked out of the Groucho Club, so unfortunately the drink was doing the driving. Jools was fine for the first 200 yards, until I took the clapped-out Roller over 60mph and the spongy steering really kicked in. In the camera-car in front, Tim Pope, the director, had his thumbs up and was beaming from ear to ear. Jools, however, saw it differently. He was, after all, sitting next to me. Let's not forget, the 1962 Corniche was an old car and it didn't have seat belts, and Jools began gesticulating to Tim drawing his finger across his throat. 'Cut, cut! Stop, this is far too dangerous, he's going to kill us all!'

That's always the way, isn't it? If you want it to look good, it helps to be dangerous.

The Groovy Fellers was only aired once, and I think we were paid for two showings, so, who knows, it may turn up on telly again without any financial benefit to either Jools or myself, but untold cultural benefit to all those who can be bothered to sit and watch it, as it was a perfect slice of life in the late eighties.

Jools: 'They only showed them the once; hopefully they will show them again.'

Me: 'When one of us dies.'

Jools: 'That'll be nice.'

The next time I worked with Jools was five years later. It was on the Sunday following the heart attack Gilson Lavis had suffered during the encore in Derby. I hadn't played the drums for four years, and there I was, back in the band. But now it was 'The Rhythm and Blues Orchestra', and a whole different ball game.

Jools remembers, 'Simultaneously, I was thinking, "Oh my God, I hope Gilson's going to be all right" and "I wonder if Rowland's about."'

17: THE GIRLS

'You were very wild. I remember you turning up and thinking, Rowland's here, give it half an hour . . .' says Jennifer Saunders.

To W2 and Jennifer's house in London. My usual lunch offer of a pie and a pint had been vetoed in favour of an evening round at Jen's with Dawn, some fine wine and a beautifully grilled chicken sandwich. How could I refuse?

After the success of the Comic Strip tour, the girls had a short run at the Hampstead Theatre Club and wanted some music in their show. Having worked with Simon and me, they approached us. We said we'd love to help and seeing as they wanted us to appear on stage, we adopted characters rather than just sit there like lemons – although two lemons might have worked just as well as characters. And so it was to be, that from that day on, if Simon Brint and Rowland Rivron appeared on stage together, they would forever more be known as Ken and Duane Bishop, the father and stepson duo that were Raw Sex.

The idea for Raw Sex had begun when we were out on the Young Ones tour. Through boredom, Simon and I would get into character as Ken and Duane. As mentioned earlier, we imagined that the band was originally called Ken Bishop's Nice Twelve. But after a tragic air accident, they had all died apart from Ken, who through a fear of flying was travelling by train. He had a stepson, Duane, who had started playing with Ken aged twelve. It was that classic thing you'd see on *Opportunity Knocks* – the pushy father on keyboard with his son dwarfed by a drum kit far too big for him. They were rubbish, but cute. We developed the backstory further. Duane didn't go to school and became feral, and after a while he and Ken morphed into Raw Sex. The name was coined by Duane, who imagined women would find it appealing.

As Raw Sex, Simon and I would go on to do two series of *French and Saunders* and a year-long national tour, followed by two weeks' residency at the Shaftesbury Theatre. We'd push the boat out most evenings, but Dawn and Jen would always know where to find the boat in the morning!

After Hampstead, there was a run at the King's Head Theatre pub in Upper Street followed, with John Sessions as support doing his one-man tour de force, *Napoleon*. I'm sure it was fantastic, but I didn't understand a word of what he was on about. John was very nervous before going on stage and had a 'calming ritual' of throwing his guts up seconds before going on stage. He did this into the small sink in the dressing room, which was in fact little more that a corridor directly behind the curtain that ran along the back of the stage. You could clearly hear the audience talking; everything was so close and intimate. Dawn remembers standing backstage, seconds before going on, and overhearing a woman talking with her friend: 'They're quite good, but not a patch on Wood and Walters.' If Dan Crawford, the guy who ran the place, hadn't already taken the chairs from the dressing room for the audience's use, Simon and I would sit in silence listening to Sessions pontificating, on the other side of the curtain, while the girls stood at small shaving mirrors endlessly curling their hair. Big hair was very in back then, and they weren't going to be denied it.

Dawn and Jenny were going down a storm, so the next predictable step was to do their first *French and Saunders* series for the BBC. They took us with them, Jennifer claims, as much for moral support as anything else, although Dawn does point out that, unlike *The Young Ones*, they didn't fancy the idea of different musical acts turning up each week. They much preferred the musical element to be variations on a Raw Sex theme. This suited Simon and I perfectly. The very first series also had a regular contribution from the Hot Hoofers, a motley crew of over-the-hill variety dancers fronted by the legendary Betty Marsden. When we first started working together, I would sit there staring at Betty, transfixed, because even I remembered her on the BBC Radio comedy series, *Round the Horne*, and I must have only been about ten years old. She also appeared in a couple of Carry On films, and was quite sexy in one of them. Everyone remembers Barbara Windsor's bra flying off as the saucy high point of the classic *Carry On Camping*, but I'll never forget Betty on a tandem opposite, or rather behind, Terry Scott, and somehow being very sexy.

After twenty-five years working with the Rolling Stones, Charlie Watts said something along the lines of it being five years playing and twenty years hanging around. It was incredibly similar with *French and Saunders* and Raw Sex. We'd spend hours sitting at the congas and keyboard watching them doing their thing in one of the vast BBC rehearsal studios in Acton. Then, on cue, we'd come alive for a few minutes to put in our tuppence worth. Don't get me wrong, I'm not complaining, and I'm sure Charlie didn't have the hump when he said what he said; quite the contrary, it was a peach of a job. Being responsible for a few minutes' 'hilarity' in an already funny show was unbelievable. I found myself in a similar situation when doing my stints as the shambolic Dr Scrote on *The Last Resort* with Jonathan Ross – none of the pressure associated with delivering a whole show, but all of the fun.

Working at the BBC in the late 1980s was, at times, bizarre. Theft was rife; rumour had it that there was a stall in Shepherd's Bush Market, just up the road from TV Centre, that sold nothing but knocked-off BBC gear. This was a time when televisions weren't bolted to the wall, but left in the corner on a table, obviously not for long. Simon and I stood open-mouthed one day as we watched gallons of lager being poured down the sink in the props room of Studio Two, where the girls recorded their show. The reason for this was that the set for Raw Sex, within the girls' show, comprised of nothing more than a length of red velour material as a backdrop, and about twenty-five pallets of lager that would be stacked up around us – heaven, we thought. But after the recording of the first show, every single pallet and can went missing. To ensure we had the same set for the following weeks, every single replacement can was opened at the bottom, emptied away and returned to the pallets with no one the wiser.

'You were very, very, very nearly handsome,' recalls Dawn French.

One day we were all in the studio and word filtered through that Jim Moir, the then head of Light Entertainment, would be paying a visit. Jim was very old-school entertainment. He often said he'd found his own 'Two Ronnies' in Dawn and Jennifer. Jim was hosting the BBC Light Entertainment Christmas party I'd attended with Rik some years earlier where, amongst other things, I'd got my knob caught in the executive lift. Dawn and Jen were aware of this, so they insisted, just for the duration of his visit, that I make myself scarce and hide in the dressing room. They didn't want Jim to spot me and think they were associating with a rowdy element. In the fullness of time, Jim came down, said hello to everyone, told them all they were doing a grand job and disappeared. I don't think we ever saw him again.

Having a resident band hanging around, the girls began trying different comedy musical ideas, the most successful being a string of pop pastiches that *French and Saunders* would become famous for. We were actively encouraged to take part. With incredible attention to detail, we'd dress up as the band ABBA and deftly take the piss out of one of their videos. The song Simon came up with, 'C'est La Vie', could have been penned by Björn and Benny, the two guys he and I played opposite Dawn and Jen's Agnetha and Anni-Frid.

Dawn and Jenny have a knack of being able to look the spitting image of whoever they dress up as. Not so Simon and me. Our take on the all-girl band the Bangles had me looking a dead ringer for the mugshot snap of Britt Ekland and Peter Sellers' daughter, Victoria, shortly after she had been arrested slightly the worse for wear. Simon's incarnation as Diane Lee to my (passable) Lenny Peters for our Peters and Lee tribute was suitably unnerving. Money seemed no object when making these videos. We took a trip down to Torquay for a Mamas & the Papas pastiche on board a yacht moored in the harbour. It was the first of several location shoots that day, and we spent a long morning wobbling about on a boat, dressed in authentic sixties clobber, freezing our bits off, miming to another of Simon's masterpieces. Only when the director, Geoff Posner, was happy we'd done the original video full justice did we stop for lunch.

Everything was packed away, people were stood down, backs were patted and we set off for the next location. Then word reached us that the camera used to capture our triumphant Mamas & the Papas pastiche had been nicked from the crew van while we were eating, along with the tape of everything we'd done still in it. Geoff visibly aged in front of us, and Dawn and Jennifer went on the local radio and TV stations appealing for the return of the camera, and if not the camera the tape at least. Nothing surfaced. We had visions of some oiks selling the camera for a fraction of its £25,000 worth, and some more oiks shooting a very poor porn video, recording over our superlative Mamas & the Papas spoof. Two weeks later, the BBC, without batting an eyelid (it was 1989), had us all back to reshoot the whole thing.

During the second series, Dawn and Jenny let us do pretty much whatever we wanted, as long as it was funny. One time, our two-minute musical slot expanded to about a quarter of the show, and there was little they could do about it. Simon and I had come up with an idea based on the Ralph McTell teach-yourself guitar books. Ken was poring over one, unable to follow the chord charts, as Ralph had omitted the little picture that showed you where you were supposed to place your fingers on the fret board. The screen went all wibberly-wobbly, and we were all daydreaming what it would be like taking Ralph to court over it. Dawn was the judge, Jen the stenographer, I the prosecuting lawyer and Simon the bloke making the accusation. Ralph was in the dock, the accused. The plan was to try and get a really famous guitarist to appear as a witness and attempt to play something from Ralph's book, only to find he was unable to as there were no little pictures of where your fingers were meant to go.

There was consternation, embarrassment and incredible excitement all round, when on the day of the recording, every one of the guitarists approached turned up. The thought was that if one or two said yes, then we'd have a result. As it was, Lemmy from Motörhead appeared, and was unable to follow the chart for 'Ace of Spades'. Mark King of Level 42 was unable to grasp 'Lessons in Love' from Ralph's book. Gary Moore was struggling with the music score for his lilting ballad 'Parisian Walkways'. Mark Knopfler couldn't get his head round 'Money for Nothing' and David Gilmour was stumped without the little finger pictures to help him play 'Another Brick in the Wall'. It was one of the most fantastic sketches I've had the good fortune to be involved in, and I thoroughly recommend you check it out – it'll be floating about somewhere on the internet. In the bar after the show, I spotted Lemmy clutching the bottle of 'Jack' he'd requested for his dressing room, and trying to cash the cheque for his appearance over the bar.

Being involved with *French and Saunders* was taking up a fair bit of time, but I was still doing the odd jazz gig here and there. One of the better ones was a Sunday lunch gig at the Latchmere in Battersea. A blindingly good sax player called Dave Bitelli was running a Latin jazz group that was infectious good fun, and one week Dawn, Lenny Henry, Simon and a few friends came along to check it out. All very embarrassing. After the gig, Dawn and Len invited Simon and me for a bit of late Sunday lunch at an out of the way, hush-hush hotel in Down Street just off Piccadilly. It was where people would stay who didn't want to be hassled.

We all turned up and were shown to the dining room situated in the windowless basement where we quickly made ourselves at home. There were a few of us and we were in high spirits. I'd just got everyone successfully balancing tablespoons off the end of their noses when the only other person in the dining room walked past to leave. It was Barry Manilow. Len had appeared on the Jimmy Tarbuck chat show earlier that week with Barry who, obviously, had come over to say 'hi' before leaving. Len felt a hand on his shoulder and looked round, still with the spoon dangling off his nose. Barry then clocked that we all had spoons swaying off the end of our noses. Of all the people in the world it had to be Barry standing there. One by one, we self-consciously removed the spoons and nodded an embarrassed 'We really weren't taking the piss, Barry, honest' hello. Through a fixed smile, he said something about how good it was to see us all having such fun, promised to catch up with Lenny some time, and left. I don't think Len ever did catch up with Barry.

The more we worked with the girls, the more time we were spending with them. Regularly after the recordings, we'd all – wardrobe, make-up, everyone – head off to a Polish restaurant on Shepherd's Bush Green called the Hat Shop. Things would really kick off in the basement with wild dancing, instigated, according to both Dawn and Jennifer, by me. I, of course, have no recollection of this happening and strongly doubt it ever did, as I have always maintained I don't dance. Unfortunately, the girls could remember it as clear as day and, without prompting each other, had the same story.

'No one would want to dance with you, it was too dangerous,' says Jennifer. With a certain amount of relish, the pair of them recounted the time I enthusiastically grabbed hold of a middle-aged make-up lady and vigorously spun her around repeatedly, Jen maintains, by an arm and a leg. Apparently her big mistake was to say yes in the first place. The consensus of opinion was that she was flattered by my invitation. Having said that, Dawn adds: 'If Rowly says you are going to dance, you have no option.'

* * *

The second TV series of *French and Saunders* had gone down a storm, and Phil McIntyre wasted no time enticing the girls out on the road. Of course, Raw Sex were invited to provide their invaluable professionalism, musicianship and portering skills. It was decided early on that I should be responsible for Dawn's bags and Simon would look after Jennifer's. The slight fly in the ointment was Wendy James,

who I was still living with at this point. To say things were
intense between thick-skinned Wendy and me would be an
understatement. Sure, I'd fallen under her spell – no sane
man couldn't – but I half-saw the tour as a means of putting
some space between us.

From the time we met, bobbing about in the Thames,
we'd not been out of each other's sight for more than a few
hours. I'm ashamed to say, this didn't go down at all well
with my then girlfriend. One minute I was living in leafy
Muswell Hill, North London, with a girlfriend who played
cello and had financed her college years doing photo shoots
for *Mayfair* and *Club International*. The next, I was bounc-
ing around a painfully trendy Notting Hill Gate, sharing a
flat with Wendy and not daring to look left or right. A tour
would afford me the chance to slow down, to take stock of
just how spectacularly my bridges were burning. The trouble was, Wendy couldn't bear to be apart, so would insist
on catching up with us at the earliest opportunity. This
would almost always be day two of any leg of the tour.
Dawn and Jen remember through gritted teeth the times the
tour bus would have to make the odd detour to pick up
Wendy from this train station or that airport – something
that she would have arranged without mine or the girls'
knowledge. Did I mention she was thick-skinned?

The way Dawn and Jen saw it was that the dynamic on
the bus was just fine with French and Saunders and Ken and
Duane. But, they now freely admit, when Wendy was along
for the ride, there was something of a 'Yoko Ono Effect'
about it. What was this young, slim, incredibly beautiful
rock chick, who could carry off a diamanté bra on her
album cover with ease, doing in their world, for Christ's

sake? Considering it was Dawn and Jenny's gig, they were amazing. They put up with her and never once expressed their wish that she would just go away and stay away. They even had a 'Welcome Back Wendy!' banner made, which would be rolled out whenever they got wind she was on her way. I did mention she was thick-skinned, didn't I?

The girls were booked into full-on theatres which we wasted no time exploiting. Raw Sex opened the show, with Simon astride a huge motorbike with sidecar, and me pushing it on to the stage. It really was the last thing the audience expected and got a big laugh before we'd even done anything. I have to take my hat off to Phil McIntyre. In rehearsals, we said we wanted a motorbike and sidecar, and we got one. It was carted all over the country for one five-second entrance gag; we didn't use it in any other part of the show.

Even when you don't include the motorbike, it has to be said Raw Sex were still 'prop heavy', including: the amp that blew up every night when I went to take a piss behind it; the Kirby wire Simon was hoisted up on for our tribute to 'The Thin White Streak Of Piss' David Bowie and his hit 'Space Oddity'; the paint pots and huge easel for my artistic tribute to Rolf Harris, complete with life-size horses' heads for the 'Two Little Boys' section; and the endless fags I 'pretended' to smoke and countless cans of beer I didn't pretend to drink both on and off stage. We had a lot of 'business'.

'Do you remember that time Jen had you by the collar up against the wall?' says Dawn.

Some nights, if I was particularly refreshed, our opening twenty-minute set would stretch to maybe thirty, thirty-five minutes. I'd be on stage thinking I was hilarious and running around like a mad thing, while the girls would be waiting in the wings for their big entrance. One night Jen just snapped. As I staggered off stage thinking I'd done a grand job warming up the audience, Jen flew at me and pinned me against the wall. Dawn wasn't one for confrontation, but Jen had no inhibitions on that front. She went ballistic, telling me to never, ever arse about like that again. I think there was a lot of swearing on her part. Dawn remembers doing her 'Don't panic' figure-of-eight pacing, accompanied by nervous laughter, as I was resoundingly told off. Then Jen calmly put me down, turned round and walked on stage in front of 2,000 people and knocked them dead.

The drinking and the madness continued, but after my brush with Jen, not so much on stage. The night after the 'up against the wall' incident, I attempted to do a show without the customary pre-show sharpeners. After the show, I distinctly remember as we came off after the encore Jen patting me on the back and saying, simply: 'See, you can do it.' She was right, I could do it, but it was like going to the seaside and not going in the sea.

Unbeknownst to me, things were being said about my excesses. My family had got in touch with Dawn. Raymond was mulling over the worst-case scenario. He was thinking of getting me committed – apparently he only needed a Justice of the Peace present and I was off. We were heading to Glasgow, to the Theatre Royal, and Ray just happened to be 'Ear, Nose and Throating' up the road in Edinburgh, so it was decided he'd come along to the gig, to see how I was doing.

Ray watched some of the show from the wings and his

first concern was not how steady I was on my feet, but how loud the music was. Apparently at times, he maintained, it was up there with a jet taking off. Rock 'n' roll! After the show, we adjourned to a restaurant and had a thoroughly good time. The show had gone particularly well and everyone was in a buoyant mood. I reckon Ray's mistake was trying to keep up with the rest of us, most definitely when we were back at the hotel and the tequila debating juice came out and the slamming began. Ray didn't fall far. He was sitting on the arm of a large Chesterfield, as I remember, and he was only unconscious for a split second, but it was enough. We all felt he'd had enough and it was time for him to head the fifty-odd miles home to Edinburgh and a good night's sleep. Herpes, the tour manager, and Ian Day, our head roadie, kindly helped me get him into a cab and reassured the driver that he was all right – 'Hey, he's a doctor!'

His wife Marilyn wasn't best pleased when he turned up at three o'clock in the morning and was violently ill. He did go to work the next day, though, spending most of the day slumped in a wheelchair, getting some fresh air, in the grounds of the hospital. There was no more mention of my mental or physical state after that visit. Everything calmed down and we all went back to work.

The tour was pretty relentless. At one point, we were all living at the Britannia Hotel in Manchester as that was a better base for the gigs than London. We had suites, which was a far cry from the first time Simon and I stayed there during the Comic Strip tour. Back then, we were sharing a room, which was fine. The money had been tight on that first tour. A lot of people were sharing – Rik and Ade, Dawn and Jenny. Our problem was that the room we'd been allocated on the third or fourth floor didn't actually have a window. There was a lovely curtain, but no sign of the great outdoors behind it. After some remonstration and threatening to produce bogus medical records detailing Simon's long history of claustrophobia, we were assigned another room with a panoramic view of the brick wall next to the hotel.

With the girls it was different: we were spoilt rotten. I was also getting hooked on the 'Is there anything I can get you?' culture that's never more than a phone call away when you are on tour. My suite quickly became the place to be after shows for an interesting selection of vodkas and a serious game of Scalextric. I had a massive set installed that ran all round the furniture in the living room and into the bedroom, where one lost sight of the cars momentarily, adding a certain excitement rarely seen in slot-car racing.

Wendy was up the day we were checking out of the hotel, and it wasn't the tour bus we had to meet but a specific train back to London. Something was happening in the capital, and I had to be there. We were woken by Phil banging on the door and telling us we had about half-an-hour to get to the station round the corner. It was all I could do to get my clothes into a few bags before we legged it to the station – Phil, Wendy and I running like nutters through the streets of Manchester. I know what you are thinking: why didn't you have a cab waiting? By the time the car had gone round the one-way system, Phil had sussed it would have been quicker for us to speed-walk it. I left about two hundred quid's worth of Scalextric and some very fine vodka in that hotel. Trouble was, it didn't occur to me at the time that I had paid for the whole thing, as most things were put down as expenses and forgotten about. 'It's okay, it's on exes,' I thought. Oh, how I got my fingers burnt.

At the end of each month Phil or this man in charge, Paul Roberts, would hand Simon and me a buff-coloured envelope that contained a breakdown of our expenses and a cheque for what we were owed that month. This usually happened on the tour bus. One time, as Simon and I were sitting opposite each other at a table, we were handed our envelopes, and I couldn't help but notice mine seemed a little bulkier than his. Stapled to the front of Simon's single sheet of paper was a cheque for about £4,000. Stapled to the first of about fifteen sheets of paper I had in my hand was a similar looking cheque, this time for £17.50. I kind of knew how Duran Duran must have felt coming home and seeing the bill after their video shoot for 'Rio', filmed on board a huge yacht off the coast of Antigua: gutted.

What I wasn't too happy about was that if, by accident, something got broken, the cost of replacement or repair came winging its way out of your exes as well, no questions asked.

At this point we were doing the south coast and had got as far as the Brighton Conference Centre. Our bed for the night was at the Grand Hotel, which had been blown up by the IRA in 1984. Alan Marke, who with Jonathan Ross was running Channel X, had travelled down from London to see the show and have a chat about some Dr Scrote commitments. By this time in the tour, I had calmed down a fair bit and there was less of the familiar cry, 'Let's all go off together after the show and be mad.' Mostly, we'd do the show and people would grab a bite to eat and a swift half and then get off to bed. So it was quite refreshing having someone with whom to enjoy a few beers. Alan was staying at the same hotel so we set up camp in the corner of the lounge bar at the Grand to eat, drink and discuss Scrote.

By about half-twelve, one o'clock, the only other people in the lounge were two couples in their mid to late thirties, obviously having a good time as things were getting steadily more raucous. If fact, they were the only people breathing any life into the place so it was fine. Shortly after more drinks arrived at their table, one of the men stood up and ambled over to were Alan and I were sitting, much to his friends' consternation. We quickly learnt that they had been along to see the show and that this chap's wife thought I was quite funny. This was all very well until he asked if I wanted to make his wife laugh some more. I politely declined his request and said maybe they should come and see the show tomorrow if they wanted more laughs, as we were on for two nights.

He said nothing and made his way back to his friends and then loudly announced that he was right, I wasn't that funny. His wife tossed over an apology for her husband's behaviour and we thought nothing of it. If he hadn't got up again, it would have been fine, but his stupid wife and friends did nothing to stop the arse coming over, this time to tell me I wasn't genuinely funny and, obviously, I could only be funny when I got all dressed up and had that other bloke to help me. All the time his friends were pleading with him to give it a rest, which of course he ignored. Alan gallantly stepped in and tried to calm things down by cajoling him back to his seat, which he eventually did. All this time it was sinking in with me that they were having a laugh at my expense so, promptly, I snapped.

RAW SEX: THE OFFICIAL
PUBLICITY SHOT . . .

TRYING TO BLEND IN WITH
DAWN AND JEN.

WITH DUANE'S GIRLFRIEND TINA BISHOP (KATHY BURKE)
AND HIS FRIEND EDUARDO (JACKO), SUPPORTING HELEN LEDERER
AT THE EDINBURGH FESTIVAL.

ON TOUR WITH THE GIRLS, DOING OUR ENCORE. NO ONE CAN REMEMBER
WHY I'M TETHERED TO A PORTER'S TROLLY.

THE 'SEX' IN FULL FLIGHT, WITH EDUARDO.

AS FASHION DESIGNER JEAN-CLAUDE VAN PLOP (PRONOUNCED 'PLOW-APP') ON *SATURDAY ZOO*. NAOMI CAMPBELL WAS A BIG HELP...

AS WIDOW TWANKEY TRAPPED IN THE FLOOR OF THE LONDON PALLADIUM. HARRY DEAN STANTON: 'WHO THE FUCK...'

NOT A TURD, BUT INCHWORM, ONE OF THE FRIENDLY 'LOVEABLE SIDEKICKS' FOR JONATHAN'S SHOW.

HAMISH THE FRIENDLY HOUSE FLY, SCARING THE BEJESUS OUT OF JONATHAN, BEN ELTON AND STEVEN WRIGHT.

WENDY AND
HER CHIRPY,
HAPPY-GO-LUCKY
BAND...

AT JONATHAN'S
WEDDING,
POSING
WITH KATIE
LANDERS'S
FIRST BORN
CHILD.
I HAD A LOT
TO LEARN
ABOUT KIDS.

AS SCROTE BROTHER RONNIE,
IN ICELAND. THE HALF PINT IN MY
HAND COST ABOUT EIGHT QUID . . .

TERRY 'THE TORNADO' SCROTE,
RENAMED 'TERRY SCROTE'
AFTER HIS FIRST FIGHT.

TARQUIN SHIRLEY STANSTEAD SCROTE, FORMER MP FOR
FELTCHCOME AND THORPE.

WITH MUM, DAD AND BROTHERS ON A RARE 'STANDING IN A FIELD ON THE ISLE OF WIGHT' DAY OUT.

MY FAMILY, INCLUDING OUR DOG CALLED BEAR THAT COST A MONKEY . . .

WITH MY NIGHT NETWORK 'CHUMS'. LEFT TO RIGHT: RICHARD COLES,
MICK BROWN, MYSELF, EMMA FREUD, TOM WATT, LEE WESTWOOD
AND PAUL THOMPSON. THIS WAS TAKEN ON OUR FIRST BIRTHDAY,
I DON'T THINK WE MADE IT TO OUR SECOND.

WITH JONATHAN AND RICHARD BRANSON. I'M ASSUMING THERE
WERE OTHER PEOPLE IN THE ROOM. IF YOU WERE ONE OF THEM,
COULD YOU GET IN TOUCH AND TELL ME WHAT THE BLOODY HELL
WE THOUGHT WE WERE DOING.

PROMOTING *GOOD STUFF.*
DAVINA IN ONE OF THE
THIRTY-SEVEN OUTFITS
SHE BROUGHT ALONG FOR
THE SHOOT. I'M SPORTING
ONE OF THE TWO TIES
I TURNED UP WITH.

APPEARING ON DICK AND
DOM'S RED NOSE DAY
IN DA BUNGALOW SHOW.
CHARITY BRINGS OUT THE
STRANGEST COMBINATIONS
OF PEOPLE (HERE, BRIAN
CONLEY, FEARNE COTTON,
SIÂN LLOYD, MICHELLE
HEATON, ED BYRNE).

Downing what was left of my large vodka tonic, I got up and ran towards the Chesterfield sofa and chairs they were draped on. I jumped up on to the arm of the leather sofa to attract their attention and asked them in no uncertain terms, 'What's red and white?' Not waiting for an answer, I declared, 'Pink! Now fuck off!'

As I did this, I put my hand out to steady myself and grasped the edge of a huge picture on the wall behind them. It was the sort of picture that is so big it has its own brass light attached to the top of it. The screaming and the picture coming away from the wall with its light still attached happened at the same time. Before I knew it, all four of them were fighting to get out from under a really quite large picture. As I was attempting to get down from the sofa, I managed to send one of the oversized table lamps positioned at each end of the Chesterfield flying. Light bulbs were popping, electrical wires were sparking and women were now crying. I left them struggling in the debris and retired for the night. I think I'd made my point and somehow I was still alive, so I left.

The next day we were checking out, as it was straight home after the gig. Phil or Paul would always be on hand when we were settling up, in case there was a problem. When it was my turn to hand in the key, I was given a folded piece of paper; on it was the bill for the food and drinks I'd had with Alan and an extra charge of £850. This was the estimated cost of the damage caused in the lounge the previous night. On closer inspection, the bulk of the cost was down to an L-shaped rip that had appeared in the red leather Chesterfield. The receptionist made it clear we were unable to leave until the bill had been paid. Phil got his chequebook out, and as he filled in the amount muttered, 'Christ, the bloody IRA didn't cause this much damage.'

18: GOOD STUFF

To Signor Zilli's, Dean Street, London, the first of Aldo Zilli's empire of restaurants. He's been selling Italian food in Dean Street for over twenty years, so he's obviously doing it right. It's a curious set-up, though, comprising two small self-contained eateries adjacent to each other: the one on the right all posh with padded chairs, thick linen, heavy cutlery, seventy-six-year-old sommelier and an illegible menu; the one on the left a clattering, cheap and cheerful cafe-bar selling, to the best of my knowledge, exactly the same food, cooked in exactly the same kitchen hidden away under exactly the same Dean Street. It's the suit-and-tie brigade to the right, T-shirt-and-jeans flotsam and jetsam to the left. The man I was lunching with owns neither T-shirt nor jeans, so I'm paying through the nose, having my wine poured for me and coping as best I can with the menu. I'm eating on the right.

It's a table for two in the window for me and the man mountain that is Derek Guthrie. A large, engaging Scot, coming in at six-four at least, Derek could have easily carved out a career as Michael Gambon's stunt double, but didn't (although I'm not sure anyone did). Instead, he opted for the more sedate but equally precarious job as a TV producer. Derek really was, and to be honest probably still is, the exception to the rule: a series producer you could go and get ruinously arseholed with. Traditionally the relationship between a presenter and a producer was always an arm's-length affair.

Kenton Allen springs to mind as a good example. Probably best known for steering Caroline Aherne and Craig Cash's *The Royle Family* to wide public acclaim, back in 1993 Kenton produced *Saturday Zoo*, the live hour-and-a-half show I had some involvement in.

Jonathan Ross and the regulars used to have a weekly Thursday meeting with the suits, producers, director and Channel Four lawyers, where we'd lock off what each of us was going to be doing on the following Saturday's show. After that, most of us would head over to the pub directly opposite the Channel X office to celebrate that fact we'd got away with it, for another week at least. Often Kenton would join us, but he never seemed to put his heart into getting fully stuck in. Even though he was a good mate and a laugh, his producer's hat would always prevent him from letting rip, getting hammered and falling over. He always left that to us.

No such problem with Derek. Quite the opposite, in fact. Such was Derek's network of friends and acquaintances in the television industry that he would often admit to booking a table at the Groucho Club for lunch and still be there at eleven o'clock that evening. I'm sure I would have bumped into Derek much earlier in my career, but for the fact he was living in New York. There he was series editor on BBC2's *Trial of OJ Simpson*, which everyone had originally thought was going to last a few weeks, but instead lasted eighteen months. Derek was pliable like that.

He was going to stay on in New York, but he'd already approached what was then Carlton TV with a pitch for a replacement show for its London arts and entertainment review, *Big City*. He came up with the name 'Good Stuff' to indicate that this was going to be about, well, all the 'good stuff' happening around town in arts, entertainment, parties, film and music. Although he was in charge of the show for only one year, he managed to create a programme that was to run for forty-two weeks a year for four years.

Then he took his encyclopaedic knowledge of television and the arts to CNN for their global arts and travel series, *The Artclub*, and a show called *Hotspots*, which ran for several years. That involved him producing a half-hour show from – and get this! – a different city in the world each week, fifty-two weeks a year! A man who likes a challenge, then.

In 1995, with Derek at the controls, *Good Stuff* arrived on our screens, as long as your screen was in the southeast, that is. Squeaky-clean Emma Forbes – every child's big-sister-they-never-had – originally fronted the show, but it quickly became clear she wasn't too happy about some of the things Derek was asking her to say. Things like, 'Coming up are the ads, so I'm going to pop down the pub and get the right side of a pint and a packet of pork scratchings – see you after the break.' He had a way with words, did Derek.

Derek's argument was that, as the show was going out at night to an adult audience, this was the sort of chat they would identify with. Emma had come from kids' TV and didn't want to offend her loyal band of eight-year-old followers, which was fair enough. She'd only ever talked their language on TV, and that certainly didn't include references to booze and pork scratchings. Having done my fair share of kids' programmes, namely playing Alf, the pizza chef, in a show called *Cats' Eyes*, the BBC's science and education series for eight-to-ten-year-olds, I can fully sympathize with Emma about wanting to protect your image. That said, I did, somehow, get the chef gig directly on the back of my stint as Duane the conga-playing, fag-smoking, pissed half of Raw Sex, so sometimes the rules don't apply.

Emma walked off the show and wrote Derek a memo explaining that she was mortified that not only did she not eat pork scratchings, but also her audience of eight-year-olds would never believe her again! Derek was very astute, took all this in and promptly hired *The Rocky Horror Show*'s Richard O'Brien to front the show, safe in the knowledge that Richard would have no problem with booze, scratchings or anything 'adult' for that matter. Richard saw out the last eleven weeks of the first series and was fabulous, treating the whole thing as a playground, which is what it was meant to be.

The studio was the only problem now. A show that was basically out and about in London was tethered to one of the smaller studios at LWT on the South Bank, and that wasn't ideal. Derek suggested doing the show from the back of a stretch limousine cruising round London. Limos at the time weren't quite the tacky monsters that they are now. By this time Fiona Phillips had been recruited to front the show, but there was a strong desire to make the show funny, as well as being informative and factual. Derek reckoned – quite rightly – that no one would pay any attention to a late-evening show that was merely information.

Clive Jones, the head of Carlton TV at the time, liked what Derek was doing with the programme and suggested he get me on to the show. I should point out that I didn't know Clive from . . . well, from Adam. In fact, I don't think I'd ever met him. Derek said he couldn't put me on the show as he already had Fiona Phillips, but Clive gave him a VHS of me doing a piece to camera, being a journo at a press conference. I vaguely remember the item on the tape, but I'd never have thought that that particular bit of arsing about would get me a foot in the door of the show I was to be involved with for two-and-a half years. It had something to do with a famous pop star . . .

In 1996, Robbie Williams had assembled the press at the Lancaster Gate Hotel on the north side of Hyde Park to make an announcement. The whole thing was geared up to happen on the stroke of midnight. Robbie was to appear and make a short statement to the effect that, as the clock ticked past midnight, he was no longer with one record company and was now with another, or something along those lines. It was to take about thirty seconds, and that was it. But rather than just turn up and be in a huge bun fight with hundreds of TV crews and journos, I got it into my head that it would be much better television to be the one reporter who got there at one minute past midnight as the applause was dying down and Robbie was leaving the stage.

The piece started with me unable to find a parking space outside the hotel and eventually just leaving the car in the middle of the road with the door open. Then there were lots of shots of me running up and down hotel corridors opening double doors into empty function rooms and screaming.

When I finally got to the right room, everyone was packing up and leaving. I was now frantically asking anyone and everyone what I'd missed, how it went, what Robbie'd said, how Robbie'd looked, what Robbie was wearing. I can't for the life of me remember who the item was for, but it must have worked because I found out later that the head of Carlton TV had a copy and was lending it to his mates.

The ultimate irony was that while I was at the hotel, I bumped into Antony Genn, a drinking friend from the Groucho Club. These days he fronts the band the Hours, but back then Antony was working with Robbie on some songs. The next thing I knew, the pair of us were up in Robbie's suite having a laugh with the great man himself and meticulously emptying his extensive mini bar. We left at about four in the morning. For a man who been hoisted aloft on a pole for public scrutiny, Robbie was remarkably normal and grounded.

Robbie later appeared on *Good Stuff* and very gamely agreed, for a reason that escapes me today, to pretend to be Elton John, or Elton 'Joan' as we christened him. It's amazing what a wig can do for a man.

He also helped me out when I was recording a pilot for Channel Five's new evening talk show. Producer Paul Jackson approached a few people to make a bunch of try-out shows for the five-nights-a-week slot that eventually went to Jack Docherty with a show imaginatively titled *The Jack Docherty Show*. (It was soon renamed *Not The Jack Docherty Show* as, towards the end of its run, Jack seldom presented the thing, as he was otherwise engaged behind the camera. I got the impression he would rather be the puppeteer than the puppet. A little-known 'puppet',

Graham Norton, sat in on a few, won an award on the back of his efforts and never looked back. Now there are no strings to hold him down.)

Paul asked me to gather some guests together for a non-broadcast half-hour that he would present to Five. I managed to secure Robbie as one of the guests and, amongst other things, we chatted about his Take That days and the pre-show rituals. He confessed that, for him, it pretty much amounted to knocking back a long glass of Pimms. We also covered how we first met, and the fact that he still owed me . . .

Let me explain. While working with Dawn and Jenny, Simon and I had got it into our heads that a Raw Sex album would be a great idea and a bit of a laugh. We'd call on all our comedy friends and cajole them into doing a number. It's common knowledge that all comedians want to be rock stars and vice versa. I don't think he'll ever be a rock star, but the Scottish comedian Arnold Brown was the first to help us out, giving a haunting and amusing version of 'Around the World', the Victor Young song. Arnold managed to bring a unique Glaswegian lilt to it, adopting the Telly Savalas spoken-singing delivery. For the same concept album, the girls also recorded Paul Simon's 'Feelin' Groovy', the lyrics of which are really, really, stupid – talking to lamp-posts and the like.

Somebody at Sony BMG got wind of it, and the next thing I knew I was being invited to dinner with one of their A&R men in a trendy little restaurant in Frith Street, Soho. We were on our desserts; he'd obviously done this a hundred times before and simply ordered a double espresso. I hadn't, so ordered a tiramisu, as I think it was the most expensive dessert they had. It also contained alcohol and I'd never had it before. When it arrived, I quickly realized it wasn't my cup of tea, so pushed it to one side; I was never a big fan of the sponge finger biscuit. The meeting was all very agreeable, and while we were waiting for the bill, three scruffy kids in their teens came into the restaurant and plonked themselves down next to us. They obviously knew the guy I was with, but pretty much ignored me and began pestering the A&R man for some money, as they wanted to go see a band who were, apparently, 'playing round the corner'.

One of them asked me if he could have some of my dessert, and I said he was more than welcome to it. He mumbled a 'thanks' and promptly got stuck into my tiramisu in a way that suggested he hadn't eaten for a while. Either that or he was a massive fan of the sponge finger biscuit. Having got what they wanted, something like a fiver each, they cheered up and sloped off. The A&R man later informed me they were three-fifths of 'new boy band sensation', Take That. Every time I see Robbie, which is almost never, he mentions the tiramisu he still owes me. One day Robbie, one day . . .

Back at *Good Stuff*, Derek found a little bit more cash from somewhere – he was good at that – and shoehorned me into the show alongside Fiona Phillips, thinking everything would be hunky dory. Like many of the decisions Derek made in his career in television, it was, of course, the wrong one. What actually happened, apparently, was something Derek maintains has never happened to him before or since. Every time I said something funny in front of Fiona, it would just go straight over her head and she would just carry on reading her prepared script. What he hadn't accounted for was Fiona's almost complete lack of a sense of humour. Heaven forbid that her reaction was as a result of the brand of humour on offer. And don't get me wrong, there's nothing wrong with not having a sense of humour – a good friend of mine openly admits to not having one, and it's really quite endearing. In fact, perversely, not having one can be quite funny in itself. It was decided that the funny stuff should still happen, but not within earshot of the bubbly and vivacious Fiona.

Derek had to make one thing clear before I was to be made a fully paid-up member of the show. It transpired that prior to Clive's tape, he had actually seen quite a bit of me on TV. There was *French and Saunders*, where I played Duane with a can of beer, *The Bunker Show*, playing myself with a bottle of Scotch, and *The Last Resort*, playing Dr Scrote clutching a vodka and tonic. He just wanted to make it quite clear that nothing untoward was going to happen on his show and that I was going to be the epitome of sharp-suited sobriety. I was able to reassure him that the lager was low alcohol, the Scotch was in fact cold tea and it was only the vodka and tonic that was indeed vodka and tonic. Two out of three's not bad . . .

* * *

The first few shows went well and it wasn't long before Derek felt confident enough to leave the helm of the *Good Stuff* ship and take advantage of a four-day junket up at the Edinburgh Television Festival. He left the show in the capable hands of Stuart Bateup, the Miles Davis 'monkey gland' researcher from my *Tube* days and now a jobbing director, and Andy Green, the show's editor. Stuart had been directing shows for Derek for some time, they seemed to have the same ideas and values when it came to *Good Stuff*, so he could be trusted.

Derek was obviously already beginning to tire of London as the backdrop of a show about London, so the following week's programme was going to feature Spain and all things Spanish. Before he left for Scotland, Derek set the show up. Robert Elms was hired to go to Barcelona with the band Pulp, film them at some festival and then cruise a few of his favourite tapas bars in Seville.

The show was going to open with Robert and me in a wine bar that thought it was a tapas bar on a street called The Cut, right next to Waterloo station. Derek's genius idea was that we'd be at the bar sipping a Spanish sherry, and I'd casually say to Robert something along the lines of, '. . . these tapas bars are becoming awfully popular. You got a favourite one then?' At which point the screen would go wibbly-wobbly and Robert would walk into a proper tapas bar in Seville, Spain. I, meanwhile, would seek out a Spanish slice of London.

Derek returned to London four days later and the first thing he did was ask Stuart if he could see the rough cut of that week's programme, to which Stuart immediately replied, 'No, you can't!'

Andy, the editor, promptly locked the edit suite door and said, 'And you can't come in.'

Derek smelt a sizeable rat and demanded to know what was going on. Stuart stood his ground and said he could only see the final edit of the show. What looked like Robert Elms and I enjoying a glass of fine Spanish sherry and going our separate ways at the top of the show was in reality the pair of us drinking pretty much a bottle of sherry each. Robert will maintain he only had two glasses, but *Good Stuff* was billed for two bottles – evidence that was to incriminate me later. The drinking wasn't too much of a problem for Robert as he was whisked off home when we were done, as his flight to Spain was the next day. I, however, had to go straight from the wine bar to the next location, a flamenco dance class.

Costa Dorada in Hanway Street, off Tottenham Court Road, remains one of London's best-known and biggest Spanish restaurant-bars. It was regarded by many as the most authentic and billed as the next best thing to actually going to Spain. The plan was to chat with the bevy of flamenco dancers who regularly perform there in the evening and then take to the floor myself. Having the restaurant featured on the show was great publicity and, to show their gratitude, the management laid on a huge buffet of tapas for our enjoyment. I seem to remember the proprietor being most insistent that we all enjoy a particularly fine rioja with the food so, not wanting to upset him, we steamed in. The Dorada has no windows to the outside world; it's the kind of place where you quickly lose all sense of time. That, and the fact that we had to hang around waiting for the dancers to show up, meant that by the time we were ready to do anything, Stuart and I were in a very jolly mood indeed, thanks to the 10 a.m. bottles of Tio Pepe and 12.30 p.m. bottles of rioja.

Derek watched the finished programme open-mouthed. In it, I staggered down the road shouting at people and stumbling into the doorway of the Costa Dorada. Once inside, there was some semblance of an interview with the lovely flamenco ladies, which amounted to little more than, 'What is it you do here, honey?', as if I was trying to pick up a hooker. They then invited me to join them on the dancefloor, something I would be very uncomfortable with when sober. As I stomped around the flamenco lovelies, laughing uncontrollably, Derek was watching with mounting horror. I then fell over and everything in my jacket pockets went flying – I never have been one for a wallet. The ladies gamely carried on clicking their heels as I crawled about on all fours beneath them trying to retrieve credit cards, phone, cash, bits of paper, a pen. And that was it; that was the *Good Stuff* item on how to enjoy a bit of Spain in London. Derek thought it was a nadir. Or should that be 'a nada'?

My idea for the link into the break after the flamenco dancing didn't go down too well, either. I had a couple of burly guys purporting to be the bouncers from the Dorada toss me on to a mound of bin-bags in the street outside the restaurant, whereupon I delivered the '. . . coming up after the break' line. Derek went mental, through the roof. Stopping just short of punching Stuart full in the face, he demanded the show be reshot and re-edited, insisting that it couldn't go out. It was a classic 'the minute I turn my back' situation. Quite understandably, Derek wanted to know what the bloody hell had happened. Stuart put it down to the day's sherry and red wine, but Derek was by now incandescent with rage, as he had apparently negotiated some licence that permitted me to have just one small glass of sherry on the show.

As Derek stormed out of the edit suite, Stuart and Andy

said they thought the film had a fun feel to it, which I don't think helped. The reality was that it was going out the next day and there was no time to reshoot or even recut the programme. Derek sat at home, seething as he watched the show go out. As soon as it finished, his phone rang. It was Clive Jones, head of Carlton TV, with tears running down his face, saying it was one of the funniest programmes he'd seen on ITV and if that was the future of *Good Stuff*, it was going to be the hit of the network. Derek graciously accepted Clive's comments, but for some reason, at the time he couldn't bring himself to pass them on to the people on the front line.

* * *

For a while the faux tapas bar in The Cut became the place to be, until the night we went there for somebody's birthday, or maybe there had just been another sacking – I remember it as a good place to drown sorrows, too. There was little or no pavement outside the restaurant so when cars pulled up outside, they would be just the other side of the window. Things were going swimmingly at our table, what with our new-found love of sherry, when one of our party mentioned they had to leave and wanted to get a cab. Being just round the corner from Waterloo station, there were loads of black cabs in the area and just at that moment a big black cab came to a halt outside with its 'for hire' light on.

From the table we were sitting at, quite a way into the restaurant, I put a couple of fingers in my mouth and let off a huge screeching whistle. This caught the cab driver's attention and he looked across at us inside the restaurant.

I held up my hand and managed to catch his eye, at which point he turned his 'for hire' light off and waited. I'd actually hailed a cab from inside a restaurant. This, of course, didn't go down well with the other customers or the management for that matter, because they came over to suggest that, 'Maybe sir has had enough sherry for the night.' We never went back.

* * *

A restaurant with fashion shows as its theme and a bloody great catwalk running through the middle of it with skeletal lovelies flouncing up and down all day . . . Bonkers or what? The Fashion Café opened, just off Piccadilly Circus, in a blaze of publicity in November 1997. What Planet Hollywood had done with the world of film, the Fashion Café was going to do with the world of fashion. Using the industry as its backdrop, this was going to be the place where you could gorge yourself on international fashion, fresh fish and fries. Claudia Schiffer, Naomi Campbell and Elle Macpherson were all going to be there for the launch, and so was *Good Stuff*. What is it with supermodels? At the end of the day, they're just attractive women who can afford to spend a week getting ready to go out. Word that Claudia, Naomi and Elle were going to be making an appearance resulted in hundreds of film crews vying for position outside the old Rialto Cinema, now fully refurbished at vast expense.

We had all been promised ten whole minutes with each of the models to ask questions carefully vetted by 'their people'. So breezy openers like 'What's it like being a restaurant entrepreneur?', 'Will you be doing any of the cooking?' and 'Surely supermodels live on fags and fresh air, not plated meals?' were out.

I've been to some fairly chaotic junkets, but this one really did take the piss. After about four hours of standing around doing absolutely nothing, a visibly flustered PR woman informed us that Elle Macpherson wasn't feeling very well (which didn't bode well for the opening of an eatery) and would not be attending. Naomi Campbell, meanwhile, would be doing all her interviews at the hotel she was staying at. Not that she had actually arrived at the hotel yet, so there was no point heading over there to try to do something constructive and get her interview knocked off.

Rumours very quickly got round that the Concorde she was undoubtedly on was probably still circling above us waiting to land at Heathrow airport. This meant only Claudia would be available for an interview and she would be arriving very shortly. Arriving very shortly? We'd already been there four hours and she wasn't even in the bloody building. It was a good six hours before I was ushered into the restaurant to meet the blonde, blue-eyed, German vision of beauty. At this point, I decided to adopt something of a protest stance; nobody should be made to hang around for six hours. Rather than ask any questions about her new restaurant and all the lovely frocks that were on display, I simply asked her what she thought I should do about a broken nail I had. She had a look at the nail, laughed and said there wasn't much I could do with it, at which point I said 'thank you' and left, much to the chagrin of the flunkeys around her.

It was early evening before we got over to Naomi's hotel,

and there was yet more hanging around. Again, when it was my turn for my ten minutes with her, I just asked what she thought I should do with the nail, as Claudia didn't have a clue, and left.

The segment was now going to be about what it's like hanging around waiting for supermodels to get dressed, put their face on and show up, with the added bonus of the best advice for damaged nails from some of the most beautiful women in the world. There would be a token nod to the stupid Fashion Café. Derek loved it, as he too could see that a six-minute film playing right into the hands of the ridiculous Fashion Café wasn't what he wanted his show to be about. As if to confirm what we already thought, the place went bust within the year.

* * *

Each week a new film release would be featured on the show. And each week we would try and build in a reference to said film. One week the film was David Cronenberg's *Crash*, and so we presented the show from a car – that one was handed to us on a plate. We thought: let's mock up a little 'accident' with the presenter and the limo. The driver's name was Alan, an ex-soldier who, rather intriguingly, would always carry with him photos of soldiers he'd stumbled upon who had been decapitated. Passing these pictures around didn't go down too well with some of the more 'delicate' guests we had in the back of the limo. It was obvious Alan had a certain blood lust, perfect for armed conflict on your average Middle Eastern frontline, but not quite so ideal in the world of genteel TV chauffeuring.

When we mentioned the *Crash* idea, his eyes lit up. So

no surprise then that he jumped at the chance of 'running me over'. In a lot of other productions, mocking up a road accident of this nature would entail all manner of forms, clearances, requests, planning, stunt men, maybe, and a large amount of rubber matting at the least. But that was the beauty of *Good Stuff* – 'Got an idea? Good. Go do it!' The fewer people – including the series producer – who knew what you were doing, the better. They'd only spoil your fun.

The idea was simple. I'd be doing the 'hello and welcome' to camera bit and then absent-mindedly walk off the pavement and be run over by Alan driving the limo. From my new position on the bonnet of the car, I'd carry on the link through the windscreen to the camera now mounted in the passenger seat. The next time you saw me I'd be in bandages and bleeding in the back of the limo, but determined to carry on. For the next link, I'd be slightly more the worse for wear, my injuries now taking precedence over the piece I had to deliver to camera. The link into the adverts I'd do with the window down while simultaneously trying to get directions to the nearest hospital from complete strangers we'd pass on the street. When we came back after the ads, I would be getting into the back of the limo, full of beans, having been fixed up by the hospital just visible in the back of shot. At this point, I'd introduce the week's new film release – David Cronenberg's *Crash*. Brilliant, right?

We headed for a quiet street round the back of King's Cross to knock off the opening piece to camera. We made it clear to Alan that he wasn't to go too fast as things always look faster, bigger and louder on camera. Unfortunately, I think the part of his brain that collates instructions must have closed down once he'd got behind the wheel. As he came hurtling down the road towards me he had a huge smile on his face; all I could see were the whites of his eyes and his teeth. I jumped up on to the bonnet as he skidded to a halt and fell against the windscreen. James Strong, the director, shouted 'cut' and I climbed off the bonnet. It worked! Not a rubber mat in sight and not a penny wasted on trifling things like insurance.

That was the exterior shot sorted. Now it was time to mount the camera in the passenger seat and do it all again, this time continuing the dialogue through the windscreen. Having done it once, with ease, it was felt that I should go for it this time as the car wouldn't need to go nearly as fast. We could really make it look like the limo has tossed me into the air and landed me on the windscreen. The side of my brain that collates common sense must have closed down at about this point. I ran at the car and launched myself on to the bonnet.

This time you could actually hear the metal of the bonnet buckle underneath me. As I slapped my hands and forearms on to the windscreen for that full 'I've just been hit by a car' effect, the dull cracking sound of a fifteen-year-old American windscreen prefaced my piece to camera perfectly. Not everyone saw it that way. Alan went ballistic. It was his car, and he had a stag do and two weddings coming up at the weekend. The dent in the bonnet was eventually pushed out by camera and sound, Rupert Binsley and Dave Pepperoni. (Pepperoni wasn't his real name but it was so similar that it wasn't worth remembering both pronunciations. I don't think Dave Pepperoni minded – soundmen always seem to be preoccupied with other things.

It's as if being a soundman, he's heard a load of things, some of which he is still coming to terms with.)

The windscreen wasn't looking too bad; I've been driven in mini-cabs that were much worse. And bearing in mind the limo was the wrong side of old, the crack in the top left-hand corner now gave the car a comfortable, dishevelled look. It was probably no longer street legal, but it looked good. Unlike Mr Cronenberg's film, I am reliably informed. After a lot of shouting in the series producer's office, the programme went out. It always puts a spring in your step when you hear there have been numerous complaints about the content of a show. More than one person actually thought I had really been run over by Alan, that I was genuinely in pain as a result and that surely it was unprofessional to let me carry on in the state I was in.

19: ASSAULTING PRINCESSES AND DINOSAURS

'First off I remember being quite frightened of being with you, because I always thought you were very funny and very cool and I thought you were just going to think I was a sort of novice idiot but you were very nice to me and very kind, so that's nice to know,' reflects Davina McCall.

I always wonder if I'm doing the right thing, arranging to meet a card-carrying AA member in a drinking establishment. In the back of my mind, I have that fear: I might find myself responsible for them falling off the wagon and back on the sauce. Then I'd watch their life, almost immediately, spiral completely out of control in front of my eyes.

I'm reminded of a regular gig I used to do in the cafe-bar at the Architectural Association in Bedford Square, London, when I was about nineteen. It was a four- or five-piece band (OK, I don't remember it *that* well) at which various musos would show up and sit in on a few numbers. One week what I thought was a quite elderly sax player whom none of us knew strolled in as we were setting up and asked if it was OK if he could sit in. The place hadn't opened its doors yet, so we ran through a couple of numbers to make sure he could play and wasn't going to embarrass the tits off us. The bloke obviously knew what he was doing, so he got the green light. He then suddenly disappeared, saying something about needing to find a better place to park his car as he was intending to be here for the duration. He seemed quite excited.

You rarely, if ever, find the same routine in television or the theatre, but the jazz gigs I did while still a teenager had a great tradition. Turn up. Set up. Sound check. Go to the pub. Come back. Go to the bar. Do the gig and, once you'd been paid, go back to the pub. I was only nineteen, playing with a bunch of guys some of whom were old enough to be my dad, so I was more than happy to go with the flow on this one. We arrived back at the cafe-bar in the Architectural Association to find our brand new friend sitting patiently, reading a paper. We had a bit of time before they 'opened shop', so we topped and tailed a few numbers, and as we were doing this, said 'shop' opened. A huge roller shutter was hoisted up to reveal the bar area with all its shiny optics, pumps and bottles. This was our cue to down tools and get stuck into the first of our free drinks before the punters turned up.

What happened next has stayed with me all these years. I clearly remember standing at the bar next to our new friend while drinks were being lined up. He began to fidget and rock backwards and forwards, oblivious to the barman's request for his tipple. Something was up. He made his apologies, packed his sax away and left. I never saw him again. The poor guy just couldn't be in the same room as a bar full of booze.

I must admit, during the six weeks I was off the beer while in training to get into shape to play Terry 'The

Tornado' Scrote in *Set of Six*, I found it almost impossible to hang out with anyone with a glass in their hand. This poor sax player had probably thought, great, a gig with no bar, I can actually enjoy myself and play. Sadly, it wasn't to be. For years after that my understanding of who an AA member was and how they lived with their problem was based solely on that poor old sax player.

So it was to be the Groucho Club for my get-together with Davina, whom I hadn't seen for an age. She gave me a hug which more than indicated she was still leading the field in the fitness video business. To her eternal credit, she was an out and proud AA member years before we first met and worked together back in 1995. I'd never known her with a drink in her hand so when I asked her what she wanted and she replied, 'I'll get'm in,' and confidently pushed her way to the front of the bar, there was the briefest of moments when I thought, 'What's this? She's parched! She's fallen! She's back on it!'

Of course, she hadn't and wasn't – it was just me hamfistedly coping with the fact she can look forward to, and enjoy, a fresh orange and soda just as much as I look forward to that first screw-top litre bottle of soave after breakfast.

Our first encounter with each other was at a small, makeshift, windowless room in the bowels of the vast ITV building on the South Bank, the location for the promotional photo-shoot for the upcoming series of *Good Stuff*. The done thing is to have two or three changes of clothing at these events – get a nice variety of pictures, make sure nothing clashes. I arrived with two suits and a handful of ties; Davina staggered through the door with what looked like the contents of her and a mate's wardrobe. She had everything: jeans, trousers, dresses and those funny baggy half-mast things that have a French name, so we in this country can distance ourselves from them. I think she even brought a selection of hats. She came across as feisty and excitable on *Big Brother*, an attitude, I can tell you now, which was not cultivated for that particular show; she was just like that from our first hello. I saw no evidence of the novice idiot she claimed to be. She really did throw herself into everything we did.

I stood, barely able to conceal my blushes, as she repeatedly stripped down to bra and 'nearly pants' and tipped herself in and out of her complete wardrobe. Heck, why bother with the cramped inconvenience of the ladies' changing room? I quickly removed the four ties I'd hung in the men's changing room and nonchalantly slung them over the long mirror in the small studio we were now sharing. First impressions are strange things. When she was virtually starkers, I couldn't help but notice the array of tattoos Davina had about her body, as if someone, blindfold, had been playing 'pin the tat' on the lady. I'm not talking big complex tattoos, full-colour pictures of Elvis or skulls, not a bit of it. These were like little 'sound-bite' tattoos dotted tastefully all over the place.

There was one tattoo which I know she's spoken openly about on TV, so I'm sure she won't mind me drawing your attention to it. To the untrained eye, it looked just like a little bunch of carrots casually tossed over one shoulder, but on closer inspection – which, to my surprise, was actively encouraged – it turned out they weren't carrots but chillies, an altogether more racy tattoo I think you'll agree. For me, carrots shout, 'Better eyesight!' Chillies, on the other hand, shout 'Hot!' And that's what I mean about first impressions. She claims that, initially, she was frightened of me, but I was equally intimidated by her hot chillies.

I often mention, when asked what I was like as a kid, that my two older brothers and I never smoked, owned a motorbike or had a tattoo, what I regard as the three symbols of rebellion. I'm almost ashamed to say it, but we simply had nothing to rebel against, as our youth was spent in an idyll. I never did find out whether Davina had a motorbike – beautiful image though it is. But having got to know her and snippets of her past, I got the impression a motorbike would have been slightly over-egging her rebellious youth. Even so, Davina and I had a fairly idyllic time together, sat in the back of the tawdry *Good Stuff* limo, taking it in turns to jump out and do a link to camera. The limo would pull up outside some impressive building and one of us would be scrambled into action.

Davina says: 'It would take me five minutes to do the link: three to learn it and two to record it. In those five minutes you would always manage to go AWOL. We'd all have to search the pubs in the immediate vicinity.'

Unlike my partnership with Fiona Phillips, Davina and I got on like a house on fire. Our inability to take anything seriously and the complete lack of one-upmanship made us ideal backseat companions. We didn't realize how lucky we were, but that was probably the best way to approach the whole thing. Start taking it too seriously and you begin to disappear up your own arse. That's my excuse, anyway.

We'd do things like seeing who could have the last word at the end of the show – that got quite silly. Or when interviewing a really important film star, we'd challenge each other to incorporate an inappropriate word like 'pineapple'. *Good Stuff* went out on a Tuesday, so we'd take childish delight in rounding off the show with, 'C U Next Tuesday!' I got the impression, talking with Davina, that she too enjoyed our time together. She remembers: 'There was never a question of: "Do you think Rowland would mind looking like a total idiot in some ridiculous outfit?" It wasn't even, "Let's ask him . . ."'

I asked Davina if she ever got hauled in to see the series producer, the boss man, over our various antics. She never was. Just me, then. She confessed to being a goody-two-shoes, very compliant, which is probably why she left me behind in the limo and went on to command huge critical acclaim throughout the land as 'Mrs TV' while my status as 'Mr TV' has yet to be pulled fully into focus. One day, Jonathan, one day. (Small theatrical spit over one's shoulder.)

* * *

I tried to be compliant, but things would always conspire against me. Jenny Agutter was a classic example.

She was doing a play in the West End, so the plan was to pop round to her house, a big one in one of those imposing squares near the Oval cricket ground, and give her a lift into work. Simple. I'd be lying if I said I didn't fancy her. I've seen two of her films, *The Railway Children*, which had her waving her knickers in the air to avert some railway disaster, and *Walkabout*, where she very quickly dispensed with her knickers and the rest of her clothes in order to, if not so much walk about, then swim about, at least.

We arrived at her large townhouse a little early, something that can throw the more self-important guest, but not Jenny Agutter. She was all, 'Come in, sit down, I'm not quite ready, make yourself a tea, coffee, help yourselves, please have a look through my pants drawer.' She didn't say the last bit, but she could have and somehow, with Jenny, it wouldn't have been out of place, such was her charming, disarming nature. I loved her; we all loved her.

We climbed into the back of the limo and I immediately launched into my grovelling apologies for the slightly tacky nature of our transportation into town, the worn leather seating, the incredibly cheap bottles of faux champagne dotted about. She wouldn't have any of it; in fact, she seemed quite excited by the whole thing, which made her even more attractive. This was going to be great. The journey wasn't that long, but the ice had already been broken in her living room so the interview could be nice and relaxed. She had a fantastic giggle that was a joy to tease out of her.

As they had a tendency to rattle in their pretend mini ice-buckets, I removed one of the incredibly cheap faux champagne bottles from the window ledge behind Jenny and laid it flat on the bench seat opposite where she was sitting and forgot about it. We eased out of the square and pulled on to Kennington Road, Jenny authoritatively suggesting nifty short cuts as we made our way into town. We didn't want to get into town too quickly so I mentioned that the limo, being the length it was, often got stuck so the longer, straighter route would be the safest bet.

To a lot more infectious giggling, I recalled the time we picked up Cliff Richard from his hotel, in full costume and make-up for his appearance in the stage show, *Wuthering*

Heights. We were going to do the interview while driving him to the theatre where he was starring as Heathcliff. He knew the route to the theatre and had got the timing down to a tee, so that he'd arrive at the stage door with just minutes to spare before going on stage. Unfortunately, the route he always took was in a normal size car, not a bloody great limo. As we chatted, I could sense him getting more and more agitated about the route we were taking – this obviously wasn't Cliff's route. Eventually he started barking instructions to Steve the driver to cut down side roads that, clearly, were no place for a thirty-eight-foot car.

Quite quickly, the inevitable happened and the limo ground to a halt, unable to make the next left turn. It was then that any chance of a lucid interview with Heathcliff went out of the window. Curtain up was a matter of minutes away and we were quite possibly miles from the theatre – I had no idea where we were. To his credit, Cliff didn't swear once; he just got out of the car, thanked us all, informed us that the theatre was in fact less than half-a-mile away and began walking quite quickly.

As we crossed Westminster Bridge, I'm convinced Jenny momentarily fell in love with me. Forget the house, we were getting on like a whole street on fire. Then it happened. The bottle of incredibly cheap faux champagne I had very carefully laid on the edge of the seat opposite Jenny suddenly came alive. The cork flew off and pretty much the entire contents of the bottle emptied into Jenny's large, open handbag she'd tucked out of harm's way, down by her feet.

To say the mood changed would be an understatement. Everything in the bag was sodden with cheap, sticky, fizzy wine, and as this was in the days of big bulky Filofaxes, it didn't look good. Understandably, Jenny's infectious giggling dried up. If only her handbag would, but it wouldn't. It would never be the same again. Something tells me leather of that quality isn't designed to cope with the 'champagne' Steve the limo driver provided for the numerous stag and hen parties he couriered round town when not working on our show.

So many of the *Good Stuff* altercations were drink-related, but this was the first where not even the smallest glass had passed my lips. Booze had cut out the middleman and was now trashing the show without my help. The last 200 yards down Shaftesbury Avenue to Jenny's theatre felt like three hours. Jenny, now stony-faced and avoiding any eye-contact, briskly did the plug for her show and climbed out of the car, unaided.

We've not kept in touch.

The one time things had gone tits up – and Davina wasn't there to witness my innocence and sobriety in the whole event. Typical.

Davina says: 'You can put this in your book. I thought that you were going to meet up with me to ask me about "AA". I thought, "There are only two reasons why Rowland would call me up. One, to offer me a job, which I very much doubt, as I hadn't seen you for years. Two, he's finally going to come to an AA meeting." I'd been saving you a seat for years.'

* * *

Rupert Camera and Dave 'Pepperoni' Sound were two of the most reliable people you could wish to work with. Although there was that one time, with Princess Diana . . .

ITV's remit to Carlton was to provide twenty hours of arts programming a year, so forty half-hour shows a year of *Good Stuff*, featuring the arts and entertainment, fulfilled that obligation perfectly. As long as you throw in the odd art gallery or exhibition, everyone's happy.

It was pretty much Her Royal Highness Princess Diana's last public appearance. She was attending a thing called the 'Tate 100' at the Tate Gallery on Millbank, now of course known as Tate Britain. I'd like to think some ageing, patriotic, sozzled gallery board-member was behind the name change, thinking it would be great fun to call it 'Tate' Britain as it sounds so much like 'Great' Britain.

We were going to do the whole show from the gallery. It would be a *Good Stuff* Tate Britain special, where we'd meet everyone, get access all areas and really get under the skin of the place. With royalty being there, the gallery insisted everyone – and I mean everyone, including camera, sound, director, runner – had to wear dinner jackets. It was white shirts, bow ties, the lot, fully suited and booted. This was fine by the James Strong, the director, and me – I'd always said it would be a great idea if the *Good Stuff* crew all wore the same sharp suits, to really create an impression wherever we went. Dave and Rupert thought differently. They saw it as a completely ridiculous idea, so they were far from happy when they learnt about the strict dress-code requirements for the upcoming Tate special.

Davina turned up at the Tate and looked stunning in a long sparkly, shimmery, sexy, slinky ball gown and a face full of 'special occasion' make-up. As a crew, we did look fantastic! Maybe my sharp-suited idea would work after all! Come the day, Rupert was now fairly comfortable with what he was wearing, an old dinner suit his father had given him. It was Dave who didn't take kindly to it – at all. I think the problem lay in the fact he didn't own a dinner suit, so he'd had to hire one. My theory is that if you don't already have a DJ, you are never going to feel good in a borrowed one. Dave looked great but felt shit, so wasn't in the best of moods.

Once we started filming inside the vast Tate Britain, it very quickly became clear that our 'access all areas' was nothing of the sort – royal security had put paid to that. From their point of view, we could have been nutters out to cause insult to Her Royal Highness. As it was, only Rupert in his fifty-year-old DJ looked like the type of nutter who might follow through with that sort of threat. Ever the diplomat, James listened carefully to their demands and assured them everything would be fine.

But as soon as they were gone, he decided to take a chance. We were going to, pretty much, 'door-step' Princes Diana and her American guest, the avid art collector and one-time funny guy, Steve Martin, as they strolled through one of the few picture rooms we were allowed in. I was to jump in front of Steve using a hand-held mic, with James operating the second camera, while Davina, Rupert and Dave, with the boom mic – a long pole with a big furry caterpillar thing on the end – were to accost Diana, the Princess of Wales. With time to kill before they arrived, we carefully rehearsed how we would go about orchestrating our chats with Di and Steve. Suddenly there was a flurry of activity that caught us all on the hop, and they were in the room. Davina lunged towards the Princess and fired off her first question. Unfortunately, Dave hadn't quite got the boom mic where he'd like it, and with one twist of the long handle he was now holding at arm's length above his head he whacked the Princess on the back of her head. This wasn't good. Within seconds, we were all ushered out of Tate Britain and told not to attempt to gain entry again.

Dave was quick to apportion the blame squarely on the stupid dinner jacket he had been press-ganged into wearing. It wouldn't have happened if he had been allowed to wear the regulation soundman's jeans, check shirt and sleeveless body warmer. Apparently, there was insufficient movement in the arms of the DJ. For his part, James, whose job it was to come back with a coherent film, wanted to 'insufficiently move' at least some of the boom mic right up Dave's arse.

We were out on the street, all dressed up with nowhere to go. I suggested we repair to the nearest pub and make a plan B. Hearing this, Davina burst into tears and plonked herself down on the front steps of the Tate. Ironically, everyone thought we were too overdressed to entertain the idea of a boozer. We had shot some stuff in the gallery with everyone in there dressed up to the nines. So all we had to do was get a bottle of fizz and a couple of champagne glasses and do the links on the steps under the pretence that it was all a bit of a squash and very hot inside so we'd come out for a bit of fresh air. It worked a treat, and from that day on we let Dave Pepperoni wear whatever he wanted.

* * *

Museums are always good fun to film in – they're so big and everything is laid out so beautifully. Programmes virtually make themselves in museums. At least, that was the theory . . .

There was a bit of a first at the Natural History Museum in Kensington: an exhibition called 'Dinosaurs of the Gobi Desert'. A couple of complete articulated dinosaur skeletons, never before seen in this country, were to be put on display for the public to marvel at. Apparently, it had taken weeks to install the things and had cost a small fortune, not least from an insurance point of view. *Good Stuff* had a bit of a scoop as we were the only show to be allowed to film the magnificent, two million-year-old skeletal beasts prior to them going on display.

The director James, camera, sound and I turned up in the morning just as they were putting the final touches to the exhibition, only to be told we wouldn't be able to film anything inside until the afternoon – basically, 'Get lost.' I got the impression the curator of the exhibition wasn't mad keen on us being there, getting in the way. As it happened, this wasn't that much of a problem, as we could spend the morning doing the exterior stuff, the 'hello and welcome' and the 'that's all we have time for'. We even spent a happy hour taunting a bunch of French students about the whereabouts of a brace of prehistoric dinosaurs. 'Avez-vous spotted deux grand dinosaurs prehistoriques, s'il vous plait?' This always works well, until you get the one foreign kid who has a slightly better grasp of the Queen's English than you do. Then, suddenly, the game's not so much fun.

It was decided we'd have an early bite to eat and be ready to roll at about one o'clock – when, we hoped, the curator of the exhibition and his team were all at lunch. You can get a lot more done when there's no one about. There are plenty of tiny, very accommodating Italian restaurants just off the Cromwell Road in North Kensington, so we had no trouble getting one to open at half-eleven in the morning for a spot of lunch. What we obviously should have done was go with what the crew wanted, a brunchy sort of meal, and not what I was angling for – a full-on lunchy sort of meal. Trouble is, I'm a big fan of the thick-linened, heavy-cutleried, plated meal, the very backbone of a perfect long lunch. If we were going to start at eleven-thirty, we could at least get an hour-and-a-half in before we had to be back at work. I got my way, which I shouldn't have.

The letter of complaint sent by the Natural History Museum to Derek, the series producer at *Good Stuff*, made no mention of anyone being drunk, thank God. Their beef was that we had gone beyond the red rope, and no one goes beyond the red rope in museums. More importantly, *no one* touches the exhibits.

Our plan of getting back to the dinosaurs while the boss-man curator was at lunch worked a treat. When we arrived, the only person keeping an eye on things was a young, willowy female assistant munching through a Tupperware box of lettuce. The dinosaur we were going to feature was set in a landscape of jagged flints, thousands of them all painstakingly stood on end. James and I talked the poor assistant into letting me go beyond the red rope and stand next to the big fella for the piece to camera. Obviously, she was not happy, but seemed keen for us to get the best results. She very kindly showed us the narrow pathway that led to the dinosaur from behind a side curtain. This was going to be great, we thought. I would appear and walk amongst the pointy bits of slate towards the beast, where I would end up face-to-face with him. The rehearsal went fine – we should have bloody shot that. It was when we were on tape that the fireworks started. As I walked toward the dinosaur, I lost my footing on some of the slates and began crunching them into the ground, each one sounding a huge CRACK as it broke.

I attempted to carry on as best I could, knowing we had to get it in the can this time. Now walking and talking, I moved up alongside the back end of the skeleton but it was no good, the carefully positioned pieces of slate had beaten me and I completely lost my balance. I reached out with a hand and grabbed hold of the dinosaur's tail to steady myself. The skeleton was suspended from the ceiling, and the bones were all connected to each other by thin wires. My grabbing the tail end sent a shock-wave through the body of the dinosaur – the whole thing looked like it was suddenly coming alive. Manically, I tried to stop the bones swaying back and forth – by this time the shock-wave had reached its head which was now moving from side to side as if to say, 'No, I wouldn't do that if I were you.'

We all heard him before we saw him.

'WHAT THE BLOODY HELL IS GOING ON HERE?'

It was the boss-man curator back from lunch. I tried to explain how I'd lost my footing on the slates, but I don't think he wanted to hear that. There was more shouting, this time at the willowy assistant. She burst into floods of tears and we left. They didn't even let us try and put some of the carefully positioned slates back in place, the ones that weren't broken that is.

It was only in the cold light of day did I notice a nasty scratch down one side of my leather shoes. That'll be the bastard bits of painstakingly arranged slate that did that,

I thought. Should I put in a claim? In the circumstance, James thought it was probably best I didn't and we'd all be better off if I just let it go. For a short while, ITV were banned from filming at the Natural History Museum. I decided not to take my kids to see 'Dinosaurs of the Gobi Desert'.

I like watching tennis on TV – particularly when they talk about the amount of unforced errors a tennis player has made. I've had many unforced errors in my life. People playing tennis often get away with about twenty unforced errors – I wasn't allowed one . . .

20: WHAT SORT OF WORD IS JUNKET, ANYWAY?

To promote their latest work, a lot of film stars head to London, capital city and all that. With Americans, it's invariably a whistle-stop tour while taking in as many European cities as their two-day window will allow. *Good Stuff* had the honour of featuring everyone who was anyone, and I had the dubious task of conducting a lot of the interviews.

It's a pretty tried and tested format. The people promoting the film rent a couple of flash suites at somewhere like the Dorchester, the hotel towards the bottom end of Park Lane (and, curiously, built at right angles to the road it's on – what happened there?). Then reporters, reviewers and presenters are all summoned to the appropriate adjoining suites, clutching their twelve questions, and told they have anything from three to seven minutes, depending on the talent's window in London, for their 'one to one' with the 'star' and left to wait and stew.

To keep us all happy, the spread the film company begrudgingly provides is always top-notch: fiddly pastries, all manner of finger food, fresh orange juice, teas and coffee. But always conspicuous by its absence, from where

I sat, was any vestige of booze. And there's probably a very good reason for that.

Sometimes, we were also sent abroad to 'meet the stars'. I'm reminded of the *Good Stuff* junket to Ireland for my 'six minutes' with Courteney Cox and Harry Connick Jr. Here's a thing: his full name is Joseph Harry Fowler Connick Jr . . . So his middle names are Harry and Fowler. Could this be a parent's nod to the cockney character-actor and voiceover veteran, Harry Fowler, noted for his juvenile roles in such classics as the Ealing comedy *Hue and Cry*, made in 1947, and the Boulting Brothers' *Lucky Jim* ten years later? Great, I had my breezy opening question! We got to the quaint hotel in Dublin, where the encounter was to take place, by about midday, only to be told, as so often, that the 'talent' hadn't as yet landed in the country, but I was to be ready the minute they showed up. Brilliant.

It got to about four-thirty in the afternoon before I was ushered into the really quite small living room of the hotel's grandest bedroom for a chat with, firstly, Courteney Cox. I forget what was actually said during the six-minute natter. There couldn't have been anything insulting. I don't think I upset her because I would have remembered. What everyone does remember was the official complaint the fragrant Courteney lodged with the film's promoter later that day. It was to do with the overpowering stench of Guinness that rapidly filled the small room she and I were squeezed into.

The trouble is that the curtains are always closed at these events – show me a cameraman who says he has no fear of natural light and I'll show you a bare-faced liar. And I seem to remember it was a particularly warm day, so naturally, on the soundman's instructions, all the windows were firmly closed. The 747 30,000 feet above us or the police car half-a-mile away might both be completely inaudible to myself and Ms Cox, but would utterly ruin the recording for any soundman worth his salt. And then let's not forget the bunch of lamps used to make everyone look so gorgeous; they can kick off a fierce heat at times.

I think what must have happened was that, during the four-hour wait on standby – that's FOUR HOUR wait – I took it upon myself to sample the local beverage. Well, I'm sorry, but you can't go all the way to Dublin and not get the wrong side of three or five pints of the local beverage. Harry was up second and if he was perturbed by the now heavy fug of Guinness in the room, he made no mention of it and I respect him for that. The Harry Fowler question did, however, leave him nonplussed.

Even without a skinful of Guinness, these encounters were usually strained, to say the least. The 'star' would always be sitting bathed in a pool of light, the sort of light that could knock fifty years off an oak tree. Then there's the coterie of very important people who would shuffle in the shadows, willing the day to go well. In these situations, the slightest thing can throw you.

Woody Harlesden was over in 1996 promoting *The People vs. Larry Flint*. Woody played Larry Flint, the seventies' porn baron. Shit, I've just looked him up – his real name is Harrelson – and I called him Harlesden for the whole time I was with him. I reduced poor Woody to a deprived area of north London best known for a large railway junction. Slouched on one of those double-height folding director's chairs in coordinated grey, he looked great – until you clocked he was wearing no shoes or socks.

What? Suddenly all you want to do is drop the 'What's it like working with naked people?' line of enquiry and pull him up on his total lack of foot apparel. Maybe I missed the fact he didn't wear shoes in the film and the studio execs had thought it a good publicity wheeze to write into his contract that, while promoting their product, he is 'to desist from any form of foot covering' – what the heck, anything to sell a film. Personally, I think it was more to do with the fact he seemed a weird bloke. A nice bloke, definitely, but to me a bit of a weird, shoeless bloke nonetheless.

It's funny how the slightest unexpected detail can throw you. Another person I found completely distracting was Morgan Freeman, a fine actor and a beautiful, warm, generous man, who exudes authority and control. I went to interview him in the Savoy Hotel in a lovely big room overlooking the Thames. Everything was going swimmingly until he stood up to offer me a drink and I couldn't help but notice that the man was wearing calliper on his leg – and an old-fashioned, clanky one to boot. That was it – my concentration was shot to pieces. All my carefully coiffured line of enquiry went sailing out of the stunning picture window overlooking Waterloo Bridge. I had absolutely no idea what to say. Biting my lip, I held back the unavoidable opening question: where the bloody hell did you get that thing on your leg, Morgan? You kept that quiet.

Then again, it can be something that's said which grinds the interview to a halt. The apparently ill-conceived remake of *The Saint* in 1997 saw Val Kilmer holed up at the Grosvenor House Hotel for his twenty-odd interviews. He must have been the only one who put his hand up when they asked, 'Who wants to play the Saint?', as I understand the film was a stinker. I've an idea he heard it wrong and thought they'd said, 'Who wants to play *a* saint?'

It's common knowledge that Val's a moody thing, and not necessarily a lot of laughs. If that didn't make things tricky enough, I have to admit that I didn't fully commit to my side of the deal. I never actually got to see the film he was promoting. I'd heard it was crap, tosh, and I think the word piffle surfaced at one point. My knee-jerk reaction when those sort of words are bandied about is not to turn up at the crack of dawn at Mr Young's Preview Theatre in Soho and sit through said crap, tosh and piffle. As it was, I wasn't that popular with the elusive Mr Young. So, if you'll bear with me, perhaps I should explain . . .

A few weeks before, I'd been asked to show my face at a painfully early kick-off screening in one of the warren of underground mini-cinemas where reviewers and the like get to see all the films a few weeks before their release. I'd been up all night and was already in Soho trying to sort out getting back to Muswell Hill in north London when the phone rang asking if I was in the cab sent to my home to get me into town for the preview screening. Of course I was already nearby, so I walked the 200 yards up the road into D'Arblay Street and slunk into Mr Young's. Shunning the pots of coffee and plain croissants on offer, I sheepishly installed myself in one of the back-row seats where no one would spot me, not 'if' but 'when' I nodded off.

I can't for the life of me remember the film we were there to watch. I do remember shuffling past Barry Norman, so it must have been a biggie. To this day, I'm not sure if it was the snoring that pissed off everyone in the room, or my phone repeatedly going off – either from my wife or the cab outside my house – that prompted someone to eventually wake me up, suggest I answer the phone and then insist I leave.

So aside from *The Saint* not being very good, that was another reason I hadn't seen the film. Val Kilmer, therefore, was going to be a challenge, but nothing ventured . . .

'How are you finding London, Val?' – can't go wrong with that, or can you?

Well, yes you can, if you're sitting opposite the moodiest Batman of them all. Dressed in an outfit of coordinated tans, he launched into a five-minute diatribe about everything that's wrong with London. At one point he actually said, 'This place was so bad, there were people on the streets that couldn't even afford coal.'

People on the street short of coal? Rather than promise to try and sort out the coal shortage amongst the homeless – those people without a home but, obviously, with a fireplace – I panicked and cut to the icebreaker.

From my coat pocket, I produced a boxed Corgi Volvo P 1800 two-door sports car, complete with *The Saint* logo on the bonnet, a scale model of the one driven by Roger Moore in the 1960s classic *The Saint* TV series. I gingerly offered it up to him. This was always a good ruse: give them a little something they can relate to. Stony-faced, he informed me that *The Saint* film he happened to be promoting that day had little if anything in common with the popular British TV show of the 1960s, apart from its name, and that surely I should have deduced that having watched the film?

Val wasn't best pleased, probably realizing that I hadn't done my homework. He inspected the toy and tossed it back to me. I reckon I would have been better off with the Corgi Batmobile. At least I saw that film.

The tension and sense of failure in the room with Val that day was nothing compared to my time with the great Gary Oldman. I was dispatched to see *Nil By Mouth*, a mind-numbingly gritty film based on his early years growing up in a rough part of town, seemingly inhabited by villains, drug-addled kids and wife-beating, drunken nutcases. Gary had written and directed the film so was, understandably, very close to the project. Even though Kathy Burke (a friend of mine) was in it, I hated the film and left before the end – something of a *faux pas*, as all the other people in the small preview cinema stayed to the bitter conclusion. If you're going to talk to the person about the film they've written, directed and tipped their very heart and soul into, it's best to watch it all the way through, regardless of how good or bad you think it is.

Unfortunately, I hadn't. But what I hadn't realized was that the junket with Mr Oldman was straight after the screening. The PR lady from the film company did little to disguise her concern that I was leaving before the film had finished. I couldn't lie, so I told her I thought the amount of violence and abuse that was unfolding on screen couldn't, in my book, be classed as entertainment. I think I might have even said something pompous along the lines of, '. . . and people are going to pay good money to watch that'. I went on to tell her I was having trouble equating the word 'entertainment' with the words 'total abject depression'.

My early departure meant I now had about forty-five minutes to kill before my audience with the great man, and as the hotel where it was to take place was just up the road from the screening in Soho Square, a sharpener at the Groucho Club in Dean Street would imbue me with the Dutch courage I was going to need this time round. At the bar I got chatting to someone about the most depressing film I'd ever seen. He, of course, knew exactly what I was on about, loved it and predicted great things for it – and he wasn't wrong, as it went on to win awards left, right and centre. He'd also worked with Mr Oldman and was under the impression that Oldman didn't suffer fools gladly. I wasn't that surprised, having just witnessed two-thirds of his wretched upbringing.

After forty-five minutes of white-knuckle 'refreshing', I was able to find an inner courage and was determined to be straight with Gary, tell him what I thought of the film, cards on the table, one to one, no beating about the bush, man to man, new best friend to new best friend. I'd be fine.

How I found myself mentioning his film and *The Flintstones* cartoon in the same sentence, I'm not sure. It must have been when I told him I thought all the characters in the film were like caricatures of people in dead-end situations and not real at all. Gary's face was a picture. Not a very nice picture – much like his film come to think of it. You could have heard a pin drop but for the communal sharp intake of breath from every one of Gary's 'suits' shuffling, now uncomfortably, in the shadows. I made a beeline back to the Groucho and sat a respectable distance from Gary's mate.

Sometimes the insult can work to your advantage, and shamefully I have to admit it only really works with me if the person on the receiving end is a lady. Alicia Silverstone was over to promote *Batman & Robin*, in which she played

Bat Girl. She was gorgeous in a 'my mate's younger sister' sort of way – she didn't look old enough to be in a Batman film, to be honest. Coming in at about four-foot-nothing, she had the appearance of an American kid who was still shedding the puppy fat. The hoody and jeans she was wearing made her look a bit like a very attractive work-experience trainee/runner. Before getting into talking about the film, the ice-breaker chat found me commenting on the hoody she was sporting – not very Hollywood actressy, I thought. She told me in no uncertain terms that she was not very Hollywood actressy and in fact pretty much lived in hoodies and jeans. This was the perfect apparel for going unnoticed to the cinema with her dogs, she told me. She would often pop to her local cinema with her dogs apparently. They were her best friends – they even slept next to her.

Things were going quite well, but at this point I had to come clean and tell her that, unfortunately, I hated dogs. Quick as a flash, she came straight back with, 'Well, I hate you.' As I went on to paint the horrible picture of some bitch on all fours licking you awake in the morning, there was a pregnant pause as Alicia and myself thought that through. As she didn't storm out of the car mid-interview, I can only assume she liked me.

At least I didn't go with the line of questioning suggested by the *Good Stuff* film researcher, Rufus Roubicek. He wanted me to ask her about the rumour that the studio executives had wanted to use a body double as she was coming over a tad too plump on some of the early footage they had seen. Even I know that mentioning weight is a no-no when interviewing a lovely lady. I think hating her dogs is fine, though. Probably pushed it a bit too far with the licking and the bed stuff. Having said I hate dogs, we have since acquired a family dog and he's not that bad – he's a dog called bear and he cost a monkey.

21: LIFE-CHANGING CALLS

I didn't realize quite how many hours I'd clocked up in the back of that old, knackered limo. I did the show for about two-and-a-half years. A couple of really major things happened whilst I sat there, cut off from the outside world behind the smoked-glass windows, gliding round London's heady West End. We waited for hours one afternoon in a lovely big square in Kensington or Knightsbridge, or it may have been Chelsea. That's part of the problem with the blacked-out windows in a limo – you're never really sure where the bloody hell you are. Wherever it was, I remember remarking how enormous the houses were and that they must have been carved up into flats, as no one would live in a whole house. Apart from Twiggy.

I had her down as at least six-foot-one. She always struck me as a tall gangly thing, so maybe she needs a lot of house to 'gangle' about in. She finally emerged through the huge studded front doors, looking gorgeous, but no more than five-foot-seven. Telly puts pounds on some people and, obviously, inches on others. So what the bloody hell was she doing rattling around it that pile? We'll never know because I completely forgot to ask her. Anyway, she folded herself into the back of the limo, and we were off.

She's a very bubbly person is Twiggy. She's happy to chat

and see the joke in whatever was happening, especially if it's driving around in a big stretch limo in the middle of the afternoon. She should be a Very Important Person off to a premiere in a car like this, not going round in circles in the sunshine, while she was forced to bang on, yet again, about her latest project, her upcoming appearance in the London stage revival of Noel Coward's *Blithe Spirit*. But that's what was required that sunny afternoon, and I assured her we were going to have as much fun doing it as possible. Twiggy is one of those people who is a peach to chat to. Over the years, she's given most things a go and didn't bat a perfectly coiffed eyelash when, for comic effect, I kept bringing the conversation back to the Swinging Sixties, Carnaby Street, the Fab Four and how, surely, she must have snogged one of them? She wouldn't be drawn, however, and I respect her for that.

We were getting on like a house on fire. It was like the magical first four miles with Jenny Agutter before the cheap champagne ruined the chat, her handbag and everything else. Then my mobile rang, which was very unprofessional. The first rule of TV is to turn your phone off when filming. There's a danger it can interfere with sound recording even if it doesn't go off, but if it rings, obviously it's disastrous. If that happens, the guilty party is fair game for a right old ribbing as they would have ruined the take.

While everyone was going over the top with their feigned disgust at my *faux pas*, I took the call. It was my brother Richard; he was with my dad who wanted to have a word. Dad sounded terrible and didn't mince his words. He was able to tell me to take care and that everything would be all right because I was a good lad. Suddenly Rich was back on the phone telling me he'd call again later, and hung up.

Dad died a few minutes after he spoke to me. He had been determined to say goodbye to all his sons. I knew he was ill and had visited him in hospital on the Isle of Wight, where my parents lived, but I had no idea how bad he was. He was seventy-five years old and had, according to the doctors, been living on borrowed time since his forties. They put this down to his experience in the Japanese POW camp when he had survived, amongst other things, black water fever, beri-beri, cerebral malaria, dysentery and jungle ulcers. Thank God I'd forgotten to switch my phone off. I couldn't imagine listening back to that 'missed call' after we'd finished filming.

It's funny, but there is some truth in the phrase that the show must go. In the face of adversity, I simply carried on. I flamboyantly switched my phone off for all to see, apologized for my unprofessional error and picked up where we left off, with no one the wiser. I don't think Dad was as concerned as Mum about what I was doing with my life; he somehow knew we'd all be OK. I wasn't in a position during that last call, the last time I ever spoke to him, to tell him things were going pretty well. Sure, I wasn't operating on people and saving lives as Ray was doing, and I couldn't put my hand up and say I'd played a part in any kid's education like Rich. I was just a jazz drummer who was currently arsing about on television in a big long car chatting to people with something to sell.

It's weird, bizarre and somehow reassuringly amusing that whenever I see Twiggy on the telly, seemingly on every other advert these days, I'm moved to think of my dad because on Wednesday, 1 October 1997, I spent the afternoon recording a great interview with Twiggy for ITV's *Good Stuff*, in the back of a big long car. The day my Dad died.

* * *

Buying your first proper house, one with its own front door, with a number on it without a letter appendage, not remotely shared and with no communal passage or areas, is a big day in anyone's book. The hoops you have to jump through to achieve it are lunatic, especially if you haven't done it before. I hadn't. Money has to be made available here, there and everywhere, things have to have arrived in certain places at just the right time, and to be honest I couldn't really get my head round it all. Things came to a pretty pass one Friday afternoon at about three-thirty, four o'clock.

Sitting opposite me in the back of the limo this time was long-lashed, cow-eyed seventies pop star, David Essex. My second girlfriend in the world was besotted with David, and I will always remember the feeling of inadequacy, sitting with her watching *Top of the Pops* when David slid on to the stage, with his curly-haired good looks and clean skin.

People had said that David didn't suffer fools gladly, so what the bloody hell I was doing interviewing him for that particular episode of *Good Stuff*, God only knows. I knew the current series producer wasn't my biggest fan – maybe he'd set it all up knowing David would 'lamp' me as soon as I started mucking about, or at least 'walk' halfway through the interview, so giving him good reason to hasten

my departure from the show. (Does that sound a little para-
noid?)

That morning I'd done my best to understand what the
various solicitors were on about over the phone. We were
in the final throes of buying a house and, foolishly, I'd
promised them that I'd be contactable on my mobile should
they need to get hold of me. When it came to the interview
that afternoon, I had still heard nothing from the solicitor,
and leaning heavily on the 'no news is good news' scenario,
I began to enjoy my time with David. I'd managed to find a
bit of common ground in as much as we had both spent
time drumming. He even showed me his drummer's 'muscle
lumps'. These appear on the back of your hand when you
squeeze your thumb and first finger together – they are
funny little muscles brought on by years of gripping drumsticks. I say 'little', but former Police drummer Stewart
Copeland has a massive pair of 'muscle lumps' on the back
of his gigantic hands. David and I were sporting a similar,
smaller pair that you could see when flexed, but which
didn't make you want to be sick when you suddenly spotted them. They were not like those of Stewart. Jesus.

As I'd promised the solicitor I'd be on the other end of
the phone, I made sure I left it switched on. But I gave it
to the driver, who was a decent enough distance from the
microphone I was wearing so as not to upset Pepperoni
Dave on sound. It was now about four-thirty on a Friday
afternoon and I'd forgotten all about the imminent house
purchase. I was also quietly relieved David had chosen not
to remember the last time I'd interviewed him, on Virgin
Radio's drive-time show, with Paul Coyte. During one of
the tracks, he simply got up and left the studio – within

seconds he'd vanished. We were never sure if he thought our chat had come to a natural end or he was sick to death of the pair of us bleating on about his 1980 film, the classic *Silver Dream Racer* – you know, the shit film about a motorbike.

Halfway through my interview in the back of the limo with David, Alan the driver held my phone up to the rear view mirror and waved it about, indicating I had a call. The glass partition between the driver and the seating meant the camera, sound and director were unaware my phone was ringing so didn't bollock me. Instead I brought the conversation to a natural pause and once Rupert Camera had uttered the words, 'Tape stop', I let everyone know my phone was ringing and said, 'I'll just be a minute, I'm buying a house.'

David was very amiable about it and sat there while I took the call. As I expected, it was the solicitor with the news that I was £10,000 short of the money to be delivered to the seller's solicitor's office. He went on to tell me that there would be a £1,000 per day charge for every day we were late with the payment. I looked at my watch – ten to five – then at David, then at the director, and then at my watch again. It was still ten to five on a bastard Friday. I needed to get ten grand over to the vendor's solicitor by five-thirty, otherwise I was looking at twelve grand by Monday, thirteen by Tuesday . . .

For a split second, I contemplated just coming straight out with it and asking David Essex if he could lend me ten big ones pretty much immediately. He wrote most of his hits, so he must have a few bob. I could take him to the nearest cashpoint and wait, praying the machine had notes bigger that just tens. I only had forty minutes. Having said that, 'Tahiti' from *Mutiny on the Bounty* was his last Top Ten hit, and that was about twelve years earlier. It is bad enough having your phone go off in the company of the guest you are interviewing; but asking them for a large amount of money as well – now that is totally unprofessional.

I came clean with everyone in the car, and told them I was just about to buy a house and I needed to make one more call. The crew took the opportunity to get out and stretch their legs, probably have a fag. David stayed put. I think he was deriving some perverse pleasure witnessing my predicament. Maybe he had totally recalled the *Silver Dream Racer* incident and was now enjoying sweet revenge.

I scrolled through the names and numbers I had stored on my phone, and as soon as I saw his initials, instinctively pressed 'call'. 'Please be in, please be in, please be . . . Hello, Jonathan, can you lend me £10,000? Now? Great, thanks! I'm a bit up against it. Can you call this number and organize a bike to get the cheque over to them by five-thirty? Brilliant! Thanks a lot, mate. Want to say hello to David Essex? Fair enough, bye!'

I didn't say that last bit about saying hello to David, but everything else is pretty much word for word. What a truly fantastic man Jonathan Ross is – and thank God he wasn't going under a tunnel when I rang. Jonathan got the money over to the solicitor just in time to save me thousands of pounds and ensure I could buy the house I am writing this in now.

With a brand new spring in my step, we finished off the chat with David Essex. As he was just about to get out of the limo, he leaned over and said, I think in jest, 'You couldn't give me your mate Jonathan's number, could you? I fancy giving him a ring later.'

22: A VIRGIN ON THE AIRWAVES

Alive in London was the drive-time show that launched Virgin Radio's new FM licence. The show, which ran from 10 April 1995 until 21 June 1996, was hosted by myself and Paul Coyte. How great is that? To meet up with someone you worked with years ago who happened to be a big fan of the popular Filofax diary . . . and what's more he kept the bastards, so was able to tell me exactly what we were doing and when! I can honestly say the time spent 'working' with Paul Coyte was one of the most enjoyable periods of my life. Like Jonathan and Jools, he was one of the few people who tolerated my jaundiced view of professionalism. I couldn't believe my eyes a few years back when I was watching the early rounds of the tennis at Wimbledon on TV and I saw Paul warming up on court number two, a lot taller than I remembered him – he was always a small man. Then his stats were flashed up on screen under the name Andy Murray. Dead ringers the pair of them, apart from the three-foot height difference and the fact that Paul liked a laugh.

Paul still works in radio today. He has a voice that was made for radio and you've got to hand it to him – he knows all the buttons, which way to push a fader and what the different coloured lights mean. It was when we were paired up, initially as an experiment, I think, to present Virgin Radio's irreverent Saturday morning *Big Red Mug Show* that his professionalism was tested to the max. He had to be 'on air' at 4 p.m. the day I caught up with him to reminisce, so lunch was to be a sober affair. Heaven forbid he should turn up for work shit-faced; he doesn't do it now, and he never did when we worked together.

It's always tricky going to a pub and not entertaining the idea of an alcoholic drink, but that's exactly what we did in the Crown and Two Chairmen. Well, that's exactly what he did in the Crown, which is a largish pub on the corner of Dean and Bateman Streets. Its great claim to fame? It's next door to the Sunset Strip Club. Sadly, it's recently undergone a facelift so the sign above the door saying 'Licensed To Thrill' in a James Bond-esque font is no longer there. It's not often you can say you have something in common with a strip club but at fifty-one I happen to be exactly the same age as London's favourite titty bar. Rik Mayall and I were once there and were told to shut up by the lady cavorting around on the little thrust stage; apparently our excitable childish banter was putting her off getting naked. Consumed with embarrassment, Rik produced a £20 note (he did that a lot) and tucked it under the elastic of her G string. Suddenly everyone was happy – we could have taken our own clothes off and I don't think 'The Mysterious Nikita' would have batted a false eyelash.

Of course, I have no idea what it's like now, but back then a bevy of beauties would take it in turns to perform to one song each in front of a motley few rows of old blokes who hid behind broadsheet newspapers until they heard the mechanical whirring sound of the electric curtains slowly drawing open. In unison, the papers would be lowered and, in reverential silence, they would take in the next three-minute 'show'. Even before the curtains had drawn to a close and the woman had picked up what few clothes she originally had on, the newspapers would already be back in place for fear of any eye-contact with one's fellow man.

Before Paul Coyte and I teamed up, I'd done the show for a year or so with Paul Ross. As both he and I had no idea or interest in how the 'desk' (the conduit between us and the listener) was run, an engineer was required, making the show slightly over-staffed and labour intensive. The fragrant Carol McGiffin was also there producing. I do remember her regularly 'producing' about four or five girly mates each Saturday morning; they'd obviously crashed at Carol's the night before, all seeming as hung-over as each other. And what with the state I was usually in, it was a blessing motormouth Paul Ross was there to drive the whole thing along. The engineer would be up the corridor in the live studio running the desk, and Paul and I would be on mics in the bar area, which they called the 'zoo' for some inexplicable reason. There would be half a dozen small round tables dotted about full of punters plied with free cans of lager – at nine in the morning. This made up our small but intimate 'live' audience that gave the show a certain frisson and kept us on our toes.

To this day Paul Ross and I fondly recount the time Herbert Lom, the internationally renowned Czech film actor, best known for his role as put-upon Chief Inspector Charles Dreyfus in the Pink Panther films, showed up as a guest. He was a very quiet, unassuming man who arrived first thing on Saturday morning on his own and slipped into the 'zoo' area unannounced. Carol was enjoying her first 'hair of the dog' lager, and I was talking to her about something when I saw, over her shoulder, Herbert approaching. She must have taken a particularly large gulp of beer and I must have said something that amused (a déjà vu Paula Yates milk moment) or surprised her – something like 'Fuck me, here comes Herbert Lom!'

Surprised or amused, we'll never know, but she turned round and in a kamikaze career move, sprayed a mouthful of lager all over poor Herbert. Carol's quite tall and Herbert wasn't a big man, so she was able to completely cover his bald head with the second-hand lager. It ran all down his head and face, dripping off his ears and nose. It was as if he was still in character as the put-upon Chief Inspector. He was surprisingly good about it, producing an immaculate white cotton handkerchief and cleaning himself up, as if this happened all the time. I think we have to count our blessings Steven Berkoff wasn't due to appear on the show that day.

Eventually, Paul Coyte was brought in and Paul Ross moved on. This meant the show could be broadcast from the live studio with Paul running the desk. Suddenly it was just Paul and I with three hours to fill on a Saturday morning. 'When it was great, it was really great. When it was bad, it was shocking. We did several pilot shows, and each one was a different disaster,' recalls Paul about our early joint attempts. The *Big Red Mug Show* was a shambolic affair, to say the least. In their belt-tightening operation, Virgin managed to get rid of not only the engineer, but the audience and pretty much all the guests. One way of solving the last problem was by leaning on my good friend John

Thomson of *The Fast Show* fame, usually via the phone although he did come in one week when we had absolutely no guests. That time, he insisted on doing the whole show as 'special guest – Tommy Vance!' and fooled everyone. It's amazing just how easy it was to dupe the audience. I'm not implying they were thick; it's just that John's impressions were so good. Each week John would invite us to phone 'Christopher Walken and his good friend Joe Pesci'. They were supposedly sharing a grotty hotel room in Paddington, and eager to do some sightseeing. We'd ask them how they were finding the city and what they were up to. People would ring up demanding to know which hotel they were staying at. Amazing.

The experiment with Paul and I must have worked as it wasn't long before we were offered the drive-time slot five days a week. We were to replace 'Little' Nicky Horne as he liked to be known. We initially billed ourselves as 'Massive' Paul and Rowland, but were quickly told to 'stop doing that' and to 'take the whole thing seriously'. Which was impossible. But God knows we tried.

'Hi, my name's Sally Field. I was in *The Flying Nun*, Paul and Rowland's favourite programme about nuns. You're listening to Virgin Radio' – *Sally Field*

Our daily pre-show routine would involve an hour or so's table tennis in the boardroom adjacent to the bar area. Paul had the same childish streak as me and, because he was the consummate professional and knew exactly what he was doing on air, he was fine about acting the giddy goat with me up until showtime. The partition wall was glass but, as and when, blinds could be deployed for maximum privacy. We'd work out all the intros to the different items and the order they went in, jot it down on a scrap of paper, highlight who was saying what and that was about it, prep for the show done. We did get really good at table tennis.

At any opportunity, we'd head off to the junkets that were always occurring around town. As in the *Good Stuff* days, these would always involve a famous person promoting something, holed up in a swanky hotel suite. We would always try and bring something fresh to the short interview we'd be granted. Diana Ross, for instance, had installed herself in a huge suite at the Ritz Hotel and was talking to anyone who would listen about her latest record, her 1995 album *Take Me Higher*. Frustratingly, all I can remember about the album is that it included a picture of Diana, aged about four, sitting in a bucket. Ring any bells? Thinking about it, what a brilliant way to sell yourself – by the bucket-full. Even as a kid, she was way ahead of her time.

Ms Ross had just opened the 1994 football World Cup, as it was being hosted by the United States that year. She was asked to sing a song on the pitch and then strut up to a ball on the penalty spot and kick it into the goal, which would explode apart – all very visual and beautifully choreographed. The song was good, she can hold a tune I'll admit, but the spot kick wasn't, and it was clear, even to me, that she didn't possess natural ball skills. She missed the goal by a mile, in fact, which was a shame. Rather than talk about her album – she was probably sick of spouting the same old PR nonsense anyway, and, to be honest, we had better ways of spending our time – it was decided we should record her having another crack at that penalty shot.

Paul opened with: 'Miss Ross, the album's great, but before we go any further, we'd just like to clear something up.'

Talk about a game old diva. Her suite was about the size of a five-a-side pitch, and she enthusiastically lent a hand moving the furniture about so we could erect a goal at one end. Paul's an avid Spurs fan, so he knows a fair bit about football. I, on the other hand, see the whole thing as a bunch of men in shorts running around, so am not as well versed in the finer points. Paul was keen to fill her in on the psychology of penalty-taking and the best way to curve a ball. I was more worried about how much her shoes cost and whether I could get away with calling room service to have a pair of football boots sent up. I liked the idea of charging a pair of top-of-the-range Adidas X Predators to Diana's record label, Motown. Her first attempt ricocheted around the room and ended up under a Louis XV chaise-longue.

Paul quickly spotted where she was going wrong; apparently, she was punting the ball with her toe and not using the inside or the outside top edge of the foot, where more accuracy could always be assured. Once she got the hang of it, there was no stopping her. We spent the rest of our allocated fifteen minutes with our new best friend Di trying to master the David Beckham bending free kick. At full time, the interview over, we thanked her and told her to work on her spot kicks. The last thing we heard her say as we were all ushered out of her suite was: 'Thanks, boys. You will mention the album, won't you?'

'Hi, my name's Danny DeVito. I was in *Taxi*, Paul and Rowland's favourite programme about taxis. You're listening to Virgin Radio' – *Danny DeVito*

So, Diana Ross got to score a goal. Paul and I got a cracking interview, and I think the album did quite well too. So everyone was happy. It's not rocket science. Talking of which, another time . . .

Tom 'I'm sorry but we're heading into name-dropping overdrive here' Hanks was over promoting the film *Apollo 13*. So on our way to the Dorchester, his hotel of choice when staying in London, we popped into Hamleys toy shop on Regent Street and purchased the classic, massive, Apollo Saturn V Airfix model rocket. Despite being set in space, Tom's latest offering was, we felt, a tad claustrophobic and to be perfectly honest a bit boring. So making the model together would, for us, throw the focus nicely. Tom was completely made up – he loved it! We were like three kids, fighting over who got to do what. At one point, Tom mentioned he was keen to put the 'decals' on; we had no idea what he was on about but, hey, he was Tom Hanks, so we let it go.

We came away with a gorgeous interview, not about the film, but about Tom Hanks and what he got up to as a kid, all thanks to the Airfix model. The boss man at Virgin went ballistic when he heard a rough edit of the interview, claiming we didn't come back with anything we were supposed to get. We didn't mention the film and we overlooked the fact that the premiere was happening that night, a missed opportunity in his eyes. We did manage to pull it out of the fire live on air, though. Paul used to do a late-night show at Virgin and would phone well-known people in the States for a chat, so over the years he had amassed quite an impressive celebrity phone book. One entry was Ron Howard, who played the slightly wet guy – because he was the only one who seemed to be still living with his parents – in the American TV show, *Happy Days*. He also happened to be the man who directed Tom Hanks in *Apollo 13*. Perfect! *Alive in London* went out at the same time that the *Apollo 13* premiere would be kicking off.

Paul dialled Ron's number live on air, and the great man answered the call while he was actually walking up the red carpet. God knows what possessed us to do what we did next, but we did it. We told him that all he had to do to win a basketball signed by some of the Harlem Globetrotters – this was true, a couple of them had been in earlier in the week and left it – was whistle their theme tune. And he did! He whistled the Harlem Globetrotters theme tune, down the phone, while walking up the red carpet to the premiere of his own film. What a great guy. I could just imagine Ron, in the cinema, sitting down next to Tom and saying, '. . . the darndest things just happened, Tom. I've just whistled the Globetrotters theme tune down the phone to a couple of guys on a radio station and won a basketball,' and Tom coming straight back with, 'That'll be Paul and Rowland. They let me put the decals on a plastic rocket we made this afternoon.'

'Hello, my name's Sean Bean. I was in *Lady Chatterley's Lover*, Paul and Rowland's favourite sexy film programme. You're listening to Virgin Radio' – *Sean Bean*

The big problem with a job that doesn't kick off until late afternoon means that unless you are incredibly motivated, you end up pissing the day away. Turning up at the Virgin studios in Golden Square refreshed after a long lunch became the norm after a while, which wasn't a good thing. At the time, of course, it was fantastic, but every now and then it got a bit out of hand. Paul would know he'd be dealing with a handful if word got to him that I'd been buying stupid presents, chocolate coffee beans and the like, for everyone. I once interviewed a chap about a book he'd written on the devil. It was a bit of an odd one – his answers weren't that forthcoming – but I persevered and after the four minutes were up, thanked him and moved on. I later discovered the poor guy had come in to sing a song. I hadn't really noticed the guitar he was carrying, and I think he must have been a little shy as he never once questioned what I was going on about, but just made valiant attempts to answer my queries about the evil one. Paul must have thought I had a master plan regarding the interview so kept shtoom – but there was no master plan. It got very confusing when the bloke who had written the devil book showed up and wanted to talk about it. By then, of course, for me the moment had passed. Perhaps we should have asked him to sing a song.

Paul knew the studio and how to work it like the back of his hand. Unfortunately, I also knew it like the back of Paul's hand – I had no idea how any of it worked. One thing we were both completely in the dark about was the state-of-the-art portable recording equipment we'd be given to do the interviews away from the studio. Each week the machine seemed to get smaller and smaller and stupidly more technical and beyond us. What are people trying to prove? Look at mobile phones, it's all gone mad. If you want to make a call, use a telephone; if you want to take a picture, use a bloody camera. I realize I'm sounding like a bit of a Luddite, but come on, it's not as if people's fingers are getting smaller and smaller or our eyesight's gradually becoming superhuman. I bet you a pound to a penny the head of Sony doesn't even know his way round a TCD-D10 portable DAT tape recorder. Nobody does – we certainly didn't. Even if you did manage to get your head round the basics, you just knew the TCD-D11 would appear any second making the TCD-D10 obsolete and dragging you right back to square one.

It was with yet another brand new bit of equipment, still boxed, that we headed over to the Union Club on Greek Street in Soho for a chat with dashing actor, Sam Neill. We were hoping against hope we'd get there before him so we could get our heads round the new bit of kit, but it wasn't to be. As it happened, arriving with a large cardboard box as if we'd come straight from an audio shop in Tottenham Court Road, didn't put him at ease. What didn't help was that for some reason he was wearing, indoors mind, one of those huge Australian Driza-Bone waxed cotton raincoats which made him look even more scary. He was sitting there in a big, padded winged armchair; it was as if we'd come to seek an audience with the devil.

In front of a stony-faced Sam, we unpacked the recording equipment and attempted to get the whole thing up and running as quickly as possible. You could see his shoulders fall as we scanned the instruction manual and nervously began pressing buttons to no avail. Paul and I started to get very hot – we always did in these situations – and, what with my nervous giggling, we really weren't making a good impression. As the machine was 'box fresh', its rechargeable batteries were fully . . . un-recharged. We considered asking Mr Neill if he had any batteries on him, but quickly thought better of it. The only thing to do was use the mains adaptor, which nobody liked doing as having a little portable recording machine tethered to the wall by a big chunky mains lead never looked very professional.

This very conveniently threw up our next problem; it didn't look like Sam was sitting anywhere near a wall socket and he was looking really comfy (if a little scary) where he was.

Deep breath.

'Sam, can we move you nearer to a wall socket? Please?' He gave us a withering look and pointed to a double wall socket we hadn't spotted. We scurried over to it.

We finally got the machine up and running, or so we thought, but unfortunately something still wasn't quite right. No amount of blowing into and thumping the microphone would get the minute record needle flickering. At this point Sam snapped, became very animated and shouted, 'Damn fools, give it to me!' God knows how, but he got it going and we managed to get the interview done. Not the best we've done, but it went out and everyone was happy. Obviously, I'm not including Sam when I say 'everyone' and Paul and I were only quite happy.

Very hot, but quite happy.

23: HOLIDAY TROUBLE

This was a nutty period of my life. I had to put my hand up to being a jack of all trades and master of none. I had moved from one Virgin to another. I went from hosting a show on Virgin Radio to being the face of Virgin Atlantic's array of 'destination films' for two or three years. From jazz drumming to comedy to DJing to travelogues; it had been quite a trip – and certainly not always in first class.

But this time I *was* travelling in style. The Virgin Atlantic gig was one of the jammiest of my career. It meant flying in some style to the most exotic destinations in the world to make films about those locations for the airline. However, there was a downside. A crew and I would head off to distant destinations with great frequency, but we rarely spent much time in those far-flung places. For instance, we once flew to Tokyo, did a four-hour shoot there, and then jumped straight on to the plane back. On another occasion, we filmed a sneak preview of the Upper Class Lounge at JFK Airport, New York, in a couple of hours and then went straight home – we didn't even need to go through passport control.

It was at this time that I realized that I'd done quite a few things similar to my father. He'd earned money playing an instrument and flying around the world. So, I just had the four years in a POW camp to look forward to . . .

My mad time at Virgin Atlantic culminated in the holiday from hell. I suppose there's nothing more entertaining than hearing tales of other people's travel disasters, so here goes. The family and I had an opportunity to go to Disneyworld in Orlando for a week. I'd been away a lot, filming, so we were really looking forward to a lovely family holiday. A peaceful, idyllic week together – what could possibly go wrong?

I'd accrued a lot of air miles working for Virgin Atlantic, so I was able to get four business-class tickets for Mon, Dan, Ella and me. The children couldn't wait for it. I had a pass to the brand new First Class Lounge at Heathrow – it was to be pampering all the way. In Florida, we'd booked a very expensive and gorgeous apartment within Disneyworld. It was called the Wilderness Lodge and was constructed like a log cabin.

Virgin Atlantic even sent a limo for us – so the wonderful, relaxing holiday started at our front door. We got to the airport in very good time at 9 a.m. and were immediately directed in to the fast-track lane.

'Mr Rivron,' the woman at the check-in desk soothed, 'there is a note here to say that you're going to be upgraded, we have four seats in Upper Class.' Mon and I looked on in stunned silence as she tagged our bags with the shiny red and gold labels. It's difficult to describe the feeling when that happens, suddenly the world's a beautiful place. We were only going for a week's holiday, but what better way to start. I presented our two passports with a 'we're upper class' flourish. Then it happened.

'Er, excuse me, Mrs Rivron,' said the check-in woman, 'your passport is two months out of date. I'm afraid you and your children can't travel on this passport. Yours is fine, Mr Rivron.'

At first, we weren't that panicked, as we thought there was bound to be a passport office at Heathrow because this sort of thing must happen quite a lot. How wrong can you be? 'No,' the check-in staff told us. 'The nearest passport office to Heathrow is Petty France in Victoria, London.' Dan and Ella, who were four and three at the time, were blissfully unaware quite how much shit was hitting the fan: 'Are we getting on the plane to see Mickey and Minnie Mouse now, Daddy?'

'In a little while, dear, we just have to pop and get something.'

The woman at the desk seemed fairly sure we could get to the passport office and back in time for another flight that left at two o'clock. This can't be too bad, I thought, just stay calm.

'OK,' I replied, 'we'll jump in a cab, go get a passport and be back in a couple of hours.' Stay calm, it's going to be fine. 'Can we leave our bags with you at the desk while we sort this out?' I politely enquired.

'No, sir, you'll have to take them with you,' came the equally polite reply.

'Oh fucking hell! Jesus fucking Christ!! Do you mean to tell me we've got to schlep all these sodding bags round with us?' There wasn't much conversation in the cab on our way into town and I think the kids began to sense there was something not quite right about our trip to Disneyland. They stopped asking why we weren't getting on the plane and changed the line of enquiry to, 'When we do get there, Daddy, can we go swimming?' Bless 'em.

We finally arrived at Petty France to discover there had been a passport staff strike, so the place was heaving. The kids and I carried the bags in while Mon legged it up the road to a train station we'd passed and noticed had a 'do-it-yourself' passport photo booth. I was appearing on BBC1's *Holiday* programme a lot at the time and it got quite a big audience, not least because it was on just before *EastEnders*. The upshot was that every so often someone would approach me as I was anxiously pacing up and down, oblivious to our predicament, and harmlessly ask for an autograph. Although flattered, now really wasn't the time but through a pained smile I obliged. When we finally reached the head of the queue Monica handed over the new picture of herself, looking a little stressed and the £17.50 for the new passport. It was only eleven-thirty; we were making good time for the two o'clock flight. Then the lady behind the glass at the counter, who was also a keen BBC *Holiday* viewer, calmly informed us, 'Your children have to have their own passports now, they can no longer be on their mother's passport. We can do that here, you just need the kids' birth certificates and their photos signed by a priest, a teacher or a solicitor.'

I stared at the woman, then stared at my watch and stared at the woman again. 'When I got up this morning we were going on holiday. Now you want me to track down a priest, get a bunch of photos taken of my kids and find some birth certificates.' Monica dragged me away from the counter before the swearing started and we all made our way on to the street for some much needed fresh air. Before we knew it we were in a cab weaving our way home, back up to Muswell Hill. Mon felt sure she knew where the birth certificates were so legged it into the house while I did my best to explain to the lady across the road, who had waved us off that morning, why we weren't 35,000 feet over the Atlantic. After a quick stop at the photo booth in Woolworths in the high street we called in on our local priest only to be told by the housekeeper that he was away at a conference, somewhere in Victoria just round the corner from Petty France as it happened. We then phoned the solicitor who'd recently helped us with our house sale but he was, successfully, on holiday.

With the possibility of catching the two o'clock flight ebbing away and my desperation mounting by the minute, I phoned Addison Cresswell, my agent. He told us to go to his solicitor's off Fleet Street. He said, 'She's never met you, but I'll tell her you're looking in, it'll be fine.' From Fleet Street we headed back to Petty France, the fare for the black cab was now getting on for £100. The old boy at the wheel was very supportive though, he kept saying, 'You can do this, it'll work, I'll get you there.' It's amazing how, with the slightest amount of encouragement from a complete stranger, you can convince yourself it's going to work. The one genius moment I'd had in the whole day was taking a ticket for the queue on leaving Petty France the first time. We had number 326, and when we got back there, they were seeing number 312. Despite this scintilla of good fortune there was no way we were going to get out to Heathrow in time for the second Virgin flight to Orlando.

I phoned the people at Virgin Atlantic and, rather cheekily, explained the situation: 'I had four upper-class tickets,'

I didn't let on they were upgrades, 'for a flight we missed this morning.' Glancing forlornly at the upper-class tags that were still attached to our luggage, I enquired, 'Could I change them for similar seats on tomorrow's flight?'

'You could if there were any available. The plane's full unfortunately,' came the far from helpful but fairly predictable reply. Then she more than redeemed herself. 'What about the Miami flight? When you get there rent a car and drive up to Orlando.' Suddenly there was a small pinprick of light at the end of the hellish tunnel. 'It leaves from Gatwick first thing tomorrow and it looks like there's a few seats left.' I quickly relayed the news to Mon and for the first time that day a smile broke out across her face. As I smiled back at Mon the woman on the phone informed me there was only availability in upper class. There wasn't enough time to process the air miles so with a frozen grin on my face I purchased fourteen-hundred quid's worth of upper-class tickets.

'Kids!' I screamed. 'Leave those luggage tags right where they are!'

We had to book a hotel in Gatwick for the night because of the absurdly early time we had to check in and I really couldn't face going home *again*. The holiday was back on track, we'd lost a day-and-a-half but that wasn't too bad. To be honest three or four days submerged in the Disney experience is enough to satisfy most people and we were looking at five.

And sure enough, within a few days we were all in holiday mode. I wasn't even letting the way you haemorrhage money whenever you're anywhere near 'the Mouse' affect me; in the back of my mind I knew I had a well paid 'gig' on the very day we got home. It was at the Comedy Store, interviewing a dozen or so comedians for a series on Channel Four. I wasn't due there until 3 p.m. so I had time to get home with Mon and the kids, have a quick shower and head into town. Perfect.

'There's a little delay on your flight,' the Virgin staff said. It was 4 p.m., and we thought we'd be off in a couple of hours. But eight o'clock came and went, and the staff were all looking very nervous – they told us there was a 'technical hitch' they needed to sort out. Eventually, at 10 p.m., we started trooping on to the plane. I was slightly concerned about the knock-on effect this would have at the other end and my commitments.

'Don't worry,' the smiley stewardess said, 'we can make up the time en route.'

As with our cab driver in London, complete strangers have an ability to put your mind at ease in a way people you know well can't. I still wasn't utterly panicking. I thought, 'Oh well, I can just go straight from the airport to the Comedy Store, if necessary.' Two hours out of Orlando, people were starting to get nicely settled. We'd had 'a couple' of drinks, the kids were in their pyjamas and were preparing to bed down for the night. With Mon and the kids fast asleep I managed to talk the stewardess into letting me have a couple of half-bottles to save me from keeping on disturbing her as it was late. As reading lights around the cabin gradually went out, I sat there thinking, 'Phew, I'll just about be able to pull this holiday off. Bit pricey but we're still all talking to each other, that's a result in my book.'

It must have been more of a shock for Mon as she was

shaken awake from a deep sleep. I hadn't dropped off so had noticed the gradual commotion building amongst the cabin crew. Suddenly, a voice came on the plane's PA and announced: 'Sorry to disturb you, ladies and gentlemen, but the captain has asked me to tell you that due to a problem with one of the engines he's requested they open JFK airport for us where we will be landing shortly.'

No, I didn't realize the airport closed at night either. Monica's a panicky flyer at the best of times and this news didn't go down well. I've been on planes when there's been a bit of engine failure and the crew always took it in their stride. It wasn't like that on this flight, there was far too much rushing about. Panic gave way to despair when, just as we were about to hit the runway at JFK, all you could see out of the plane's windows were fire engines, loads of them, with their red lights flashing away as they hurtled along at the same speed as the plane. The kids loved it . . .

When we ground to a halt, a load of suits came on board and told us: 'Because there's no passport control open at this time of night, nobody can disembark. We'll bring another plane alongside this one, so you can transfer straight on to it.'

It was getting later and later and my Comedy Store interviews were looking more and more under threat, and because I was trapped in a plane the whole time, I couldn't even phone Addison to keep him up to speed with events and tell him it didn't look like I was going to make it.

Dan was awake and taking it all in. 'Dad, if we're in New York, can we go and look for Spiderman?'

I took a deep breath, finished the last dregs of the second half-bottle of red straight from the neck, checked the time again, and said, 'I don't see why not, son. Let's go and ask the captain.'

We landed at Heathrow just after 3 p.m. and finally got through customs and baggage reclaim around 4.30 p.m. My mobile phone lit up with twenty increasingly furious messages from my agent. Unbeknown to me, it had been John Thomson's fortieth birthday party the night before – he had hired a boat for a piss-up down the Thames. My agent assumed I'd got hammered with John and was still passed out in Greenwich. When I did get to speak with Addison he was so wound up, he still wouldn't have any of it. I then drew his attention to a news report of a Virgin plane making an emergency landing in the middle of the night at JFK Airport after three – that's THREE – of the four engines had failed, but it was too late, the damage had been done. I didn't get paid, and as everyone knows, a 'no show' is a 'no show'. It really doesn't matter what the reason is, you'll be forever known as the bloke who didn't turn up. Bloody holidays.

24: BACK TO REALITY

In the last ten years reality TV has arrived and, like a horrible virus, slowly seeped into every aspect of the medium. In most people's opinion, it has dragged television kicking and screaming downmarket. More recently, wherever there's a reality show, there's invariably a celebrity version sniffing around, eager to steal its thunder. Rather than come up with original programmes for performers and entertainers to appear in, broadcasters have opted for hijacking established shows with motley crews of 'celebs'. A crass and unforgivable approach to making television, to be sure – unless, of course, you are taking part. I'm ashamed to say I've taken part in more than my fair share.

It was 2006 and I had completely missed the first two series of *Come Dine with Me*, so I had no idea what the woman was on about at the other end of the phone. 'We'll be round, there's about ten of us, at about eight, eight-thirty in the morning, have a look at the house and do a quick chat on camera – it'll be how you're feeling, what you're going to cook, that sort of thing. Then we'll film you shopping for all your ingredients, and in the afternoon we'll set up the kitchen and dining room, cover you preparing the meal and the house, then everyone will arrive and you'll present the meal. We'll cover that, the guests will have a mooch round the house and make comments. Then, lastly, the other diners will take it in turns to score your meal out of ten. We should be finished by no later than eleven-thirty.' Great, so just a fifteen-hour day, then – heck, why do in two days what you can, really uncomfortably, just about shoehorn into one? Welcome to television in the twenty-first century.

The whole thing was made slightly worse, but in hindsight better, by the fact I was to be the first to create a meal for my four other 'celebrities'. There was 'Challenge' Anneka Rice, 'journalist' Toby Young, 'How Clean Is' Aggie MacKenzie, and the 'Bird of a Feather' Linda Robson.

Shitting myself wouldn't be overstating it. I had no idea what I was doing but, thankfully, Mon pointed me in the right direction, namely page seventy-six of Nigel Slater's *Real Food* cookery book and his twenty-year-old recipe for 'Coq au riesling' which was basically 'Coq au vin' with knobs on from what I could see.

The programme started with the best intentions and ended, gone midnight, with me trying to get everyone to play an old and favourite drinking game of mine which involves lifting the dining table at one end and seeing whose wine glass falls off it first. Aggie's face was a picture. Not really a game when you're sober, but hilarious when you're hammered, and I'm fairly sure we all were.

The one flaw with our series was that the dinners happened on consecutive nights. After the second or third show, we had all run out of conversation and pretty much the will to eat. So we retreated into the better and better bottles of fine wine the hosts were providing in an attempt to outdo the previous soirée. Things came to a head at Anneka's beautiful Thames-side house in Barnes.

I *think* it was paella and I *think* it was fantastic. After the meal I suggested that, for old time's sake, it would be great to see Anneka in one of the *Challenge Anneka* trademark lycra jumpsuits. She had mentioned, over cocktails when I arrived, that they were all upstairs in her wardrobe and what's more, 'They still fit me perfectly!' She said she would do it, but not alone, someone else had to climb into one, too. Aggie maintained she would have trouble filling a lycra jumpsuit, Toby made his excuses and disappeared to the loo, and Linda flatly refused, commenting, 'I'm a bit pissed and afraid I might rip the arse out of it.'

Anneka was right, she did still look great in her bright yellow one-piece. 'Very *Kill Bill*,' observed a beaming Aggie. I really didn't look great in the mauve one Anneka had picked out for me. With its lycra properties valiantly performing to maximum capacity, I looked a twat. Toby made an observation I've chosen to forget, and Linda, too embarrassed, couldn't bring herself to look at me; the jump-suit was leaving nothing to the imagination. The scoring for the show takes place in the black cab the guests take home, and I think it was Toby who put the cat amongst the pigeons by daring me to try and hail one outside Anneka's.

I sauntered out into the night followed by the camera crew. It was freezing and the cold night air filling my lungs suddenly brought home to me just how arseholed I really was. I was sure a bit of fresh air would have the opposite effect, clear my head, but not a bit of it. I stood at the side of the road and then in the middle of it, wolf whistling as loudly as I could at any car that passed. Suddenly, from behind me, I heard someone tapping on a window. It was Anneka's neighbour, twitching behind a bit of net curtain. She seemed quite perturbed. I gave her a friendly wave, ambled over and mouthed to her that I was trying to get a cab and did she have any numbers, at which point she quickly pulled her heavy drape curtains closed. The black cab that had been booked and was waiting round the corner then appeared while I was happily dancing in and out of the traffic. I spotted it, waved it down and flamboyantly jumped in.

I'd actually done my scoring of Anneka's food – easily an eight – returned the jumpsuit, intact, and was well on my way home when the police, lights flashing, finally arrived at her door, so I missed all the excitement: two police cars and a van apparently, and there was even talk of blocking the road off. Anneka also told me the biggest bunch of flowers were sent round to 'Mrs Twitchy Net Curtain' in an attempt to placate the poor woman and build some neighbourly bridges.

* * *

'And coming up at ten-thirty on Channel Four, *Extreme Celebrity Detox* where we catch up with *Rough Guide* reporter Magenta Devine, *Loaded* magazine publisher James Brown, presenter Lisa I'Anson and, er, Rowland Rivron stuck up a Himalayan mountain quite literally shitting themselves at a yogic detox retreat.'

And it bloody worked! The process, apart from the yoga, involved drinking your own wee, projectile vomiting gallons of warm water daily, flossing your nose, and finally drinking too much salt water and waiting for the world to fall out of your bottom. I know you want to try only one of the above, so here's how it's done. The trick with the morning glass of widdle is to catch it mid-flow and it must be the first piss of the day. Then don't hang around – it has to be knocked back warm and fresh as it begins to ferment fairly swiftly. Well, mine did, anyway.

The Hindu elders who were looking after us explained that we would be restored to a blank canvas and we'd have to gently reintroduce things to which our bodies had built up tolerance. They performed this procedure on themselves twice a year which probably went a long way to accounting for them looking forty but being in their sixties.

We took their word for it and, amazingly, when we got back to the hotel in Delhi after ten days living on pulses, beans and warm water, I took one largish swig of red wine at dinner and was instantaneously pissed, even to the point of slurring my words. Before I went to India, on a good day, I could polish off four bottles of wine and still conduct a conversation, and here I was unable to accept a top-up. In the past, whenever being poured wine and asked by the host or waiter to 'say when', I would always reply, 'Next Tuesday, thanks,' such was my constitution, but ten days up a mountain and I couldn't handle *one* glass. I'd also lost two stone, the whites of my eyes had returned, my skin looked fantastic and I was addicted to yoga – I was a mess.

I did witness one truly amazing spectacle while in India. Part of our voyage back to civilization involved a seven-hour journey in a beaten-up old jeep they laughingly referred to as a cab. James had made arrangements to travel by train – he obviously knew something I didn't. So it would be Magenta, Lisa and myself putting our lives in the hands of a driver who, when it got dark, would only turn the lights on if he saw another car coming towards him – he was convinced the battery would run flat otherwise.

I sat in the front and spent several minutes explaining to our driver the role of the dynamo in a car, while Magenta and Lisa sat in the back and chatted, seamlessly, for SEVEN HOURS!!! And, no, there wasn't a bloody radio in the sodding car. Think about it: it would have put far too much strain on the battery.

I'm quietly proud of the fact I've never turned down any offers of work – I came close once. Addison tried to talk me out of hosting a New Year's Eve show as it was on the Playboy Channel, which he thought wasn't a good 'product' to be associated with. At the time, I was already sitting at my computer checking out just what the Playboy Channel had to offer – so I told him I was on a mobile, he was breaking up and anyway I was going into a tunnel.

When I got a call asking if I fancied appearing on *Celebrity Masterchef* and could I cook, I said, 'Yes, I'd love to and, yes, of course I can cook,' which I can't. I honestly thought that as it was a 'celeb' version of the show, it wouldn't be taking itself too seriously. Wrong.

What a lovely, jolly man Gregg Wallace is. He's the bald presenter of the show with a good line in slightly filthy jokes. John Torode, his Aussie counterpart, is a different kettle of kangaroos. He approached me shortly after I arrived at the studios, introduced himself and then said, 'So Rowland, you're a bit of a funny man so I hear?'

His headmaster approach put me on the back foot. 'Well, now and again,' I replied, piling on the humility.

John then took one step towards me, so we were now far too close to each other and, with our noses nearly touching, said, in a spell-it-out way, 'Well, don't fuck with the food.'

I offered a hollow smile, and he just turned and walked away. There and then would have been the best time to come clean and confess to not being able to cook but he was gone. I thought, 'OK, the pressure's on, might be a struggle to get a laugh round here.'

The atmosphere wasn't to last, as the two people I was up against entered the room – comedienne Helen Lederer and weatherman Ian McCaskill. I don't think John did the 'sweary headmaster' bit with Helen – that would have got her into even more of a tizz than she usually is. As it turned out, we did have a laugh and not at the food's expense. Ian came across as a Mister Magoo character, often facing in the wrong direction or wandering around in the background when John and Gregg were doing their thing. I think poor Ian was slightly out of sorts due to the accident with his mobile phone.

He was in the make-up room having a black eye concealed – like you do – and it was taking a little time. So he'd removed his huge, ancient brick of a phone from his pocket and propped it against the mirror in front of him. The make-up artist must have brushed against the phone, accidentally, as it became propped against the first of the light bulbs that ran round the mirror. When Ian took off the smock everyone wears when they're being made up, he must have absentmindedly placed it over his phone and left for the studio along with everyone else. During the two or three hours we were all in the studio, Ian's phone had moulded itself round the hot light bulb.

The light bulb was carefully removed from its socket, but the phone remained firmly attached. It was obvious Ian wouldn't be making any more calls with that mobile. He sat cradling his phone in disbelief, turning over in his mind the chain of events that had led to this catastrophe. The producer was very apologetic and dispatched a runner to go and buy a brand new phone immediately.

Helen and I sat with Ian during lunch, commiserating as best we could. We learned that it was the only mobile phone he'd ever owned; he'd had it four or five years and it had never let him down. As he was reminiscing, the runner arrived with his new mobile. It was a state-of-the-art affair, about the size of a cigarette lighter, but we could all see he wasn't a happy man. The runner chipped in with, 'It's got a camera, Ian, a radio, Bluetooth, I think it's an MP3 player as well.' Ian thanked him, smiled the sort of smile that says 'What's the bloody point?' and carefully placed it back in the box.

* * *

'And this Saturday at eight o'clock it's a special *Celebrity Total Wipeout*, which sees a bunch of Olympic medallists itching to expand their TV profile and appear far from past their prime, compete alongside Margi Clarke, Cheryl Baker and Rowland Rivron.'

What a nightmare and, try as I might, I was unable to find *one* British Standards Kitemark on any of the equipment we were told to throw ourselves about on.

'Or over on Channel Five, *Celebrity Holiday Reps*. Follow DJ Brandon Block and, er, Rowland Rivron as they either drink far too much or mercilessly rip the piss out of surprise holiday rep, Paul Burrell, and find they are . . .'
Stop! Stop!! Stop!!!

EPILOGUE:
THE ACCIDENTAL COMEDIAN

Comedy chose me – I didn't choose it. My career happened to me almost by accident. While I was experiencing my Adrian Mole crisis of faith about my drumming, the situation was softened by the 300 people I was warming up for Ruby Wax, with a degree of success – hey, I wasn't sacked. I didn't have a joke in my body, but people were still laughing. Something must have been working.

I'd lost my love for drumming. As I left my very expensive 9-ply Sonor drum kit and mint-condition Zildjian cymbals in the forest wilderness of jazz music, the kestrel of comedy was there to swoop down and gently grasp me in its talons, soar into the sky and drop me carefully in the comforting nest of televisual Light Entertainment. Sorry, that won't happen again: I'm obviously out of my depth with metaphors. I'll leave that to the French feller with the football. Anyway, Light Entertainment was a soothing place – executive lifts, apart. Getting your knob caught anywhere for comic effect is not clever and it's not funny – all right, it was quite funny.

Even though I stumbled on to my current career path quite by chance, I haven't got a bad word to say about it, although get back to me when the work dries up – I might have a different answer. A lot of people in entertainment use the word 'career' – that makes it sound more planned than it was with me. I saw it much more as a series of opportunities that it would have been foolish to ignore. There is much to be said for being in the right place at the right time, and as long as you've got the balls, you'd be mad not to give it a go. Obviously, you'll need your all-purpose get-out clause – as I've mentioned, I've already nabbed 'You know, I'm actually a jazz drummer.' Then, the world's your Oyster Card – assuming they don't send a cab. Sharing the bill with the exceptional performers on *Saturday Zoo*, for example, made me realize that some people approach their craft with a wholly different degree of dedication. They executed their craft with pinpoint accuracy – I just turned up and had a laugh. They saw it as showbusiness – I saw it as showing off. They were playing the long game – I was playing the fool.

I've had my fair share of *Catch Me If You Can* moments. And like Frank Abagnale Junior, who spent many years as a fake airline pilot and was played by the very talented Leonardo DiCaprio in the aforementioned Steven Spielberg movie, I've often found myself at the controls of something that I have no idea how to fly. There have been a few occasions where I've been on the flight-deck of someone's show with no real clue how anything works. The BBC1 drama series *Paradise Heights* springs to mind. I found myself queuing up for lunch and swapping pleasantries with some of the best-known actors in the country – Neil Morrissey, Charles Dale, Pam Ferris and David Troughton. The creator Ashley Pharoah wrote the role of a fraudulent vet in the show. He must have thought the actor who had played the bogus GP Dr Scrote would be perfect for the fake veterinary surgeon Dr Woodman. What Ashley overlooked was that while I brought very few thespian skills to the Scrote Brothers, Dr Woodman required rather more in the way of acting.

I remember a scene in a nightclub with Charlie Dale, who was playing a character called Clive. Dr Woodman was going to supply Clive's casino with some illegal exotic snakes. Concentration has never been my strong point and I couldn't recall the name of the animal I was supposed to be procuring. This was odd, as I'd read most of the script in the cab on the way to the set. For apparently no reason, I alighted on the word 'monkey'. To Charlie's professional acting credit, this did not faze him in the slightest, and he carried on faultlessly with his lines.

Dr Woodman: 'I've got the, er, monkeys in the car outside.'

Clive: 'Great, so that's two pythons, a rattlesnake and a puff adder, as agreed. Any luck with the spitting cobra?'

Perhaps Ashley had missed my attempts at acting in the first series, as for reasons best known to himself he resurrected the character of Dr Woodman for the second. I did, however, notice that my contribution the second time, although doubtless pivotal, was nowhere near as demanding. A couple of one-liners and the odd reaction shot, as I recall.

The thing was, when I was in my twenties and didn't know any better, I thought I'd put all my eggs in one basket with drumming, but discovered I was able to earn a living acting the giddy goat on stage, television and radio. I never felt comfortable calling myself a comedian. I saw myself more as 'the accidental comedian'. Who wouldn't, when sharing the stage with the likes of Dawn and Jenny, Alexei Sayle, Steve Coogan, John Thomson, and Rik and Ade?

I could never confess to being the image of my father, having learnt over the years about the immense sacrifices that made him the man he was. In the same way, I'm sure my fifteen-year-old son is right to distance himself from a father who's earned a living by disguising himself as a fly, interviewing people in the Thames, setting fire to himself for comic effect, wandering naked along Hadrian's Wall, juggling fireworks, dressing up as a woman and projectile vomiting for cash. Sadly, the list goes on, but I'll stop there for fear of upsetting people. Did I live up to my dad's expectations? He died while I was in a stretch limo, lording it like a good 'un with the one and only Twiggy. All right, I'm not performing life-saving medical procedures or educating the nation – my brothers Rich and Ray have comprehensively cornered those markets – but I think I've done all right. My pint pot has always been half-full rather than half-empty. Unfortunately, in the Himalayas during the detox programme it was, of course, half-full of my own piss!

To this day, I'm trying to justify not turning up for my A levels or finding employment on a par with those cornerstones of life, teaching and medicine. And to this day, my family still don't know exactly what I do for a living. In the early days it was debatable, but as time has gone on, I think they've been slowly won over. Having made an appearance on just about every celebrity-based show going, I think they've made the assumption that I must be a player in the frothy nonsense world of celebrity.

But as we know, most things are only in the eye of the beholder. I'm sure when some people hear my name today, they say, 'Oh yeah, Rowland Rivron? As funnymen go, he's a really good jazz drummer.'

extracts reading groups
competitions books new events
discounts extracts extracts reading groups
competitions extracts discounts
books new events
new events books reading groups
events extracts books new
new titles reading groups
interviews events
events extracts extracts events new books
discounts interviews new books extracts
new books events events
events new interviews new books extracts
discounts extracts discounts books

www.panmacmillan.com

extracts events reading groups
competitions books extracts new